THE RETURN F

CW00958460

'With the publication of The Return From Silence, the field of near-death studies has finally gained a volume that competently introduces the general reader to the near-death experience . . . This most welcome book is unquestionably a major contribution to the field. We should be darn happy to have it and that Scott Rogo took the trouble to write it. Frankly, I don't know of anyone who could have done it better.'

— Dr Kenneth Ring

By the same author
BEYOND REALITY
LIFE AFTER DEATH
MIND OVER MATTER
PSYCHIC BREAKTHROUGHS TODAY
THE INFINITE BOUNDARY
THE POLTERGEIST EXPERIENCE

THE RETURN FROM SILENCE

A Study of Near-Death Experiences

D. SCOTT ROGO

THE AQUARIAN PRESS

First published 1989

British Library Cataloguing in Publication Data

Rogo, D. Scott
The return from silence: a study of near-
death experiences.
1. Man. Near-death experiences
I. Title
129

ISBN 0–85030–736–8

The Aquarian Press is part of the Thorsons Publishing Group, Wellingborough, Northamptonshire, NN8 2RQ, England.

Typeset by Burns & Smith, Derby
Printed and bound in Great Britain by Mackays of Chatham PLC, Kent

3 5 7 9 10 8 6 4 2

Preface

During the last several years, the scientific study of the near-death experience (or NDE) has come to the forefront of both psychology and medicine. This interest has resulted, in part, from the public's growing concern with death and the experience of dying. Since 1975, several books on the subject have been published, mostly trying to show that the NDE constitutes proof that personal consciousness survives death. The reason why these books have been so popular and successful is that research into the NDE has been a scientific endeavour. This research has demonstrated that the survival of the soul is a problem science can cogently and successfully explore. It need not remain merely a religious belief to be taken on faith. Through the study of the NDE, psychology and science have shown that even the mysteries of death and the Great Beyond can be evaluated with scientific rigour.

Since Raymond Moody's best-selling *Life After Life* was published in 1975, other researchers have written books on their own NDE research. The problem with these (often excellent) volumes is that they tend to be limited in scope. Sometimes they have dealt with only a few aspects of the NDE and fail to offer the reader a general overview of the complicated issues that emerge from NDE research. This problem is complicated by the fact that these researchers invariably focus on their own surveys and rarely integrate them with the research and findings of their colleagues.

The Return from Silence represents the first comprehensive overview of NDE research specifically written for the general public. The goal of the book is to summarize the best available research on the subject, and then point out both the strengths of and the problems with the evidence. For example, it is not generally known that some people experience terrifying nightmarish NDEs during clinical death. Not every percipient experiences rapturous joy or a comforting Great White Light. There are also several drugs known in psychopharmacology that can produce psychedelic 'trips' closely resembling classic NDEs. Before coming to any conclusions on the NDE, these types of experiences must be integrated into more survival-orientated research.

This book is designed to offer the reader a survey and evaluation of many aspects of near-death encounters—including those elements that point to life beyond death, evidence that is inconsistent with this belief, and some evidence that the NDE is perhaps either a psychological or neurophysiological experience. The book is structured in the form of an internal debate in which the objective vs. subjective reality of the NDE is fully explored.

My personal bias is that the study of the NDE cannot be divorced from the study of out-of-body states in general. From that standpoint, it seems likely that NDE research provisionally supports the stance that such experiences point to mankind's immortality. But coming to this conclusion is not easy for the researcher. The study of the NDE is a complicated pursuit, and many features of the experience must be left unexplained. So, in the long run, each reader will have to come to his/her own conclusions on the subject. Does the NDE point to survival after death, or is it merely a hallucination? No matter what conclusion the reader draws, the NDE represents a fascinating phenomenon, and studying its byways can be highly rewarding, both intellectually and spiritually.

D. Scott Rogo
June 1988

Acknowledgements

I have been interested in the near-death experience for several years, during which time I have often benefited from my talks with other researchers. I would therefore like to express my gratitude to many researchers whose work has been included in these chapters. Dr Kenneth Ring and Dr Michael Grosso have always been sources of encouragement, while Dr Glen O. Gabbard and Dr Melvin Morse have been consistently kind in answering my enquiries on their work. I am especially grateful to Dr Ronald Siegel for our talks and for his willingness to help me better understand the strange byways of psychedelic drugs, even though I criticize his opinions in this book. I am also much indebted to Dr Bruce Greyson, who has helped me innumerable times over the years, and has supplied me with some of his unpublished papers on the near-death experience.

Since this book has included a great number of cases and extracts, I would like to acknowledge the publishers that permitted me to present material from their books.

Extracts from several publications originally appearing in *Anabiosis—the Journal for Near-Death Studies* are published with the permission of the editor and the International Association for Near-Death Studies.

Quotations from Margot Grey's *Return from Death* (1985) are used with the permission of Routledge and Kegan Paul.

Material from Raymond Moody's *Life After Life* (1975) and *Reflections on Life After Life* (1977) by Raymond Moody, appears with the permission of Mockingbird Books.

One case from Kenneth Ring's *Life at Death* (1980) is reprinted with the permission of Berkley Publishing Co.

The case from Kenneth Ring's *Heading Towards Omega* (1984)

is reprinted with permission of William Morrow & Co.

An extract from Susy Smith's *Life is Forever* (1974) is used by permission of G.P. Putnam's.

Several extracts from Michael Sabom's *Recollections of Death* (1982) appear with the consent of Harper & Row.

Material from Peter Stafford's *Psychedelics Encyclopedia* (1983) is used with the permission of J.P. Tarcher, Inc.

The case from William O. Stevens's *The Mystery of Dreams* (1950) is reprinted by permission of Unwin Hyman.

Several extracts from Carol Zaleski's *Otherworld Journeys* (1987, Oxford University Press) are printed with the permission of the copyright holder.

While the author has tried to obtain permission to republish extracts from previously copyrighted material, apologies are extended for any omissions that could have slipped through.

Contents

To Gary Johnson
— friend, mentor, and colleague.

1.

Confronting the NDE

Everyone reading this book probably knows what a near-death experience (or NDE) is. People suffering close calls with death sometimes suddenly find themselves floating out of their bodies, often watching their bodies being resuscitated (by physicians, paramedics, or whatever) with curiosity or detachment. Sometimes the witnesses will suddenly be transported to a heavenly world, the realm beyond death, before finally returning to the body. But not many people realize just how forcefully and fully the NDE has entered popular culture.

I learned this lesson myself two years ago when I stopped by my neighbourhood bar while I was running some errands. It was late in the afternoon and not many people were there—a fact that didn't bother me, since my interest was merely in gulping down a soft drink before getting on home. The establishment usually caters to those of us in the area, so I was somewhat unnerved to see two rough-looking men sitting together drinking beer. Because of their dress and demeanour, it didn't take long to realize that they were members of a motorcycle gang—i.e. people here in California who like to live nomadically and often tussle with the law. I became more uneasy when a third patron walked up to them and began pointing at me!

The tension mounted when the heavier of the two bikers looked over at me silently. Then he offered an almost imperceptible smile and cocked his head in the direction of the other patron.

'Do you know anything about people who die and come back?' he finally asked.

The third patron spoke at this moment. 'Yeah, he does. Go ahead and ask him.'

The biker then asked me what I knew about people

resuscitated from death, so I briefly explained what psychology had learned about the near-death experience. The man then opened up completely, since he felt he really had to talk to somebody. It seemed that, a few months previously, a friend and fellow gang member had been involved in a motorcycle crash. The rider had nearly been killed, but his life was saved by the emergency team at a local hospital. When he finally recovered, his left leg remained paralysed and the doctors didn't know whether he would ever regain control of it. Despite this threat to his mobility and life-style (it was doubtful whether he would ever ride a motorcycle again), he seemed unusually serene when his friend visited him. The patient finally explained why he wasn't bothered by his obviously serious predicament.

While still confined to bed, the partially paralysed man told his friend that when the accident occurred, he found himself floating down a bright tunnel. The tunnel seemed endless and the light illuminating it became brighter and brighter until it engulfed him. While he couldn't see anyone near him, he sensed that he was in the presence of God. It was a kindly presence, a presence that loved him and accepted him completely and without judgement. Much to his surprise, the crash victim wasn't intimidated by the being, even though totally awed by it. Then the presence spoke to him and explained that everything would be all right and he would live. They also apparently discussed his life experiences and what changes he would make upon his recovery.

'They just talked,' the biker said to me. 'Just like you and me, like friends. It was really great.'

At this point in the conversation, the biker's companion spoke for the first time. 'Yeah,' he said while sipping from his beer bottle. 'He said that God was really cool.'

I could hardly keep from laughing when this remark was made, since I appreciated the innocent sincerity in which it was offered. It was a refreshing change from the flowery language people usually use to describe cosmic experiences.

The reason for the crash victim's serenity became clear later, when the two bikers talked further. The patient explained that the presence warned him that some paralysis would be left in his leg, but gave the exact date when it would lift. The experience was so real that the injured man didn't question the information and was casually waiting for the healing. From what my informant said, the paralysis did spontaneously heal right on schedule and his friend recovered completely.

From the standpoint of scientific evidence, this case is little better or worse than many published in the popular press. What so impressed me, however, was the obvious impact of the experience. Not only had it radically eased the pain and suffering of the injured motorcyclist, but even more stunning was the way the story impressed his friend. Motorcycle gang members do not habitually concern themselves with metaphysical issues, yet this man felt compelled to consider deeply the spiritual implications of his friend's experience. He wasn't willing to reject the story, but felt obliged to explore it further. He had been discussing this incident in the bar before I showed up that day. The other bar patron had directed him to me, knowing of my interest in the paranormal.

This little story shows how deeply the subject of near-death experiences has entered into the language of popular culture. Everyone is learning about them, and the topic often materializes in rather curious places! Even popular television shows have used them in story plots, often in sensitive and insightful ways. An episode of the once popular comedy *One Day at a Time* (which concerns the problems faced by a divorcée raising two teenaged girls) used the NDE for an unusually serious and thoughtful show. The plot revolved around the family's building superintendent, who experiences an NDE as a result of a serious injury. The focus of the show dealt with the psychological impact of the experience and the way it transformed the handyman's previously shallow life. A much less serious poke at the NDE was recently included in an episode of NBC-TV's *Night Court*, which depicts an evening session of a zany New York court. In this episode, the bailiff nearly gets killed by a lightning bolt. When he recovers, he describes a typical NDE in which he spoke to God—only to learn later that it was the building electrician yelling to him!

While these two shows ranged from the serious to the ridiculous, it was clear that the writers and producers expected their TV viewers to know what an NDE entails, and to know that people really have them.

More evidence testifying to the impact the NDE is having on popular culture comes by way of a Gallup poll conducted from early in 1980 to September 1981. It was published in full the following year. This survey dealt primarily with the American public's belief in life after death. One of the survey questions, however, was phrased as follows:

> Here is a question about unusual experiences people say they have had when they have been on the verge of death or have had a 'close call' such as experiences of continued life or an awareness after death. Have you, yourself, ever been on the verge of death or had a 'close call' which involved any unusual experiences at that time?

Of course, the phrasing of this question was extremely open-ended and vague. But despite the totally non-directive wording, 15 per cent of those polled responded in the affirmative. On the basis of their sample size and selection methods, the Gallup team estimated that millions of people have had NDE-style experiences.

The 1982 Gallup poll did not stop with sheer numbers, however, since the pollsters also tried to determine what kind of people report NDEs. So the survey asked about each respondent's race, education, place of residence, chronological age, religious background, and occupation. The Gallup people failed to find that *any* of these factors earmarked people reporting NDEs. So whatever the nature of the NDE, the experience seems to be inherent to mankind or to our culture. The Gallup poll also explored the purely personal side of the near-death experience. When the pollsters asked their informants to describe the incidents specifically, they found the volunteers reporting a wide spectrum of experiences. While 11 per cent reported only subjective sensations of inner peace or a flashback review of their early lives, 9 per cent reported classic out-of-body experiences. Eleven per cent had the feeling that they had been transported to another realm of existence. Another 8 per cent felt a spiritual presence nearby during the encounter, while lesser sub-populations perceived a blinding light or saw a tunnel. Only 1 per cent reported negative or frightening ordeals.

These percentages may seem small, but remember that the Gallup organization was talking with hundreds upon hundreds of people. The fact that even this number of people reported NDEs is impressive, since the percentages represent large total counts.

Defining the near-death experience
What exactly is the near-death experience?

There has, in fact, been a great deal of confusion both in the scientific literature and in the press concerning what is and what isn't an NDE. I think this issue should be clarified before we proceed any further, since the expression 'NDE' has often been used as a makeshift, generic term for a wide range of experiences people sometimes report. Over the past decade, I have seen the expression 'near-death experience' especially used haphazardly to describe the following types of experiences:

1. A subjective sense of calm and peace in the face of death or while momentarily dead.
2. A curious feeling of detachment or emotional flatness in the face of a life-threatening mishap, such as falling from a cliff.
3. A vivid flashback of the person's past earthly life, often called a 'panoramic review'.
4. Seeing spiritual forms, often recognized by the dying person as his deceased friends or relatives. These forms tend to be seen standing by the patient's bedside or elsewhere in the room.
5. Becoming completely enveloped in a blissful but intense light.
6. Experiencing the sensation of leaving the body and suddenly functioning outside of it.
7. Entering into a physical but transcendental location, obviously separate from the normal world.

To my own way of thinking, this list is rather too all-encompassing. While each and every one of these experiences or sensations is interesting and should be carefully studied by researchers, the conceptualization of the NDE we'll be employing in the following chapters will be more concise. I believe that the expression 'near-death experience' should be used only under certain circumstances. For the rest of this book, the term will only be used to describe those experiences which meet two basic criteria:

1. The witness must either be close to physical death, threatened by death, or *perceive* him/herself to be in such danger.
2. The person should either experience him/herself out-of-body sometime during the episode, or his/her observations should imply that he/she is functioning in such a state.

By employing these criteria, the sensations listed 1–5 in the previous list—if experienced by themselves—would not constitute true NDEs. Such experiences might be incorporated into an NDE, but would not constitute the phenonemon itself. Only those experiences categorized under 6 and 7 would be considered true NDEs. This little discussion might seem laboured, but I have listened many times to psychologists and scientists debating the nature of the NDE—only to realize that they weren't really discussing the same phenomenon.

This lack of semantic precision sometimes even clouds the technical literature on the subject. For example, in 1986 the highly respected publication *Anabiosis—the Journal for Near-Death Studies* published a paper entitled 'The Darkness of God: an account of lasting mystical consciousness resulting from an NDE' by John Wren-Lewis. Dr Wren-Lewis's paper tells of a mystical, LSD-like experience he underwent when he perceived himself to be poisoned. The experience transformed his life, and his sudden change in consciousness lasted even when he recovered. But while the paper is interesting, I don't think that he experienced anything remotely resembling a true NDE. Since he never perceived himself to leave the body, his use of the term in the title seems misapplied and inappropriate.

Some examples of 'real' NDEs

Let's take a look at the following experience, reported in 1980, when scientific research into the NDE was just beginning. The report was submitted by Tracy Lovell, whose experience took place when she tried to kill herself. She was a college student at the time, and succumbed to the pressure of final examinations mixed with too much alcohol. She tried to commit suicide by overdosing on some medication she was taking.

> I walked around campus for a while. At this point my memory is very hazy, but with the help of some friends, I have reconstructed the event. Apparently I visited some friends and continued my walk and eventually ended up at my dorm where my resident advisor decided something was wrong and called an ambulance. At this point three hours had elapsed. I was taken to the emergency room and all I remember is hitting the doctor for trying to pump my stomach. I was then taken to the intensive care unit.
>
> My memory ended with me feeling pretty high walking around campus, and a short painful memory of the emergency room. The next thing I remember is seeing my body on a hospital bed with a doctor and nurses around. The feelings I had were some that I've

never had before or since. Words do not do them justice. I felt so peaceful and I had no questions about the scene I saw. It was so clear, more real than reality. I felt I was where I was supposed to be. The room was white, but there was a brightness all around me that was different from the room. I felt as though I was in the room (in the corner) but at the same time I was in open space. Everything was beautiful. There was no pain at all. I have no idea how long it lasted, but I will never forget it. Everything was so peaceful, calm and okay.

The next thing I remember is waking up in the room in my body. My mother was next to me with her hand on my forehead. The next few weeks are pretty hazy. But the memory of that experience is very clear.

Or consider the following experience published five years later in England by psychologist Dr Margot Grey. This case constitutes a true NDE, since it precisely meets the two criteria outlined previously: (1) the subject was both threatened with death and (2) experienced an out-of-body episode in response.

I was very ill and had great difficulty breathing. One evening I woke about nine o'clock from sleep realising something was prompting me to wake up and I realised I could not breathe. My eyes were popping out of my head and I was aware I was being asphyxiated. I can remember trying to rouse my sister who was asleep in the same room with me, but as I couldn't breathe this wasn't possible. I told myself to relax and accept that I was unable to breathe and just lay there waiting to die. By this time I was unable to close my eyes. Then I realised that I was starting to move upwards towards the ceiling and I thought I was going to bang myself on the ceiling at any minute and turned to avoid hitting the ceiling and as I did so I saw myself lying on the bed and I thought I looked very ill, terrible with great bags under my eyes. I felt weightless and I somehow moved through the ceiling which was no longer important. I was aware of going faster and faster. I wasn't frightened, but I wondered where I was going. Suddenly I heard a stern male voice above me which said, 'Get back, get back in there.' With that I found myself back in bed in a split second. I have no idea how I got there but I gasped for breath and sat up coughing blood. I managed to rouse my sister and told her what had happened but she said it was obviously because I was feverish. But I know the experience was totally real.

Sometimes near-death experiences represent simple episodes such as these, but this isn't to say that every NDE is so relatively uninvolved. Sometimes a series of highly structured experiences or visionary episodes will be sparked by the out-of-body phase.

Just such a complicated NDE was reported in 1979 by a young man named Rick Bradshaw, whose NDE occurred when he was 18 years old. While working as a grocery boy in Peoria, Illinois, he was struck by a car when he was loading a customer's car. He was momentarily crushed between the two vehicles and was later rushed, bleeding, to a local hospital. His last conscious recollection was hearing the physician-in-charge calling for a blood transfusion. Rick then experienced the following:

> Sometime later there was a sudden flash of light and I found myself floating just above my physical body. I could see the surgeons working on me. There was also a nurse seated in front of me, directly above my head.
>
> The next sensation I had was when I felt someone place their hands on my shoulders. I got the impression that I was sitting on something which moved me through a tunnel guided by the hands on my shoulders. There were profound colors in the tunnel which streaked by us as we ventured through it. I soon found myself in a room which had form but no real substance. It was enveloped by mist. In the room to my right was everyone I had ever known that had died. In front of me was an object that resembled a podium; there was also a desk and what looked like bookshelves.
>
> Some of the people in the room were moving about. Their movement can best be described as floating from place to place—they weren't walking. I also remember beautiful music which filled the room and came in from all directions. I had a truly wonderful feeling as if I had no cares in the world. It's a hard feeling to describe; never before or since have I had any feelings which compare to that.

This initial portion of the NDE represents the common out-of-body sensation, followed by some sort of otherworld journey. But the next phase in the young man's experience took on a more personal meaning. A person radiating a sense a spiritual peace and power entered the room and cryptically asked him for a 'decision'. The remark made considerable sense and Rick realized he had to return to his earthly life—back to those people whose goodwill had helped and supported him. When he mentally made this decision, the being showed Rick a vision 'as if the sky had opened up and revealed to me all things of the past and present'. The experience was both overwhelming and nuministic, but Rick was brought back to his momentary reality by the being, who warned him that his peek into the future would be largely forgotten. He would only prevision the future,

the being explained, just before it took place. Rick later concluded his report by writing:

> I was then taken back through the tunnel and experienced another
> short moment of complete darkness. I awoke in my bed in the inten-
> sive care unit of the hospital. My father, a doctor, and a nurse were
> present when I regained consciousness. In my excitement and en-
> thusiasm afterward, I tried to tell them about what had just occurred.
> I found it impossible to talk because of the respirator which I was
> hooked up to. They thought that I was confused so they tied my arms
> down to the bed.
>
> It then occurred to me—I realized what the being meant with his
> words. It would be a mistake for me to go around telling everyone
> about this because I would surely be regarded as crazy. Much later
> after my hospitalization, I found out that others have had similar ex-
> periences during serious physical injury. It feels real good to know
> that I am not the only one. Needless to say, I am not the same person.
> My experience was beautiful and profound and has changed my life.

These three cases illustrate the two most commonly reported
forms of the NDE. Earlier writers have called them 'autoscopic'
and 'transcendental' near-death experiences respectively, though
perhaps uncircumspectly. Since the term 'autoscopy' has been
used in psychology to describe the pathological experience of
seeing a *doppelgänger* (i.e. a phantom form resembling the self),
it should be rejected. I think more appropriate terms for these
types of experiences would be 'simple' and 'eschatological' NDEs.
Simple NDEs would refer to those short experiences in which the
percipient momentarily leaves the body during a life-threatening
crisis. Eschatological NDEs would subsume those experiences in
which the patient or witness experiences some sort of otherworld journey, in which he/she perceives the final resting place
of the soul. (Eschatology is that branch of theology which deals
with the final state of the soul.)

Not every NDE can be placed within either of these categories,
though. Some people have 'mixed' NDEs in which the out-of-
body state is implied rather than directly experienced. These
episodes may lead to an incipient otherworld journey, though to
what realm is not clear.

The following case was reported by a heart attack patient in
1987 and illustrates this grey zone of the NDE. Mr Daniel Armore
of Bradford, Connecticut, experienced his close call with death
when he checked himself into a local hospital upon experiencing

severe chest pains.

> I did not expect to live through the night, and the doctors did not expect me to survive.
>
> At one point, I felt as if I was losing 'control' over myself. My head was shaking from side to side, and I could not regain control of myself. It was then that I felt myself drifting, drifting away into darkness. It was a tremendous feeling of no pain at all, peacefulness, a tremendous high I was on. I felt myself being rushed into this darkness of warmth, peace, love, just a wonderful, wonderful, peaceful feeling came over me. As I went further into this darkness, I was not afraid and wanted to keep going forward; I saw a vision, nothing I've seen before. I saw a vision of white objects dancing all around me, and I was being drawn closer and closer to those dancing figures. It was a tremendous feeling; you couldn't believe it. I was getting closer to these dancing figures, and when I got 'close' enough, they appeared to be angels in white gowns, dancing all around me. The feeling was warm, loving, peaceful, serene. I did not want to leave this place of peace. I wanted to keep going forward into my journey, as I was still being pulled into this darkness, except for those angels who were there.
>
> At this point I felt myself being rushed backwards through darkness again and being pulled back into my body with excruciating pain. I do not remember anything that happened that night, or why.

Mr Armore also mentions that 'it should be noted that when I awoke in the hospital, a priest did not want to know if I saw anything or if anything happened'.

I have chosen these examples of fairly typical NDEs since they represent three extreme forms of the phenomenon. They also represent the prime dilemma the researcher faces when trying to explain the NDE. This dilemma can be best called the 'boggle' problem, which is a wonderful term coined by Renée Haynes, a British writer and scholar on the paranormal. Ms Haynes has suggested that each of us harbours a personal 'boggle threshold', a point to which we can believe in the preternatural before our logical minds and biases take over. We tend to reject any phenomenon that trespasses the boggle threshold, usually by refusing to believe it exists without further consideration.

Many people face their own personal boggle threshold while trying to make sense of the NDE phenomenon. Some of them would probably have little difficulty evaluating experiences such as Tracy Lovell's momentary disembodiment. Because of our religious and cultural upbringing, her out-of-body reaction in the face of death seems believable to us. Certainly *if* mankind possesses a soul, such an essence might leave the body when we close in on death. But when it comes to eschatological visions or otherworld journeys, divine presences, visionary revelations and the like, that seems to be a different matter! It is just a little too mind-boggling for most people. So the same people willing to believe Ms Lovell's story might balk at Rick Bradshaw's testimony. The benign sceptic might label it a vision, to be kind, or an hallucination, to put it more bluntly. Taking such a stance towards *any* form of the NDE would be a mistake, however. From a perfectly rationalistic standpoint, no type of NDE experience is really any more mind-boggling than the next. The simple fact remains that NDEs come in many guises, some more complex than others, and we have little right to seriously consider some NDEs while rejecting others. No theoretical explanation for the NDE can be considered complete unless *every* form of the experience can be subsumed by it.

A final justification and classification
The definition and criteria for the NDE proposed in the previous sections have not been arbitrarily based. I have chosen this conceptualization because it seems to represent the way the NDE is generally understood by the public. While NDEs have been reported in the scientific and parapsychological literature for years, it wasn't until 1975 that the subject first splashed into public knowledge. That year saw the publication of a short and unpretentious little book entitled *Life After Life* by Raymond A. Moody, Jr. Dr Moody was a former philosophy teacher then studying for his medical degree. The book's goal was merely to present several first-hand NDE accounts without dogmatizing about them. The book soon became a paperback best-seller and sparked the interest of several medical researchers and social scientists, who proceeded to explore the subject further. The upshot of these studies was the founding of the International Association for Near-Death Studies in 1981.

For the most part, Dr Moody included clear-cut NDE cases in his book, from which the criteria outlined earlier were drawn. It was only later that some researchers began to expand the definition until the term 'near-death experience' lost its original meaning. Early in his book, Dr Moody presented an example of a prototypical NDE, which incorporated most of the commonly reported 'stages' or experiential components of the phenomenon. This prototype for the NDE has been widely reprinted by other writers on the subject, oftentimes to the point of redundancy. But it may be wise to keep it in mind, since it focuses us back to the specific phenomena we'll be discussing in the coming chapters. Table I is a chart in which I have broken down Dr Moody's typical NDE into its components, and the reader should keep them in mind while reading the rest of this book.

This components list for the typical NDE has probably never been improved, although since 1975 some researchers have shown that other features may crop up. Probably the most notable discovery is that some people experience a hellish or nightmarish world while clinically dead. Dr Moody himself expanded his components list in 1977 by including the following: the person may perceive cities of light during the NDE and/or may be given a 'vision' of knowledge. Rick Bradshaw reported this kind of incident, in which his future was presented to him.

Despite the highly structured and sometimes predictable nature of the NDE, keep in mind that each near-death report is different from the next. No single report will include every component listed in Table I nor—with the possible exception of the disembodied state—is any feature universal to the NDE. The stages or components of the NDE might also be experienced in different order by each individual.

Nobody today studying the oftentimes strange byways of the NDE would challenge the fact that Dr Moody's seminal work sparked off the scientific study of the phenomenon. But this isn't to say that neither medicine nor psychology considered such experiences before. So before exploring what science has learned about the NDE since 1975, let's begin by examining what religious scholars and some psychologists knew of it in previous years.

Table I
Component Features of the Prototypical Near-Death Experience

1. The NDE may begin when the dying individual hears a strange noise in his/her ears, such as a buzzing or rushing.

2. The subject is next taken over by a deep sense of calm or inner peace.

3. The dying person either leaves the body or suddenly finds him/herself looking down at his body from a disembodied perspective.

4. Since the patient's sense perceptions still function, he/she may overhear what is taking place in the body's environment. The subject, for example, may see and hear doctors and nurses trying to resuscitate the body.

5. The patient might notice that the 'soul' is enveloped in its own spiritual body, which can be moved merely through willpower.

6. The patient or witness next experiences a paranormal review of his/her entire life.

7. Having completed the review, the subject enters a dark (but unintimidating) void or floats through a tunnel.

8. Either at the end of the tunnel or while making the journey, the dying person perceives a great but comforting light.

9. The light may envelop the person, or it might catapult him/her into a realm of surpassing beauty. This realm is often compared to the paradise of the Bible.

10. The dying individual might next encounter a spiritual being. This being may be a deceased friend or relative, or might be God or a godlike figure.

11. The beings might either order the witness back into the body or ask him/her whether he/she wishes to stay or not.

12. Sometimes the person feels that this decision has been made for him or her, and returns reluctantly.

2.

NDEs Through the Ages
I. *Early Religious Testimony*

Since near-death experiences are common human encounters, it isn't surprising that they've been reported since time immemorial. These early accounts represent an extremely important body of literature, for by examining them the student of near-death research can determine whether such experiences tend to be reported differently in disparate societies or remain constant from culture to culture. *If* such reports do not reflect the particular culture which gave rise to them, then we are probably dealing with some sort of universal experience common to mankind. If these experiences were due, for example, to the percipient's religious upbringing or cultural expectations, we would expect to find NDE reports reflecting such influences. One might expect to find the early Christians, for example, reporting traditional angels during their otherworld journeys and so forth.

Probably the oldest and most celebrated case of an NDE was reported by the famous Greek philosopher Plato (427–347 BC) in his *Republic*, in which he cites the case of Er, a soldier reportedly 'killed' in battle. While the soldier's body lay on the battlefield, his soul took flight. Accompanied by the souls of several fellow soldiers, Er's soul experienced an otherworld journey to a strange land, where they were judged. He saw other souls choosing their subsequent incarnations and then drinking from the River of Forgetfulness, in order to obliterate their past memories. Er was forbidden to drink and later blacked out only to revive, just in time, on his funeral pyre.

Students of the near-death experience like to point to Plato's story, suggesting that it proves the universality of NDE reports. Their point is well taken, since the story of Er includes several components of the classic eschatological NDE. It includes the commonly reported out-of-body experience followed by an otherworld journey, and later ending with a resuscitation from death. But note, too, how differently this case reads from similar episodes reported today. The entire tale is cluttered with elements borrowed from Greek cultural traditions. Reincarnation or transmigration of the soul was taught in some Greek mystery schools, and this element is conspicuous in the report. This same theme is patently missing from contemporary NDE accounts. (There is a notable exception to this rule, which will be discussed in a forthcoming chapter.) Notice also that the typical command for the witness to 'return' to earth is transformed. Er doesn't receive it literally, but if forbidden to drink from the River of Forgetfulness—a thinly disguised reference to the river Lethe (in Hades, which obliterates all memory) of Greek mythology. So the story of Er teaches us two important lessons about the NDE: while several components of the experience remain consistent over historical time and culture, some of its components are significantly influenced by the culture in which it takes place.

Now it could, of course, be argued that Plato took a brief story once told to him and transformed it. Perhaps he elaborated what was originally a simple NDE report, and then imbued it with mythological and cultural features to make it more believable to his readers. Or perhaps he simply invented the whole thing because of its allegorical significance. The story of Er is, in fact, a little morality play since the soldier returns to life with a lesson for mankind: we must live an exemplary life in pursuit of wisdom in order to gain our eventual rewards. Plato was fond of allegory and often used the device in his writings, so Er's otherworld journey might simply exemplify the philosopher's penchant for such symbolism.

Whether some early NDE reports represent real stories or simple allegories is not only a problem we find in the story of Er. The same problems crop up when we start looking at medieval Christian literature on the NDE. This body of religious writing has been recently surveyed by Dr Carol Zaleski, a lecturer in religion at Harvard University. She has presented the results of her findings in her book *Otherworld Journeys*, which traces the NDE as a part of Christian visionary literature. The basic thesis Dr Zaleski promotes is that the modern NDE is an extension and reworking of the medieval Christian visionary experience, linked

with early religious eschatology. She also suggests that these early NDE reports were sometimes deliberately manufactured
and/or restructured by the Christian establishment to serve as
religious propaganda.

Dr Zaleski's premise is certainly well taken and reasonable, if
not totally convincing. NDE reports and eschatological visions
were often recorded by ecclesiastical writers between the seventh
and fourteenth centuries. Perhaps they didn't completely invent
them, but took real-life NDE accounts reported by the public and
used them as the basis for their allegories. The general public was
illiterate during the Middle Ages, so people were dependent
upon the clergy to make their experiences more widely known.
These reports may have given the Church Fathers an opportuni-
ty too good for them to pass up. Ecclesiastical propagandists
often took common forms of psychic experience and redrafted
them in the form of Christian teachings. They often used accounts of post-mortem apparitions, for instance, to support the
doctrine of purgatory, the intermediate state before the soul's
transition to heaven.[1]

It shouldn't be thought that these early Christian writers had a
franchise on NDE reports, though. Even in these early times
similar accounts were known and referenced in Jewish literature.
Despite the fact that medieval Judaism had little interest in
eschatology, the NDE motif appeared later in Hasidic writings.
(Hasidism was then a form of experiential Judaism emphasizing
prayer over ritual. It is based on the teachings of the Baal Shem
Tov, a Ukrainian Jew born in 1698.) Studying the classic book *In
Praise of the Baal Shem Tov* today, the student of religion reads
that 'in earlier days when people revived after lying in a coma
close to death, they used to tell about the awesome things they
had seen in the upper world'. Even older stories have been found
in ancient Egyptian traditions, which often focused on death and
spiritual resurrection.

But let's get back now to early Christian visionary literature,
which serves as the precursor for so many NDE studies being
made today.

Early in her study Dr Zaleski makes the observation that

---

[1]For a detailed discussion of how these narratives were treated, see *Ap-
pearances of the Dead* by R.C. Finucane (Buffalo, NY: Prometheus Books, 1984),
which is a 'cultural history' of ghosts and phantoms back to ancient times.

'strange as it may seem, the Christian otherworld journey does not depend directly on the pattern of Christ's death, resurrection and ascension'. Dr Zaleski seems to be saying that early Christian NDE reports, or eschatological visions, were not based solely on historical Christian traditions but seemed to inexplicably transcend them. This remark suggests to me that the early NDE-style narratives reported between the fourth and fourteenth centuries were partially independent of Christian culture, perhaps—I would like to suggest—because they really were based on true accounts. Dr Zaleski breaks down these early Christian stories into four different traditions, and we'll follow her lead.

1. The otherworld journey as apocalypse

The very roots of Christian belief speak to the issue of the otherworld journey, classically represented by Christ's own descent to the underworld upon his resurrection. Some scholars trace the apocalyptic tradition in eschatological literature back to St Paul and his celebrated letter to the church at Corinth. St Paul's testimony reads like some sort of NDE or NDE-like experience which occurred under unknown circumstances. While the testimony was given by the saint in the third person, it is widely believed that Paul was reflecting on his personal experience. The account appears in the Second Epistle of the Corinthians, chapter 12. He emphasized how fourteen years previously, a Christian was taken to the third heaven, 'whether in the body or out of the body I do not know, God knows. And I know that this man was caught up into paradise—whether in the body or out of the body I do not know, God knows.'[2]

At this point in the story, the witness's experience (or St Paul's vision) matches many contemporary NDE reports even more closely. For like so many people today who often refuse to talk about their experiences, St Paul or his informant 'heard things that cannot be told, which man may not utter'. Whether these cryptic remarks refer to some secret or coming cataclysm, or merely reflect the ineffability of the experience, will never be known. It is clear, though, that the experience entailed some sort

---

[2]St Paul's reference to the third heaven is an allusion to the Jewish belief in multiple heavenly realms. The third (or sometimes the seventh) was the highest, thereby making it comparable to paradise.

of out-of-body episode followed by the classic otherworld journey.

Why St Paul did not wish to reveal that he was reporting a personal experience remains a mystery. The standard interpretation is that, since the vision was a grace from God, he did not wish to boast of it. My own interpretation of this biblical passage is different. We know from modern NDE reports that some people see visions of the future during their experiences, often involving the fate of the world. These people are sometimes reluctant to disclose these premonitions, considering them too personal to be shared with anyone else. It could be that Paul wanted to keep his otherworld observations a secret, and camouflaged the incident so that the Corinthians wouldn't pry into the incident further.

Whatever the reason, his plan backfired badly. Such a provocative story soon excited the imagination of later Christian writers, who by the third century were circulating 'true' versions of what St Paul 'really' saw. These apocryphal and obviously invented tales elaborate on the basic spiritual message implied by the saint's letter. The later writers transformed the simple narrative of the Epistle to the Corinthians into an intricate preview of the soul's ultimate fate. Dr Zaleski explains that the oldest reinterpretation of the verses casts Paul into the role of prophetic visionary, in which he journeys to heaven to witness the soul's plight. She writes in her book that, in later times, it was the content rather than the experiential nature of Paul's journey that gained importance. She explains that:

> For medieval readers, however, much of the Vision's glamour derived from its vivid depiction of the experiences that are in store for individuals at death and in the period before the final judgment. Although Paul himself does not die, he observes the departure of three souls from their bodies and witnesses their journeys after death; the soul of a just man exits his body in the company of shining angels who defend him against the hostile powers of the air and escort him to the heavenly court to be vindicated and welcomed by God; a wicked man is dragged roughly from his body by 'angels without mercy,' harassed by his animating spirit, claimed as a fellow traveler by the hostile powers, and consigned to torment in the outer darkness; a second wicked man, after spending seven days before his trial on a forced tour of the cosmos, faces conviction when his own guardian angel turns state's evidence, producing a manuscript record

of his sins and bringing forward the souls of those he had murdered or betrayed.

Later in her discussion, Dr Zaleski notes that subsequent commentaries on St Paul's experience focused on hellish visions rather than on pleasing previews of heaven. The emphasis soon centred on the Final Judgement, which so consumed ecclesiastic writers in the Middle Ages. This tradition partially broke away from the emphasis on spiritual rewards and blessings promised by earlier Christianity.

2.   The otherworld journey as miracle story

This second interpretation of the NDE/otherworld journey stems from the sixth century, and Dr Zaleski traces it back to Gregory the Great (AD 540–604), whose writings were often concerned with miracles and visions. His celebrated book of miracles, the *Dialogues*, includes an entire chapter which tries to prove the immortality of the soul. It includes 42 tales of the preternatural, of which 4 seem to represent NDE accounts. The first of them tells the story of a hermit revived from death, who reports on his experience to his friends. The poor man's otherworld journey is truly frightening since he sees several powerful men tormented by fire. The scene is finally interrupted by a shimmering angel, who orders him to return to earth—suggesting, of course, that he make good use of his privileged observations! Pope Gregory's second story centres on similar themes, where a businessman named Stephen witnesses the torments of hell during a close encounter with death. Pope Gregory claimed that he personally investigated the story and interviewed the businessman. When they met together, explains the churchman, the businessman explained that he survived the NDE because he wasn't supposed to die. It seems that his journey through death was a mistake since it was really fated that Stephen *the blacksmith* was scheduled to die.

This was an interesting development in the case, and Gregory claims that he checked into the matter. He subsequently learned that a blacksmith named Stephen really did expire while Stephen the businessman was experiencing his pseudo-death.

The third story which Pope Gregory reports in his *Dialogues* is even more revealing, for by this time it becomes clear that Gregory either invented some of his NDE narratives or reworked them from the original in the form of morality plays. This fascinating incident purportedly came from a soldier revived from death the same week as Stephen's pseudo-death took place. Pope Gregory asserts that the soldier saw both the torments of hell and the pleasures of heaven, cast in the form of a beautiful meadow saturated with exquisite perfumes. He watches as earthly souls try to pass over a bridge leading to the paradisiacal realm. The wicked inevitably fall into the murky waters below, where demonic figures submerge them in unspeakable horrors, while the righteous pass without difficulty. While making these elaborate observations, the soldier claimed to have seen Stephen the businessman's trials. We read in the *Dialogues*:

> He also saw a certain pilgrim priest approach the bridge and cross it with as much self-command in his walk as there was sincerity in his life. On the same bridge, he claimed to have recognized that Stephen of whom we spoke before. In his attempt to cross the bridge, Stephen's foot slipped, and the lower half of his body was now dangling off the bridge. Some hideous men came up from the river and grabbed him by the hips to pull him down. At the same time, some very splendid men dressed in white began to pull him up by the arms. While the struggle went on, with good spirits pulling him up and evil spirits dragging him down, the one who was watching all this was sent back to his body. So he never learned the outcome of the struggle.

The fact that this part of the story is bogus seems obvious, though it is possible that Gregory interpolated it into a genuine account he had really been told. In any event, toward the end of the tale he offers his 'conclusions' on the report, in which its moral is conveniently pointed out:

> What happened to Stephen can, however, be explained in terms of his life. For in him the evils of the flesh contended with the good work of almsgiving. Since he was dragged down by the hips and pulled up by the arms, it is plain to see that he loved almsgiving and yet did not refrain completely from the carnal vices that were dragging him down. Which side was victorious in that contest was concealed from our eyewitness, and is no more plain to us than to the one who saw it all and then came back to life. Still, it is certain that even though Stephen had been to hell and back, as we related above, he did not completely correct his life. Consequently, when he went out of his body many years later, he still had to face a life-and-death battle.

Before leaving the subject of Pope Gregory's *Dialogues*, there are two aspects of his writings that deserve some additional comments. To begin with, note that by the seventh century the NDE had already been secularized. No longer was it seen as the special privilege of the saints or early holy men of the Church. Pseudo-death visions became the property of common people living outside the religious establishment. It is also interesting that Pope Gregory tried to show that such experiences could be objectively proved. Notice how in his second and third stories (i.e. the pseudo-death of Stephen the businessman and the soldier's later corroboration of it) the focus is on the *evidence* behind the story. Gregory the Great therefore might be considered Western culture's first psychical researcher, eager to find proof for the supernatural stories that perhaps were regularly told to him. Shedding a less flattering light on him, perhaps the great saint also became the field's first fudger!

3. The otherworld journey as a conversion story

This tradition of NDE/otherworld journey stories is traced by Dr Zaleski back to the Venerable Bede's *Ecclesiastic History of the English People*, written in the eighth century and still read today.

Bede (AD 673–735) includes the tale or perhaps real-life testimony of Drythelm, a family man from Northumbria, who died after a brief but severe illness, only to revive spontaneously the following day. The fortunate man explained what took place to his wife, who repeated the story to a monk. It was the monk who purportedly brought the account to Bede, who in turn put it in writing. When the tale begins, Drythelm meets a shining being who takes him to the realms of the otherworld. They walk through a valley populated with lost souls either fighting fire or enduring icy coldness. The terror of the scene is lessened by the guide, who explains that this is merely a temporary state before the souls can be saved through the prayers and fasts of the living. Later, while travelling through the otherworldly regions, Drythelm sees the literal hell, complete with fire and evil spirits ever eager to grab souls into a flaming abyss. Next he and the guide journey to more pleasant regions before he returns to earth.

The message inherent in this story is, of course, the conversion of sinners. It is presented not because of its personal importance to the experiencer, but for its greater religious implications. Dr Zaleski says simply that such eschatological reports were important 'primarily for [their] power as a model for conversion and [their] usefulness in advertising the cause of particular religious institutions and ideas'. But the eminent scholar isn't willing merely to dismiss the story, for she suggests that Bede took a possibly real NDE report and transformed it into a piece of religious fiction. Similar accounts crop up in ecclesiastical writings from the tenth to the thirteenth century. These later eschatological stories were permeated by such themes as taking religious vows, changing previous life-styles, and seeking penance for sins.

4. The otherworld journey as a spiritual pilgrimage

The last religious tradition possibly linked to modern NDE accounts can be traced back to the famous *Treatise on the Purgatory of St. Patrick*, written in the twelfth century by an English Cistercian monk. (The Cistercian order was founded in the eleventh century in France and was a strict monastic group that forbade the eating of meat and emphasized simple living.) This colourful treatise was inspired by a sacred site that existed in Lough (Lake) Derg, County Donegal in Ireland and was widely believed to be a portal to the next world. It was a popular place of pilgrimage and St Patrick converted the local pagans through his own (purported) otherworldly experiences there. The 'portal' itself was supposedly located in a cave on a barren island in the lake's reddish waters. It was common for pilgrims to be locked in the cave, so that their journeys could be extended into the spiritual realms through visions. Such experiences had the purported power to purge the pilgrim of his sins. The cave had a continuous spiritual heritage up until the eighteenth century, when it was destroyed. The site is still in existence today as a popular tourist attraction and shrine for religious penitents.

The elaborate experiences of the *Treatise's* hero, the Knight Owen, is similar to the type of conversion narrative discussed in the previous section. The protagonist is an Irish knight returning to Ireland after a successful campaign who seeks forgiveness for his sins. He has himself locked into the cave where he retreats down a deep tunnel towards a distant light. There he meets some cloistered monks who urge him to turn back, but failing, leave him to his fate. After a frightening earthquake rocks the ground, the Knight Owen is shown the otherworld complete with sinners who suffer torments before being damned to hell, which is depicted in the form of a bottomless pit. Next the penitent travels down a river of fire and sulphur, over which a bridge extends to a paradise environment of dazzling sunshine. There the knight comes upon two ecclesiastics who guide him through the heavenly realms where wondrous music pleases his ear. The guides explain that the true realm of God extends beyond this lovely sphere and urge him to make religious observances upon his return to earth. The knight would have liked to stay forever in this realm, but he is forced to return. The experience is transformative, though, and he takes up a religious life when his king, with whom he consults, orders him to serve the Cistercian monks.

Even though the story included in the *Treatise* is meant as a literal (bodily) descent into the otherworld, it is clear that many components of the modern NDE can be found in it. Such experiences as crossing a boundary to the next world, meeting spiritual guides, hearing wonderful music, and returning to earth only reluctantly, characterize the contemporary pseudo-death report as well. The fact that the knight's experience is initiated by travelling through a tunnel towards a light is too classic for comment!

The primary message embedded in this type of eschatological narrative was the importance of conversion, and such tales were promoted by several religious orders for blatantly self-serving purposes. Dr Zaleski shows in her book that the *Treatise on the Purgatory of St. Patrick* was specifically used by the Cistercians to boost their own selfish interests. (Note that the Knight Owen was told by his king to help them build a new abbey in Ireland.) But such accounts also had a more universal importance to the medieval intellect, as Dr Zaleski explains in her study:

Another remarkable feature of the story of Owen, as of all accounts of St Patrick's Purgatory, Cistercian or otherwise, is the way in which it dramatizes one of the central religious conceptions of the Middle Ages: the idea that life is a pilgrimage. It is well known that the high Middle Ages witnessed a virtual craze for pilgrimage discourse. After the lull in the barbarian invasions of the ninth and tenth centuries, travel became somewhat less dangerous, and interest in the symbolic value of pilgrimage kept pace with the increasing number of pilgrims on the road. This is not to say that pilgrimage as a metaphor was a medieval invention. The early Fathers often spoke of the church as a pilgrim or exile in the world, embarked on a collective journey through the *saeculum* to the day of judgment. In the high Middle Ages, however, pilgrimage became a symbol for the individual's journey through life and death. Romance and legend celebrated the solitary seeker; the desert hermit, the Irish seafaring saint, the knight on a quest, the courtly lover, the traveling penitent.

So like those near-death experiences reported today, even during the Middle Ages these stories spoke of deeply spiritual issues—issues which have concerned mankind since the beginning of time.

The literature on medieval eschatological journeys is complex and can only be sampled in this short chapter. For further information on the subject, the reader should carefully study Dr Zaleski's scholarly but extremely readable book. I only hope that I have successfully communicated the essence of these religious traditions in the foregoing section. But why should these traditions be so important to us? Simply because embedded within these primarily literary accounts rest the roots of the contemporary NDE report. Just about every feature of the near-death experience crops up in them. This may not be blatantly obvious to the reader, since these early characteristics are often buried below religious and romantic overlays. But if we extract the religious fluff from the reports, several core components of the true NDE are continually exposed.

While studying the material collected and codified by Dr Zaleski during her doctoral work, I began graphing out the characteristics of these medieval narratives. By charting their common components I gradually constructed Tables II and III. Note that eight specific similarities exist between medieval eschatological vision accounts and contemporary NDE stories. The initial out-of-body experience is usually implied rather than described, which is followed by an otherworld journey that transforms the witness's life. The final phase of the vision focuses on the witness's reluctance to return to earth. Against these similarities, however, several differences remain that reflect either some sort of literary (and invented) religious overlay or possible cultural effects.

It is more than revealing that most of the differences between modern NDEs and medieval eschatological narratives specifically concern religious dogmas. The emphasis of the latter body of literature speaks of damnation, judgement, and purgatory, while

Table II
Similarities between Early Christian Eschatological Visions and Contemporary NDEs

Visionary experiences	NDEs
1. The visionary often experiences an apocalyptic look into the future.	The NDE witness sometimes is shown either his own future or the future of the world, including great cataclysms.
2. The visionary is escorted through the otherworld by a saint or angel.	The witness is shown the afterlife by a spiritual guide or deceased friend or relative.
3. Such visions are experienced while out-of-body.	The experience begins when the individual has an out-of-body experience.
4. The traveller sees some sort of boundary, such as a bridge, between the earth plane and the otherworld realm.	Some type of boundary, such as mist or water, divides the earthly plane from the afterlife.
5. The visionary undergoes a religious conversion because of the experience.	The subject is spiritually transformed by the experience.
6. The visionary feels depressed when returning to the body, cast away from the vision.	The NDE witness returns to the body reluctantly through a sense of duty, still drawn to the otherworldly realm.
7. Those who return from death demonstrate increased intellectual powers.	On rare occasion, NDE survivors report that they suddenly developed new intellectual skills or showed increased capabilities.
8. Sometimes the visionary develops psychic gifts upon recovery, such as knowing when people will die.	Many NDE survivors report increased psychic sensitivity in their day-to-day lives.

Table III
Differences between Early Christian Eschatological
Visions and Contemporary NDEs

Visionary experiences	NDEs
1. The witness usually experiences visions of hell and damnation.	Only on rare occasions is the NDE witness taken to a nightmarish environment.
2. The subsequent report by the experiencer is very elaborate.	NDE reports tend to be short and matter-of-fact.
3. The visionary is usually given a message to bring back to society. The experience tends to speak to the witness's culture not to the individual.	No specific messages are given, though they may be implied. The experience is usually deeply personal to the individual.
4. The visionary does not experience a panoramic review of his life.	The witness often undergoes a review of his former life.
5. The account includes several allegorical features.	Allegories are rarely included or suggested by the encounter.
6. The experience has a specific moral to it.	While the experience may draw a moral from the NDE, specific moral messages or judgements are never forced on the percipient.
7. The theme of the experience implicitly supports Christian theology including such dogma as purgatory and punishment for sins.	Most NDE percipients see their experience as supporting a non-denominational spiritual view of the world.

the purpose *behind* the experience is to teach moral (i.e. specifically Christian) lessons to the witness's entire community. This is an important point to consider and one to which I will return shortly. So how can we explain both the similarities *and* the differences between these two bodies of literature? There are four theories:

1. It could be that NDEs are simply the current expression of a primarily spiritual experience inherent to mankind. The characteristics of the experience are archetypal and therefore arise in different cultures and times.
2. Modern-day NDEs are hallucinatory experiences moulded by popular cultural traditions similar to the same Christian beliefs that evolved during the sixth to the fourteenth century. (Perhaps similar to the way some psychotic delusions will often revolve around religious themes, and Christian themes in particular.)
3. Medieval otherworld journey stories were bogus inventions created by the early Christians to promote religious dogma. The similarities between those accounts and current NDE reports are merely coincidental.
4. These same propagandists could have heard real 'return from death' accounts upon which they based their tales.

Choosing between these mutually exclusive theories often becomes a matter of bias, but I think we can reject the idea that the similarities outlined in Table II result from coincidence. On the other hand, scholars of modern NDE research simply don't agree which of the three other theories is the best. Dr Zaleski prefers the first explanation outlined in this short list. She concludes her book by arguing that NDEs represent the extension of the eschatological Christian tradition into our own secular times. While she rejects the notion that such present-day reports prove the objective existence of an afterlife, she doesn't totally reject the possibility. She even posits the possibility that both eschatological visions and modern NDE reports point to some sort of future existence. NDEs might be symbolic journeys, she suggests, which represent an *expression* of such a realm—a realm impossible for us to reach in life, even while close to death. We may instead perceive a symbolic representation of this sphere of future existence because knowledge of it is already buried within the psyche.

By proposing this provocative model for understanding both eschatological visions and NDEs, Dr Zaleski is offering a conceptual model similar to the 'coded' experience paradigm first introduced in the mid-1970s. This theoretical model originally surfaced when scientific interest in the NDE first evolved, though a similar explanation had been put forward in the 1920s.

The 'coded' experience theory has been most prominently promoted by Czech psychiatrist Dr Stanislav Grof, who began studying transpersonal experiences in the 1960s. Basing his views on the research he conducted with psychedelic drugs both in Europe and in the United States (to which he emigrated in 1967), Dr Grof suggests that the NDE is an experience genetically coded into the brain. It remains there unperceived until it surfaces during unusual or stressful circumstances. The psychiatrist shows in his book *The Human Encounter with Death* (which he wrote with anthropologist Dr Joan Halifax) that NDE reports include features that crop up, disparately, within an entire range of unusual mental states. Features of the typical NDE can also be found in psychedelic drug experiences, during mystical or 'peak' experiences, and in popular mythology. Whether or not these coincidences point to a literal spiritual realm is left unresolved by Dr Grof.

While these interpretations of the near-death experience are provocative, there remains strong evidence that the true reason why eschatological narratives reported from the Middle Ages resemble modern NDEs so suspiciously is simpler. My feeling is that the early ecclesiastical writers *really were* basing their miracle stories on genuine NDE reports, as I've suggested earlier in the chapter.

As pointed out earlier, during these dark times the public was not generally educated. Most of the populace were illiterate and life was too hard for them to be concerned with intellectual pursuits. Only the scholars and churchmen were capable of making permanent records of any unusual experiences, such as accounts of psychic phenomena, that they might have to report. It isn't difficult to believe that upon hearing NDE accounts, these chroniclers exaggerated them for their own purposes. We even have some excellent evidence that the early Church scribes freely altered texts they were copying, especially if such changes could serve a good purpose. It is well known that early versions of the New Testament were 'revised' by well-meaning copyists, who liked to incorporate 'personal touches' into their work. This tendency to elaborate some biblical narratives can best be illustrated by placing those reports concerning Christ's resurrection in the chronological order in which they were written. The stories become more exaggerated with time, each rewriting more impressive than the preceding version. What was clearly a relatively simple event (if it really happened at all) became more complex the more it was transcribed.[3] Something similar could have happened when the Church Fathers first began recording NDE accounts reported by the common masses.

This general theory becomes more believable the more closely Christian eschatological literature from the seventh to the fifteenth century is examined. For deeply buried within these mythological and literary tales, some strikingly unadulterated NDE reports occasionally crop up. Probably the most impressive of these purportedly first-hand accounts examined by Dr Zaleski comes from Salvius, a holy man who lived in Gaul during the sixth century. Salvius began with a career in law but later became a monk. He lived the austere life of a hermit, but left this solitary life when he was made a bishop. He is best remembered today for his work with the poor. Salvius died in AD 584 while helping Gaul's plague victims, when he too contracted the disease.

Salvius' purported experience occurred close to the time when he became a bishop. After suffering from some undetermined sickness, he was taken for dead and spent the night on a funeral bier. When he revived from his pseudo-death, the following story was written down:

> Four days ago, when the cell shook, and you saw me lifeless, I was taken up by two angels and carried up to the height of heaven, and it was just as though I had beneath my feet not only this squalid earth, but also the sun and moon, the clouds and stars. Then I was brought through a gate that was brighter than our light, into a dwelling-place where the entire floor shone like gold and silver; there was an ineffable light and it was indescribably vast.

Salvius was enjoying the delights of heaven, with its wonderful perfumes, when a spiritual presence interrupted him. It manifested in the form of a disembodied voice saying, 'Send this man back to the world, since he is necessary to our church.' This command is very similar to what we read in many reports published today, in which the percipient is told to return because his/her work is not yet finished. This difference between Salvius' ex-

---

[3]For more information on this subject, refer to *Death and Eternal Life* by John H. Hick (San Francisco: Harper & Row, 1976).

perience and more modern reports illustrates how minor cultural influences are found in NDE reports—perhaps similar to the way in which Er in Plato's *Republic* sees the souls of the departed choosing their next incarnations.

The sixth-century monk ends his brief but remarkable report by bitterly complaining:

> Alas, alas, Lord, why have you shown me these things, if I was to be cheated of them? Behold! Today you are casting me out from your face, to return to the perishable world, so that in the end I won't have the power to come back here.

With such testimony on record, it's hard not to believe that real and impressive NDE reports had been placed on file by the Church before the eighth century. Reports such as these could easily have served as the basis of much eschatological literature. Even Dr Zaleski herself, while rejecting the notion that NDEs are objectively real events, comments in her book that it's difficult to separate early NDE-like reports from their religious and literary trappings.

The sceptic will, of course, still suggest that this entire issue resolves into a sort of chicken/egg paradox: did NDE reports give rise to eschatological traditions within the Church, or did these literary traditions give rise to NDE stories? Can this issue really ever be resolved?

Because experiences like that of Salvius date back to early Church history, probably around the seventh century, it seems to me that NDE-like narratives predate the rise of much Christian eschatological literature. Note how many features of Salvius' experience, taken separately, appear in modern NDE reports. (The reader may wish to refer to Tables II and III above and compare them with the monk's experience.) It seems obvious that the eschatological vision of the Middle Ages was, in fact, a traditional NDE over which a religious framework was placed. Note that each and every difference between the present-day NDE and the medieval eschatological vision speaks to specifically Christian concerns. These ingredients were probably invented to give early NDE accounts more religious 'punch'. If Salvius or his chronicler had been illiterate, who knows what form his experience would have taken when transcribed by his fellow churchmen.

Remember, though, that this point only demonstrates the experiential reality and consistency of NDE reports through the ages. Such a discovery has little bearing on the specific on-tological nature of such encounters. That is an issue to which we'll return later in the book.

3.

NDEs Through the Ages:
II. *Secular Reports*

During the Middle Ages, the study of the paranormal or super-natural fell under the aegis of the Church. It was the responsibility of the ecclesiastical establishment to decide if a person's psychic or visionary experiences were sacred, demonic, or delusional. The notion that such experiences could be natural human potentials played little role in early religious thought. But this limited attitude towards the paranormal would change by the early eighteenth century, when Prospero Lambertini wrote his *De Canonizatione*. Lambertini, who later became Pope Benedict XIV, was fascinated by the miraculous and wrote his treatise to guide the Church in its endeavour to evaluate these holy events. He was the first to consider seriously the possibility that some psychic experiences were neither sacred nor demonic, but the result of natural faculties in mankind. The writing of his *De Canonizatione* represents the first important 'secularization' of psychic experiences. Gradually the study of the paranormal became an intellectual pursuit rather than a purely religious one.

It would be nearly impossible to trace the NDE through secular history. The earliest collection of such reports was probably made by Dom Augustin Calmet, a Benedictine of the congregation of Saint-Vannes, who died in 1757. Calmet was enthralled by the psychic world and collected reports of apparitions, both good and evil, and other supernatural visitations. In his two-volume work *The Phantom World*, he reports on several 'return from death' stories. Some of them read surprisingly like present-day NDE narratives. Moving ahead several decades, we find that NDE reports also played a role in the Church of Jesus Christ of the Latter-Day Saints in the United States during the nineteenth century. The early Mormons were certainly aware of NDE phenomenology and used such accounts to bolster their religious convictions. These early views and cases were recently extracted from Mormon literature by Dr Craig R. Lundahl (from Western New Mexico University) and Harold A. Widdison (from Northern Arizona University), who published a paper on the subject which appeared in *Anabiosis—the Journal for Near-Death Studies* in 1983.

Mormon cosmology begins with the assumption that mankind possesses two bodies: a physical form which plays host to an incorporeal spirit, capable of leaving the body when death occurs. This concept of the spirit body is similar to the Spiritualist and theosophical doctrine of the 'astral' body. According to nineteenth century Mormon teachings, the spirit realm is also similar to that of the Spiritualists: the beautiful realm so often reported by people who have NDEs:

> [this spirit world] is here on the very planet where we are born; or in other words, the earth and other planets of like sphere have their inward or spiritual spheres, as well as their outward, or temporal. The one is peopled by temporal tabernacles, and the other by spirits, A veil is drawn between the one sphere and the other, whereby all the objects in the spiritual sphere are rendered invisible to those in the temporal.

Drs Lundahl and Widdison explain further that in Mormon belief 'the world of the spirits is so glorious in comparison to ours that no words exist in any language to describe it'.

Despite the plethora of references the two scholars found in early Mormon literature, they do not report many first-hand NDE testimonies in their paper. They report only one—an experience reported by a man named Jedediah M. Grant, who told it to early Church leader Heber C. Kimball. The experience probably took place towards the end of the nineteenth century. Kimball reports how his friend first came to him:

> He said to me, Brother Heber, I have been into the spirit world two nights in succession, and of all the dreads that ever came across me, the worst was to have to return to my body, though I had to do it.

During the episode itself, Grant had the typical experience of seeing his deceased friends and relatives:

> He saw his wife, she was the first person that came to him. He saw many that he knew, but did not have conversation with any but his

wife Caroline. She came to him, and he said that she looked beautiful and had their little child, that died on the plains, in her arms, and said, 'Mr. Grant, here is little Margaret; you know that the wolves ate her up; but it did not hurt her, here she is all right.'

Like the previous studies of Augustin Calmet, it seems that the early Mormon leaders preferred to use secular testimony to support their own religious doctrines. This is a tendency that has lasted up to today, where NDE reports have been used to 'validate' everything from Fundamentalist Christianity to New Age spirituality—strange bed (or deathbed) fellows, indeed!

The rise of the psychical research tradition
The rise of scientific interest in the NDE can be traced back to the close of the nineteenth century. The Victorian era was a rapidly changing culture that threatened to undermine the Christian religious *status quo*. This *status quo* had guided European culture for many centuries. With the rise of science and industry, European society began to seek answers to its problems in discovery, not religion. This secularization process was further fired by the publication of Charles Darwin's *The Origin of Species by Means of Natural Selection* in 1859 and later by his *The Descent of Man*. These classics offered a self-consistent theory of mankind's evolution without recourse to religious dogma. Darwin's findings ushered in Victorian materialism, and society turned from the religious outlook which many people now found irrelevant to their everyday concerns. It didn't help much either when 'form criticism' was introduced in Germany which showed that it was impossible to take the Bible literally.

These brief remarks only summarize the great upheaval of society that upset the Christian establishment in the nineteenth century. These decades represented the beginnings of the secular society, from which modern American culture grew and matured.

Because of these cultural changes, it wasn't surprising that counter-movements to this secularization soon evolved. The most notable took place in the United States and especially on the East Coast, where many novel religious movements sprang up. Spiritualism, Mormonism, and Seventh-Day Adventism were the best-known of these sects, whose power lay in their emphasis on personal spiritual experience instead of blind dogma. Great Britain was not immune to these influences either. The birth of the Spiritualist movement in 1848 in the United States brought widespread public attention to the existence of psychic phenomena. Poltergeists, table-turning seances, and phantasms of the dead were just a few of the experiences people began to report publicly. These accounts eventually came to the notice of several British scholars, most of whom were educated at Cambridge University. These scholars joined forces with several Spiritualist leaders in the hope that, by studying such stories, they could re-establish a spiritual model for mankind. While not explicitly stating their goal in these terms, the first psychical researchers wanted to use the possible existence of psi[1] to support a primarily Christian view of the world. They eventually founded the Society for Psychical Research in 1882, and a branch was later organized in the United States.

The Society for Psychical Research soon gained a reputation for its fierce dedication to intellectual honesty and for the rigorous (and sceptical) way it investigated reports of psychic phenomena. The primary founders of the movement in England were Professor Henry Sidgwick, a philosopher from Cambridge University, and his student F.W.H. Myers, an educator and scholar in his own right. They were joined in their work by Edmund Gurney and Frank Podmore, lesser scholars who enthusiastically committed themselves to the SPR's work. The movement's guiding light in the United States was William James, the revered philosopher-psychologist from Harvard University.

While interested in the problems of religion, the leaders of the psychical research movement were not biased by their religious backgrounds. They set themselves up primarily as investigators, for before drawing any far-reaching conclusions from their studies they first had to scientifically demonstrate that psychic phenomena even existed! So they began by focusing on the experimental study of telepathy and collecting accounts of personal psychic experiences from the general public. Many of these accounts pointed to the possible existence of an afterlife, so they studied those reports especially closely to see what conclusions could be drawn from them. (This general subject later became known as survival research.) The researchers were primarily in-

[1] 'Psi' is a shorthand term for psychic phenomena widely used in parapsychology today.

terested in reports of crisis and post-mortem apparitions—i.e. phantoms resembling dead or dying people simultaneously seen miles away by their friends or relatives. But the more cases they collected, the more they widened the scope of their investigations. Soon they were studying several gifted psychics they had discovered both in England and in the United States.

Early research on deathbed vision cases

The first psychical researchers were also interested in the experiences of the dying, and paid special attention to the visions they sometimes reported. Deathbed visions do not represent NDEs as such, and they should be considered a separate order of phenomenon. (Many writers today tend to lump NDEs and deathbed visions together, which has contributed to the semantic confusion I discussed in the first chapter.) Deathbed visions can be defined as *those unusual perceptions sometimes reported by the dying that explicitly point to survival.* Most commonly, the dying person will 'see' his deceased friends or relatives by his bedside coming to 'take' him away. Deathbed visions are different from the classic NDE in two major respects:

1. The dying patient is usually lucid when making the observation and doesn't make the report upon recovering from pseudo-death.
2. The vision takes place while the witness's consciousness remains 'inside' the body.

Deathbed visions are similar to the classic NDE, however, since they share some of its characteristics:

1. The patients often see their deceased friends, relatives, or spiritual guides coming to greet them.
2. The patient may glimpse the realm of the afterlife. While not experiencing a literal otherworld journey, sometimes the dying see panoramic scenes of great beauty.

There is also a third difference between NDEs and deathbed experiences, even though it's a provisional one. People who experience deathbed visions usually see these figures welcoming them *into* the afterlife. Of course, this could be a false difference, since we don't know whether some people momentarily 'dead' don't get sent back and decide to stay on the other side for good!

But just why should we be interested in these visions if they don't represent true NDEs?

My answer is that we cannot separate the study of the NDE from related death phenomena. The primary issue raised by the NDE is whether such experiences prove the existence of an afterlife. We can't confront this question without studying other related forms of psychic experiences that either bear on it or resemble it. Any conceptual model we formulate to explain the NDE should also be capable of explaining deathbed visions. So for the next several pages let's examine this second subject before returning to the main study of the NDE.

Even before the rise of nineteenth century psychical research, stories of deathbed visions had come to the public's attention, and the first booklet reporting such a case was published in 1864. The pamphlet was entitled *Daisy Dryden—A memoire by Mrs. S.H. Dryden* and was privately printed in California. The report constituted a detailed look at several deathbed visions experienced by little Daisy and recorded by her parents.

Daisy Irene Dryden was born in Marysville, California, on 1 September 1854 and died in San José when she was 10 years old. She was the daughter of a Methodist missionary and her experiences began when she was convalescing from a fever. She seemed to be improving when she entered what appeared to be a trance. Her father was by her bedside. Since her wide eyes were staring into space, her father asked her what she was seeing. The young girl replied, 'It's a spirit. It is Jesus. He says I am going to be one of His little lambs.' Since her father spoke approvingly of the visitation, Daisy explained gleefully that she was soon to die and would join the welcomer.

This vision heralded four days during which Daisy constantly saw visions before her eventual death from enteritis. She suffered terribly, since she couldn't take food or water. But during those days she sometimes became extremely lucid, and when these episodes occurred she would speak of her otherworldly glimpses. It seemed that her illness opened the curtains between this world and the beyond. It is also interesting, in retrospect, that her description of the afterlife didn't conform to the Sunday school depiction she probably knew. Two days before she died, in fact, the superintendent of her Sunday school came to see her while she was enjoying a lucid period. As he was leaving, he turned to her and said, 'Well, Daisy; you will soon be over the dark river,' obviously referring to her imminent death.[2] Daisy appeared puzzled by the reference.

'There is no river,' she replied, 'there is no curtain, there is not even a line that separates this life from the other life.'

She then stretched out her hand and said, 'It is here and it is there; I know it is so, for I can see you all, and see them there at the same time.'

Later when a neighbour came to visit, Daisy welcomed her and saw the apparition of her deceased son from whom she delivered a message. She also heard wondrous music, similar to the 'music of the spheres' sometimes reported by NDErs. She specifically saw angelic beings by her bedside, which surprised her since they didn't sport wings and looked like everybody else. (Note again that this isn't the type of remark to be expected from a child hallucinating on the basis of prior religious upbringing.) Mrs Dryden also recorded the appearance of her deceased son, who had died from scarlet fever seven months previously:

> I was sitting beside her bed, her hand clasped in mine. Looking up so wistfully at me, she said, 'Dear Momma, I do wish you could see Allie; he's standing beside you.' Involuntarily I looked around, but Daisy thereupon continued, 'He says you cannot see him because your spirit eyes are closed, but that I can, because my body only holds my spirit, as it were, by a thread of life.' Then I inquired, 'Does he say that now?' 'Yes, just now,' she answered. Then wondering how she could be conversing with her brother when I saw not the least sign of conversation, I said, 'Daisy, how do you speak to Allie? I do not hear you or see your lips move.' She smilingly replied, 'We just talk with our think.' I then asked her further, 'Daisy, how does Allie appear to you? Does he seem to wear clothes?' She answered, 'Oh, no, not clothes such as we wear. There seems to be about him a white, beautiful something, so fine and thin and glistening, and oh, so white, and yet there is not a fold, or a sign of a thread in it, so it cannot be cloth. But it makes him look so lovely.' Her father then quoted from the Psalmist: 'He is clothed with light as a garment.' 'Oh yes, that's it,' she replied.

Daisy greeted her death with pure joy since she had nothing to

---

[2] This may sound like a terrible thing to say to a child, but remember that death was an integral part of nineteenth century life. Certainly it was much more familiar to children then than it is in our contemporary culture. Children also seem to know when they are dying and have little problem openly discussing it. For more information on this subject, the reader might like to consult *On Children and Death* by Dr Elisabeth Kübler-Ross (New York: Macmillan, 1983).

fear from it. She merely waited, snuggled up against her father's shoulder, for her brother to take her away. She died peacefully and painlessly.

Mrs Dryden ends her narrative with the uplifting yet poignant statement, 'There was a solemn stillness in the room. We would not weep, and why should we?'

Despite scattered reports such as the Dryden case, the first systematic case collection of such experiences was made by Frances Power Cobbe in an essay she included in her book *Peak in Darien—With Some Enquiries Touching Concerns of the Soul and Body*. The book originally appeared in 1882, although the essay from which the title was derived was published earlier. Miss Cobbe's report on deathbed visions entails only 22 pages of the book, but it is the only section that is remembered today. (The other chapters deal with popular social issues of the times.) The writer collected several cases in which the dying saw welcoming figures at their bedsides or in their sick rooms. Miss Cobbe was probably the first student of the subject to notice something quite extraordinary about some of these incidents. Sometimes the dying reported seeing deceased friends or relatives they *didn't previously know were dead*. It wasn't unusual for her witnesses to see people who had only recently died, and sometimes this information had been deliberately kept from them. Miss Cobbe realized that simple hallucinations could not explain these special cases, which she called 'Peak-in-Darien' cases after the lines in John Keats's poem 'On First Looking into Chapman's Homer' which describe the wonder Cortez felt upon first catching sight of the Pacific Ocean, similar to the surprise the dying feel upon glimpsing the afterlife.

Despite the historical importance of her brief study, the standards of evidence Miss Cobbe employed in her essay were hardly critical. She even neglected to provide her readers with specific names, dates, or any supporting testimony. Even though the study was terribly flawed, it did spark the interest of several early psychical researchers, who began ferreting out similar cases and publishing the better examples—especially those falling into the Peak-in-Darien category. Some of these cases were published in the official periodicals of the Society for Psychical Research.

Perhaps the most classic of these cases was originally collected by the Rev. Minot J. Savage, a Unitarian minister in Boston who wrote extensively on psychical research in the 1890s and early

1900s. He not only collected reports of psychic phenomena but also investigated them. The following case concerned two childhood playmates who contracted diphtheria in 1889:

> In a neighbouring city were two little girls, Jennie and Edith, one about eight years of age and the other but a little older. They were schoolmates and intimate friends. In June, 1889, both were taken ill of diphtheria. At noon on Wednesday Jennie died. Then the parents of Edith, and her physician as well, took particular pains to keep from her the fact that her little playmate was gone. They feared the effect of the knowledge on her own condition. To prove that they succeeded and that she did not know, it may be mentioned that on Saturday, June 8th, at noon, just before she became unconscious of all that was passing about her, she selected two of her photographs to be sent to Jennie, and also told her attendants to bid her good-bye.
>
> She died at half-past six o'clock on the evening of Saturday, June 8th. She had roused and bidden her friends good-bye, and was talking of dying, and seemed to have no fear. She appeared to see one and another of the friends she knew were dead. So far it was like other similar cases. But now suddenly, and with every appearance of surprise, she turned to her father and exclaimed, 'Why, papa, I am going to take Jennie with me!' Then she added, 'Why papa! you did not tell me that Jennie was here!' And immediately she reached out her arms as if in welcome, and said, 'Oh, Jennie, I'm so glad you are here!'

Nor was this impressive case undocumented, for the Rev. Mr Savage placed the pertinent names and those of the witnesses on file with his colleague, Professor James H. Hyslop. Professor Hyslop was a faculty member at Columbia University, a position he dropped when he later reorganized and breathed new life into the American Society for Psychical Research in 1907.

It was, in fact, Professor Hyslop who first tried to make a comprehensive study of these curious deathbed vision cases, which led him to write his celebrated paper 'Visions of the Dying' in 1907. This paper first appeared in the Journal of the recently restructured American Society for Psychical Research, and it was later incorporated into his book *Psychical Research and the Resurrection*. The indefatigable researcher was not, however, content merely to recount these provocative experiences. He wanted to make some parapsychological sense out of them by determining their relationship (if any) to purely hallucinatory experiences. The ex-Columbia University philosopher eventually concluded that deathbed visions were not true hallucinations but objectively real occurrences perceived by the dying. Like so many other researchers both before and after him, Dr Hyslop was ultimately drawn to Peak-in-Darien cases because of their obvious importance.

It is unfortunate that Professor Hyslop never achieved his goal of comparing deathbed cases to obviously pathological visions. He finished his research by simply urging the psychical investigators of his day to be more actively involved with the study of hallucinatory experiences in general. He specifically suggested that physicians and nurses be on the lookout for deathbed cases, and urged the Society for Psychical Research to conduct a survey on the subject. Professor Hyslop was also the first scholar to realize that his colleagues should be collecting all types of deathbed experiences—whether or not they seemed to be the product of genuine psi or just brain intoxication. It is also interesting that, perhaps prophetically, the professor proposed that his colleagues study what people report when they recover from close calls with death.

It is unfortunate that it took the parapsychological community some 50 years before following up on these recommendations.

While the insightful researcher never claimed in his paper that deathbed visions proved the soul's survival, his bias was clearly in that direction. This was the inclination he shared in common with both Frances P. Cobbe and Rev. Minot J. Savage. It is rather strange that his conclusions were so conservative, for by 1907 he was an ardent believer in survival. (This belief was due primarily to his earlier research with trance mediums, and he doggedly supported the survival theory for the rest of his life.) But later on he pointed to these deathbed experiences as the key evidence in the case for survival. When he issued his last book, *Contact with the Other World*, in 1919, he wrote that such cases 'deserve a first place among spontaneous incidents in favor of survival'.

Not everyone shared Hyslop's obvious enthusiasm for such cases, however, and both the psychical research community and the medical establishment offered non-survivalistic theories for them. Some years before Hyslop's seminal work was published, for instance, Dr Edward H. Clarke, a physician in the United States, had published his study *Visions: A Study of False Sight*. Twenty pages of the book were devoted to deathbed visions which Clarke suggested were probably the result of brain dysfunction. His primary thesis was that such visions were merely projected daydreams, though he considered it possible that future research might prove him wrong.

While Dr Clarke was grappling with the meaning of such experiences in the United States, similar consideration was being given to the subject in Europe. Charles Richet was then France's leading psychical researcher, as well as a Nobel Prize-winning physiologist. While the French scientist believed in the existence of psychic phenomena, he never came to believe in the soul's survival. But despite this bias, Richet had to admit that deathbed vision cases constituted strong evidence not only for survival, but even for spirit return. The subject does not figure largely in his writings, but in 1905 he respectfully submitted that:

> Facts such as this kind are very important. They are much more explicable on the spiritistic theory than by the hypothesis of mere cryptesthesia. Among all the facts adduced to prove survival, these seem to me to be the most disquieting (i.e., from a materialistic point of view). I have therefore thought it a duty to be scrupulous in mentioning them.

These candid remarks were published in Richet's celebrated book *Thirty Years of Psychical Research*, in which he betrays his obvious ambivalence towards such reports. For after making these favourable remarks, he goes on to ignore such cases for the greater part of his book and never again mentions their importance.

Charles Richet wasn't the only researcher who rejected the notion that deathbed visions proved survival. One popular counter-explanation offered in these early years was that the dying really did hallucinate 'take away' figures. But those researchers promoting this theory suggested that the dying sometimes use extrasensory perception to reinforce the hallucination. When these welcoming figures are produced by the unconscious mind, they suggested, perhaps the psyche simultaneously uses ESP to learn if anyone important to the patient has recently died.

This theory was both practical and ingenious but it didn't remain unchallenged for long. Other researchers suggested that, if the delusion/hallucination theory were correct, the dying patient should more commonly see the living and not the dead. But it seems to me that the issue is rather moot. We simply don't know enough about the psychology of dying to second-guess the process, even today.

The research of Sir William Barrett

The most significant contribution to the study of deathbed visions in these early years was made by Sir William Barrett. Barrett had begun his career in physics and taught for several years at the University of Belfast. Spiritualism was all the rage during his tenure, and he gradually became interested both in the religion and in extrasensory perception. It was Barrett who first suggested that the Society for Psychical Research should be formed, and he is often considered one of the organization's founders. Later in his life his interests began to focus more on the survival question and less on telepathy, and shortly before his death, he embarked on a special study of deathbed visions. It is most unfortunate that he never completed his study, and his book on the subject was left unfinished when he died in 1925. While he never completed his theoretical discussion on these cases, the rest of the manuscript was published the following year. *Death-bed Visions* is primarily a collection of unusual reports and little more, but the collection is impressive for its scope and for the way it successfully synthesizes a large body of literature. *Death-bed Visions* isn't a classic in what it says about these reports; it is a great book because of the framework in which they are placed. So before continuing with this historical review, let's examine Barrett's study in more detail.

Death-bed Visions is divided into five chapters, each one devoted to a specific type of deathbed experience. The first chapter concerns Peak-in-Darien cases, the most impressive being reported by Barrett's own wife, who was a physician. Lady Barrett had witnessed the incident while one of her patients was dying in childbirth. The setting was Mothers' Hospital, in Clapham, London, and the date was 12 January 1924. The woman couldn't be saved but she died peacefully, thanks to a remarkable vision she experienced right before the end. The following statement was provided to the Barretts by the hospital matron:

> I was present shortly before the death of Mrs. B., together with her husband and her mother. Her husband was leaning over her and speaking to her, when pushing him aside she said, 'oh, don't hide it; it's so beautiful.' Then turning away from him towards me, I being on the other side of the bed, Mrs. B. said, 'oh, why there's Vida,' referring to a sister of whose death three weeks previously she had not been told. Afterwards the mother, who was present at the time, told me, as

I have said, that Vida was the name of a dead sister of Mrs. B.'s, of whose illness and death she was quite ignorant, as they had carefully kept this news from Mrs. B. owing to her serious illness.

This brief report was corroborated by the more detailed testimony of the patient's mother, who wrote to Sir William Barrett as follows:

I have heard you are interested in the beautiful passing of my dear daughter's spirit from this earth on the 12 day of January, 1924.

The wonderful part of it is the history of the death of my dear daughter, Vida, who had been an invalid some years. Her death took place on the 25th day of Dec., 1923, just 2 weeks and 4 days before her younger sister, Doris, died. My daughter Doris, Mrs. B., was very ill at that time, and the Matron at the Mothers' Hospital deemed it unwise for Mrs. B. to know of her sister's death. Therefore when visiting her we put off our mourning and visited her as usual. All her letters were also kept by request until her husband had seen who they might be from before letting her see them. This precaution was taken lest outside friends might possibly allude to the recent bereavement in writing to her, unaware of the very dangerous state of her health.

When my dear child was sinking rapidly, at first she said, 'It is all so dark; I cannot see.' A few seconds later a beautiful radiance lit up her countenance; I know now it was the light of Heaven, and it was most beautiful to behold. My dear child said, 'Oh it is lovely and bright, you cannot see as I can.' She fixed her eyes on one particular spot in the ward, saying, 'Oh, God, forgive me for anything I have done wrong.' After that she said, 'I can see father; he wants me, he is so lonely.' She spoke to her father, saying, 'I am coming,' turning at the same time to look at me, saying, 'Oh, he is so near.' On looking at the same place again, she said with rather a puzzled expression, 'He has Vida with him, turning again to me saying, 'Vida is with him.' Then she said, 'You do want me, Dad; I am coming.' Then a very few parting words or sighs were expressed—nothing very definite or clear. With great difficulty and a very hard strain she asked to see 'the man who married us'; this was to her husband, who was standing on the opposite side of the bed. His name she could not say; it was the Rev. Maurice Davis, of All Saints, Haggerston, E., and he was sent for. He had known my dear child for some years, and was so impressed by the vision that he quoted it in his 'Parish Magazine' for February last.

It is tempting to suggest that these experiences represent the opposite side of the classic NDE, during which the patient encounters similar guides while out-of-body. Perhaps these guides are summoned when a person is dying, which might explain their habit of appearing in hospital rooms or at bedsides. When a person merely experiences clinical or pseudo-death, perhaps this 'call' doesn't occur, which is why the percipients travel to the otherworld before meeting them—only to be ordered back to earth!

Of course, this is a blatantly survivalistic interpretation of both the NDE and deathbed visions, but it seems appropriate to mention the possibility.

The second chapter of Sir William Barrett's study is less interesting and concerns 'Visions Seen by the Dying of Persons Known by Them to be Dead and Deathbed Visions Seen by Others'. The most interesting section of the chapter regards rare observations sometimes made by the patients' friends. We know that the dying see spiritual guides coming to take them into death, but what if people visiting the dying also see these radiant phantoms? While such cases are rarely recorded today, Barrett found a few of them in which this claim was made and incorporated them into his short book. The following well-documented case, for example, was published by the Society for Psychical Research in 1889. It is extremely evidential since three people saw the figure. The primary testimony was given by the patient's niece:

> My aunt, Miss Harriet Pearson, who was taken very ill at Brighton in November, 1864, craved to be back in her own home in London, where she and her sister Ann (who had died some years previously) had spent practically all their lives. I accordingly made the necessary arrangements, and had her moved home. Her two nieces (Mrs. Coppinger and Mrs. John Pearson), Eliza Quinton the housekeeper, and myself did the nursing between us. She became worse and worse. On the night of Dec 23rd Mrs. John Pearson was sitting up with her, while Mrs. Coppinger and I lay down in the adjoining room, leaving the door ajar to hear any sound from the next room. We were neither of us asleep, and suddenly we both started up in bed, as we saw someone pass the door, wrapped up in an old shawl, having a wig with three curls each side, and an old black cap. Mrs. Coppinger called to me, 'Emma, get up, it is old Aunt Ann!' I said, 'So it is; then Aunt Harriet will die to-day!' As we jumped up, Mrs. John Pearson came rushing out of Aunt Harriet's room saying, 'That was old Aunt Ann. Where has she gone?' I said to soothe her, 'Perhaps it was Eliza come down to see how her old mistress is.' Mrs. Coppinger ran upstairs and found Eliza asleep. Every room was searched—no one was there;

and from that day to this no explanation has ever been given of this appearance, except that it was old Aunt Ann come to call her sister. Aunt Harriet died at 6 p.m. that day.

The way this sighting relates to the study of deathbed visions is clearer from the housekeeper's testimony:

We searched in every room but could not find anyone in the house. Miss Harriet died on the evening of that day, but before that she told us all that she had seen her sister, and that she had come to call her.

If these cases can withstand critical scrutiny, they will be of considerable importance to our understanding of both NDEs and deathbed visions. They propose that the spiritual guides and figures seen by the dying have some sort of objective existence. The sceptic might suggest that the witnesses 'picked up' on the dying patient's hallucination by extrasensory perception, and subsequently 'saw' it for themselves. But this theory fails to explain why the witnesses saw the same figure carrying out the same manoeuvres. Nor can it explain why they saw the figure before the patient did.

The last three chapters of *Death-bed Visions* concern several experiences loosely related to deathbed visions—i.e. visions seen of people still living, reports of the 'music' heard by the dying, and the claims of people who clairvoyantly 'saw' the soul taking flight.

Probably the most interesting chapter pertains to the strange subject of deathbed music. People undergoing classic NDEs and patients close to death often report hearing beautiful music. Sir William Barrett collected several accounts where the dying person's visitors also heard this music. Once again, these reports tend to be rare, and it isn't easy to evaluate them. But they suggest that some of the characteristics of both the NDE and deathbed visions represent some sort of objective reality. The first reports of this strange phenomenon were collected by the founders of the Society for Psychical Research. When Edmund Gurney and his colleagues prepared their first spontaneous case study for publication in 1886, they included the experience of a Mrs L., who had died in 1881. Several friends had gathered at her bedside shortly before the end. With the exception of the patient's son, each of the visitors heard the strange music. The following is the report of the chief witness, a close friend of the dying patient. It was given to Edmund Gurney on 28 July 1881 when the events were probably still reasonably fresh in her mind:

> Just after dear Mrs. L.'s death between 2 and 3 a.m., I heard a most
> sweet and singular strain of singing outside the windows; it died
> away after passing the house. All in the room [except Mr. L.] heard
> it, and the medical attendant, who was still with us, went to the win-
> dow, as I did, and looked out, but there was nobody. It was a bright
> and beautiful night. It was as if several voices were singing in perfect
> unison a most sweet melody which died away in the distance. Two
> persons had gone from the room to fetch something and were com-
> ing upstairs *at the back of the house* and heard the singing and stop-
> ped, saying, 'What is that singing?' They could not, *naturally*, have
> heard any sound from outside the windows in the front of the house
> from where they were at the back.

This testimony was corroborated by the patient's physician, who
also heard the music though in a different form:

> I remember the circumstances perfectly. I was sent for about mid-
> night, and remained with Mrs. L. until her death about 2.30 a.m.
> Shortly after we heard a few bars of lovely music, not unlike that
> from an aeolian harp—and it filled the air for a few seconds. I went
> to the window and looked out, thinking there must be someone out-
> side, but could see no one though it was quite light and clear.
> Strangely enough, those outside the room heard the same sounds, as
> they were coming upstairs quite at the other side of the door [house].

The fact that the patient's son didn't hear the music implies
that the sounds weren't from the street, but represented some
form of psychic process. Other people have occasionally heard
this type of music right in the patient's room. Several of these
cases were published by Ernesto Bozzano, an Italian student of
the paranormal, in 1923. (Bozzano was also fascinated by
deathbed reports and wrote extensively on the subject, but little
of his work has been translated into English.)

Even though experiences such as these don't seem to be
reported in today's more sophisticated times, I don't think we
can simply dismiss them. There may be two reasons for the lack
of similar contemporary accounts:

1. Dying was a much more intimate matter towards the end of
   the nineteenth century. Between 70 and 80 per cent of the
   general public now die in the clinical surroundings of a
   hospital. Back in Victorian times people tended to die in their
   homes, making the transition in the company of their friends

and family. Perhaps this more relaxed setting is better for giving rise to remarkable psychic phenomena banned by the impersonal conditions of a medical facility.

2. Cases of deathbed music may simply not get reported because few researchers look for them. I think this is a real possibility. I began searching for such cases myself in 1968. After writing letters to two popular psychic publications, several people wrote to me of their experiences with this music. (My original letters merely stated my interest in the subject and requested readers to contact me if they had ever experienced the phenomenon.) Some of these reports were similar to those originally collected by Barrett and a few other researchers.[3]

Despite the posthumous publication of Barrett's *Death-bed Visions*, the study of these cases never really caught on within psychical research, and it wasn't untill the 1960s that further work on the subject was undertaken.

Research on pseudo-death experiences
Even though many early psychical researchers were fascinated by deathbed reports, few of them were correspondingly interested in pseudo-death experiences. While scattered reports of more typical out-of-body experiences were published by the Society of Psychical Research, they were never studied in much depth. Two of these cases, however, exemplify what would today be considered simple NDEs.

The first of these cases was reported by Dr A. Wiltse, a physician from Skiddy, Kansas, who published it in 1889 in the *St. Louis Medical and Surgical Journal*. The Society for Psychical Research took an interest in the case and republished it in 1892 with depositions from the primary witnesses. Dr Wiltse's report is so long that it can only be summarized in this chapter. The NDE occurred when the physician contracted typhoid fever. He knew he was dying and even said goodbye to his family before entering a coma. It was during this 'unconscious' period that the incident took place. Everybody at his bedside thought he was

[3]I reported these cases in two of my previous books, *NAD: A Study of Some Unusual 'Other-World' Experiences*, and *NAD, Vol. 2: A Psychic Study of the 'Music of the Spheres.'* (Both books were published, in 1970 and 1972 respectively, by University Books.)

dead; even the physician-in-attendance concurred when a needle jab into Wiltse's body failed to evoke a response. Dr Wiltse reports that he blacked out only to find himself cataleptic but lucid. He was fascinated by the state, which resolved into a typical out-of-body experience:

I came again into a state of conscious existence and discovered that I was still in the body, but the body and I had no longer any interests in common. I looked in astonishment and joy for the first time upon myself—the me, the real Ego, while the not me closed in upon all sides like a sepulchre of clay.

With all the interest of a physician, I beheld the wonders of my bodily anatomy, intimately interwoven with which, even tissue for tissue, was I, the living soul of that dead body. I learned that the epidermis was the outside boundary of the ultimate tissues, so to speak, of the soul. I realized my condition and reasoned calmly thus. I have died, as men term death, and yet I am as much a man as ever. I am about to get out of the body. I watched the interesting process of the separation of soul and body. By some power, apparently not my own, the Ego was rocked to and fro, laterally, as a cradle is rocked, by which process its connection with the tissues of the body was broken up. After a little time the lateral motion ceased, and along the soles of the feet beginning at the toes, passing rapidly to the heels, I felt and heard, as it seemed, the snapping of innumerable small cords. When this was accomplished I began slowly to retreat from the feet, toward the head, as a rubber cord shortens. I remember reaching the hips and saying to myself, 'Now, there is no life below the hips.' I can recall no memory of passing through the abdomen and chest, but recollect distinctly when my whole self was collected into the head, when I reflected thus: I am all in the head now, and I shall soon be free. I passed around the brain as if I were hollow, compressing it and its membranes, slightly, on all sides, toward the center and peeped out between the sutures of the skull, emerging like the flattened edges of a bag of membranes. I recollect distinctly how I appeared to myself something like a jelly-fish as regards to color and form. As I emerged, I saw two ladies sitting by my head. I measured the distances between the head of my cot and the knees of the lady opposite the head and concluded there was room for me to stand, but felt considerable embarrassment as I reflected that I was about to emerge naked before her, but comforted myself with the thought that in all probability she could not see me with her bodily eyes, as I was a spirit. As I emerged from the head I floated up and down laterally like a soap-bubble attached to the bowl of a pipe until I at last broke loose from the body and fell lightly to the floor, where

I slowly rose and expanded into the full stature of a man. I seemed to be translucent, of a bluish cast and perfectly naked. With a painful sense of embarrassment I fled toward the partially opened door to escape the eyes of two ladies whom I was facing as well as others who I knew were about me, but upon reaching the door I found myself clothed, and satisfied upon that point I turned and faced the company. As I turned, my left elbow came in contact with the arm of one of two gentlemen who were standing in the door. To my surprise, his arm passed through mine without apparent resistance, the severed parts closing again without pain, as air reunites. I looked quickly up at his face to see if he had noticed the contact, but he gave me no sign, only stood and gazed toward the couch I had just left. I directed my gaze in the directon of his, and saw my own dead body. I was lying just as I had taken so much pains to place it, partially upon the right side, the feet close together and the hands clasped across the breast. I was surprised at the paleness of the face. I had not looked in a glass for some days and had imagined that I was not as pale as most very sick people are. I congratulated myself upon the decency with which I had composed the body and thought my friends would have little trouble on that score.

The physician could see several of his friends standing by his body, especially two women weeping and kneeling by his side. Dr Wiltse stated, 'I have since learnt that they are my wife and my sister, but I had no conception of individuality.' He tried to gain the attention of the bystanders, but failed. Both confused and a little annoyed, he simply left the room and the house. Next he walked down the street while taking careful note of everything he saw. The subsequent phase of his out-of-body experience seemed to be an incipient otherworld journey, for he explains:

Suddenly I saw at some distance ahead of me three prodigious rocks blocking the road, at which sight I stopped wondering why so fair a road should be thus blockaded, and while I considered what to do, a great and dark cloud, which I compared to a cubic acre in size, stood over my head. Quickly it became filled with living, moving bolts of fire, which darted hither and thither through the cloud. They were not extinguished by contact with the cloud. I could see them as one sees fish in deep water.

I was aware of a presence, which I could not see, but which I knew was entering into the cloud from the southern side. The presence did not seem, to my mind, as a form, because it filled the cloud like some vast intelligence ... Then from the right side and from the left of the cloud a tongue of black vapor shot forth and rested lightly upon either side of my head, and as they touched me thoughts not my own entered into my brain.

These, I said, are his thoughts and not mine; they might be in Greek or Hebrew for all power I have over them. But how kindly am I addressed in my mother tongue that so I may understand all his will.

Yet, although the language was English, it was so eminently above my power to reproduce that my renditon of it is far short of the original ... The following is as near as I can render it:

'This is the road to the eternal world. Yonder rocks are the boundary between the two worlds and the two lives. Once you pass them, you can no more return into the body. If your work is complete on earth, you may pass beyond the rocks. If, however, upon consideration you conclude that ... it is not done, you can return into the body.'

The thoughts ceased and the cloud passed away, moving slowly toward the mountain in the east. I turned and watched it for some time, when suddenly, and without having felt myself moved, I stood close to and in front of the three rocks. I was seized with a strong curiosity then to look into the next world.

Dr Wiltse saw several entrances through the rocks but hesitated to cross the boundary. He realized that he had reached the point of no return. Another blackout occurred and Dr Wiltse revived back in his sickbed.

The second famous case reported during these years was contributed by the Revd. L. J. Bertrand, based on the testimony he originally gave to Professor William James. The Rev. Mr Bertrand was climbing in the Alps with a guide and some students when he nearly froze to death. Because the trek was so exhausting, the clergyman had stayed behind the rest of the party. He tried to light a cigar but found himself paralysed when the cold overcame him. Soon he left his body and perceived himself to be 'a ball of air' in the sky, 'a captive balloon still attached to the earth by a kind of elastic string and, going up, always up'. Below he could see his physical body frozen in the snow. Despite the fact that he was nearly dead, the Rev. Mr Bertrand felt vibrantly alive in his disembodied state and could see his party's further climb up the mountain from his elevated perspective. To his dismay he saw them taking the wrong path, and became understandably annoyed when the guide proceeded to eat the lunch he (Bertrand) had packed. Stealing some of his wine was the final straw!

The Rev. Mr Bertrand's experience didn't end with these simple observations. Next he found himself transported through space, where he saw his wife and some other people in a carriage heading towards Lucerne. While making these observation he felt a 'pull' back to his body. The other climbers had returned and they were reviving him by rubbing snow into his stiffened body. The Rev. Mr Bertrand later astonished the guide by mentioning his purloining of the lunch and the wine, and later still corroborated the observations he had made concerning his wife's carriage trip.

It is strange that few of the first psychical researchers connected these reports to the growing literature on personal survival. Even F.W.H. Myers, whose research specifically focused on the survival question, made only a loose connection. The researcher set aside several pages in his (posthumously published) *Human Personality and Its Survival of Bodily Death* to a discussion of out-of-body experiences, but failed to realize their connection to deathbed reports. He treated out-of-body experiences more as mystical or visionary episodes than psychic experiences. Included in this monumental two-volume offering, however, was a classic NDE/otherworld journey narrative. What makes this report so fascinating is that the percipient was not close to death when it took place, nor did he even perceive himself threatened.

The case was reported to Myers by the chief witness, Mr J.W. Skilton, who worked as a railway engineer in Florida. The pseudo-NDE (to coin a new term) occurred when Skilton was unloading fir trees from a boxcar. Some sort of spiritual guide suddenly materialized by his side, clothed in white and beaming with a bright countenance. The apparition placed its hand on Skilton's shoulder and the otherworld journey began.

> We moved upward, and a little to the south-east, with the speed of lightning, as it were; I could see the hills, trees, buildings and roads as we went up side by side till they vanished out of our sight. As we passed on, this glorious being that was with me told me he was going to show me that bright heavenly world. We soon came to a world of light and beauty, many thousand times larger than this earth, with at least four times as much light. The beauties of this place were beyond any human being to describe. I was seated by the tree of life on a square bunch of what appeared to be a green velvet moss, about eighteen inches high; there I saw many thousand spirits clothed in white, and singing heavenly music—the sweetest song I have ever heard. I here told my attendant that it was the first time I had ever been perfectly at rest in my life. They did not converse by sound, but each knew the other's thoughts at the instant, and conversation was carried on in that way, also with me.

After enjoying this realm for a while, Skilton told the guide that he wished to see his deceased mother, sister, and child. The wish was granted and Skilton suddenly saw his relations standing before him, but he wasn't allowed to talk with them. Then the heavenly guide said they had to return to earth:

> I wished to stay, but he (the guide) told me my time had not come yet, but would in due time, and that I should wait with patience. At this we started back, and were soon out of sight of that heavenly land. When we came in sight of this world, I saw everything as it looked from a great height, such as trees, buildings, hills, roads, and streams, as natural as could be, till we came to the car that I had opened the door of, and I found myself there in the body, and he vanished out of my sight. I spoke then (just as I opened my watch and found it had been just twenty-six minutes that I had been engaged with that mysterious one), and said I thought I had left this world for good. One of the men said, 'There is something the matter with you ever since you opened the car door; we have not been able to get a word out of you,' and that I had done all the work of taking out everything and putting it back into the car, and one item was eight barrels of flour I had taken off the ground alone and put back in the car, three feet and a half high, with all the ease of a giant. I told them where I had been and what I had seen, but they had seen no one.

What can we make of this strange story, a story that perfectly matches more conventional NDEs reported today? Since Mr Skilton wasn't close to death, his experience certainly wasn't a true NDE even though it shared every characteristic of one. So this case shows that NDEs (despite the rubric) do not necessarily take place *only* when the percipient's life is at risk. They can occur under separate circumstances. This is an important topic to which we'll return in a later chapter. Particularly intriguing is that Mr Skilton's experience took place while his body continued working—certainly a change from most individuals who experience NDEs while comatose.

Reading Mr Skilton's report today, it's tempting to compare his experiences to some bizarre forms of seizure disorders. Epileptics don't necessarily have *grande mal* seizures, in which they fall and thrash about in uncontrollable fits. There are many forms of epilepsy and some epileptic behaviour can be rather subtle. During an episode of psychomotor epilepsy, for instance, the patient will become unconscious while his body continues to perform intelligent behaviour. (Note how closely this form of epilepsy matches Skilton's report.) When electrical seizures take place in the temporal lobes of the brain, the patient sometimes undergoes strange hallucinations—perhaps another possible link to the Florida engineer's experience. The more we look into Skilton's experience, in fact, the more it appears to support the 'coded' experience explanation for the NDE. Please recall that this theory was first formally proposed by Dr Stanislav Grof, whose model was briefly summarized in the last chapter. While experiences like Skilton's don't prove this particular model, they do suggest that the NDE is a more complicated subject than some researchers seem to believe.

It should also be mentioned that the psychical researchers weren't the only scholars grappling with such cases. Several members of the psychological establishment were also beginning to take an interest in NDE-like experiences. Back in 1881, for example, the French psychologist Ribot discussed the observations of near-drowning victims in his *Les maladies de la mémoire*. Some years later Professor Albert Heim issued a report on people who nearly died from falls. While not undergoing NDEs *per se*, some of them reported experiences such as the 'panoramic' life-review or heard exquisite music. The core feature of the classic NDE case, the out-of-body episode, was not part of such experiences, however. For this reason Professor Heim's subjects can't be said to have undergone NDEs, even though many researchers today link his work with Raymond Moody's and NDEs in general.

Research on deathbed visions and NDEs, 1960–1975

Despite the fact that the early psychical researchers were not uninterested in deathbed visions and NDEs, the subject was never central to the field's concerns during these seminal years. What little interest these experiences generated literally evaporated from 1930 to 1960 when the field's focus significantly changed. Between 1882 and 1930 the field had been mainly concerned with research into the survival question. Studying the psychic experiences reported by the general public was also pursued, but not with the same enthusiasm. But with the rise of purely experimental parapsychology in the 1930s, these earlier traditions gradually ebbed. Dr J.B Rhine showed through his research at Duke University that parapsychology could gain better scientific recognition by entering the psychology laboratory.

Rhine was not personally uninterested in religious and spiritual issues, but he found that experimentally studying extrasensory perception was the most profitable method for exploring psi. Because of the importance of his famous Duke research, and his spectacular success there, he took most of parapsychology with him. It wasn't for many years that the survival problem made its formal comeback within the field.

The project that heralded this return was conducted by Dr Karlis Osis, who was then working with the Parapsychology Foundation in New York. Previously impressed with the pioneering research of both Barrett and Hyslop, he decided to conduct a scientific survey on deathbed vision reports. So in the late 1950s he sent questionnaires to 10,000 physicians and nurses in which he asked them to talk about their experiences with the dying. The feedback the Latvian-born psychologist received wasn't great, since only 540 responses were collected. But that was enough for Dr Osis to use, and in 1961 he published his monograph *Deathbed Observations by Physicians and Nurses*. This report was packed with findings that upheld those of his two predecessors: many of the respondents had seen their dying patients 'greeting' welcoming figures. Nor did it appear that these patients were hallucinating or were delirious. Dr Osis actually presented five important points in his report:

1. Shortly before death, terminal patients often exhibit inexplicable periods of bliss or even exaltation.
2. They may see apparitions coming to greet them, and they report such figures more commonly than hallucinations are reported by the public in general.
3. Based on the medical information provided by the respondents, neither the effects of the patients' illnesses nor their medication could explain these visions.
4. The apparitions usually represented the patient's deceased friends or relatives, although religious figures and people still living were sometimes seen. Beautiful otherwordly landscapes were also reported by the dying.
5. Many of the patients realized that these figures were coming to take them into death.

It should also be noted that few of the patients were frightened by their experiences, which seemed to comfort them. The truly impressive nature of Dr Osis's study becomes more obvious, however, when the statistical graphs included in his monograph are examined. The great majority of the patients (close to 80 per cent) were not medicated when they experienced their visions, so the visions were obviously not caused by drug intoxication. Similar percentiles were found for the occurrence of pre-death mood elevation, nor were most of the patients suffering from hallucinogenic illnesses. Fifty-two per cent of the patients understood the spiritual mission of the figures, while smaller patient groups felt them to be bedside visitors or simple memories. What impresses me the most, however, is that these apparitions seem to show up right before the patient's death. While some terminal patients will have repeated experiences with the phantoms within a week of their deaths, the visions tend to occur most commonly within the hour before death. In Figure 1, I have graphed out the temporal relationship between such sightings and death based on Dr Osis's report.

There was also suggestive evidence that seeing these figures wasn't related to the patient's religious background or education.

Figure 1
Temporal Relation Between 'Take Away' Visions and Death

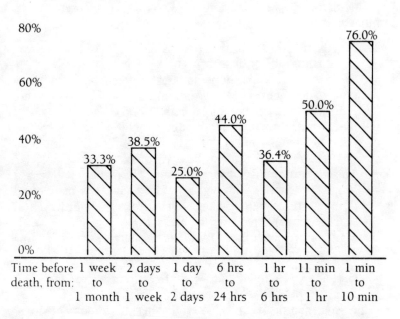

It should be obvious that Dr Osis's 1961 findings closely parallel the case study findings of earlier researchers. Only one major difference can be found between this modern survey and the research conducted in psychical research's heyday. Dr Osis found that some patients reported religious figures or representations of the living in their sickrooms. Such cases played little part in the collections published by Sir William Barrett and Professor James H. Hyslop, but this difference can be explained easily enough.[4] These earlier researchers were only interested in impressive individual cases, while Dr Osis conducted a more sweeping analysis of the subject. Naturally he found and published a wider range of cases than his predecessors had.

Dr Osis was not, however, satisfied that his 1961 report was the final word on the phenomenon. Still of interest to him was the possibility that deathbed visions are a cultural product. The idea that we're greeted while dying by our deceased relatives or friends is suspiciously consistent with our Judaeo-Christian heritage. Could this heritage be conditioning us into seeing these hallucinations when we die? Because this issue is so important, Dr Osis decided that he needed to conduct a similar survey in a non-Western culture. The psychologist had to put the project on hold for several years, however, since the Parapsychology Foundation closed down its research division in 1962. Dr Osis thereupon became research director for the American Society for Psychical Research, but funds for survival research did not become available for several more years. It wasn't until 1971 that he could begin to put his plan into operation.

Dr Osis's second survey was undertaken in collaboration with Dr Erlendur Haraldsson, a psychologist and parapsychologist from the University of Reykjavik in Iceland. Together they arranged a field trip to northern India where they surveyed a large number of medical personnel. Their primary finding was that deathbed cases reported from India conform to the same patterns as those in the West. Only two significant differences occurred between the two surveys. Dying patients in India more commonly report seeing religious figures coming to take them into death, and they fear these visions more often than people in the West.

---

[4]Barrett included a chapter in his book on 'visions' seen of the living. But these were cases of travelling clairvoyance or remote viewing, in which the dying seemed to 'travel' to the homes of other people.

It is not clear, however, whether these Eastern patients really saw religious figures or *interpreted* their sightings within a cultural framework. (For example, perhaps some of the Indian patients really saw deceased friends at their bedsides, but mistook them or reported them to be 'yamdoots'—their version of the Irish banshee.)

To be sure, the findings of Drs Osis and Haraldsson never proved that deathbed figures literally represent the return of the dead. But the two researchers have demonstrated that such visions represent cross-cultural experiences. Whatever they are, such encounters and visions seem inherently linked to the psyche.

While Dr Osis and his colleague were busy investigating deathbed visions, there was some interest within parapsychological circles to further explore out-of-body experiences. But little of this research specifically bore on the NDE. The most sytematic research conducted between 1960 and 1970 was probably that of Dr Robert Crookall, a British geologist who retired from his post to study reports of the phenomenon. Crookall eventually published two books filled with classic out-of-body reports, which he collected either from other books or from his own non-random surveys. (A third book was to be published in 1972.) His first case collection was issued in 1960 in his *The Study and Practice of Astral Projection*, which contained 153 first-hand reports of the phenomenon. Thirty of these cases were what might be more formally called NDEs. Four years later he published a second collection in his *More Astral Projections*, which increased his total accumulation of accounts to 285 cases. 43 additional NDE-linked out-of-body experiences were included.

Most of these cases could be considered simple NDEs, such as the following report sent to Dr Crookall in 1960 by a British ex-soldier:

> As a young soldier, forty years ago, I was drafted to the Sudan. One morning, the boys and myself went swimming in the river. Having gone half-way across, I decided to come back, the whole distance being too great for me. I started to swim back, got cramp and could not move arms or legs. I told my friend to get help. He swam back to the shore, but in the meantime down I went in twenty-seven feet of water.
>
> As I lost consciousness, *certain things in my life came in front of me.* This was followed by a queer sound of music and the next thing *I*

was suspended in mid-air and looking at them bringing my body out of the water and trying artificial respiration. I was very happy and free and wondered why they were doing that when I was here!

At that moment I was transported to my mother's room. I stood beside her as she was by the fire in an easy chair, trying to tell her I was all right and happy.

Afterwards, I was back looking at my body, when a brilliant light shone around me and a voice said, 'it is not your time yet—you must go back. You have work to do!'

Immediately I began to come down to my body and the lads around it. *Then everything was dark* and my eyes opened. They all said, 'He's alive!' I got up and went back to the hut, with everyone amazed.

Cases of otherworld journeys were also included in the collection, but consisted of a limited number of incidents. Note how in the following account, the patient saw a symbolic instead of a literal presentation of the life review:

In 1953 I was rushed to hospital on the verge of collapse. A few hours later I collapsed. At times I came round and then went unconscious again ... *I saw a book giving account of all things I had done in the past, good and bad* ... I floated up towards a heavenly gate on the right; to the left were three loved ones dressed in blue and coming towards me through a blue haze, smiling and calling, 'Come along, Mummy! It's lovely up here!', I answered, 'I'm coming'. Imagine how disappointed I was to come to earth!

The late Dr Crookall commented prolifically on his cases, suggesting in a series of subsequent books that out-of-body experiences, in general, point to the existence of an afterlife. Crookall worked independently, however, and his non-random surveys and collections had little influence on the rest of the parapsychological community. The subject of the out-of-body experience was not especially popular within the field in the 1960s and only made its comeback in 1973. Between 1973 and 1975 there were several attempts made to study the experience in the laboratory. While these projects did not specifically concern the NDE, the results of this research have some bearing on the subject. This research will be discussed in an upcoming chapter.

Both public and scientific interest in the classic NDE was stirred, however, in 1971 when two physicians in Canada published a case in a Canadian medical journal. While the publication of this interesting report received some comment in the press, it served mainly as a harbinger of the Moody revolution of 1975. The 1971 report was, however, the first to force the medical establishment to examine the phenomenon seriously, and it will be discussed in the next chapter.

This chapter has been concerned with two related but disparate subjects—i.e. classic NDEs and a range of possibly related deathbed experiences. Deathbed visions have been sometimes (erroneously) called NDEs, but they cannot be properly subsumed under this rubric. But since the study of NDEs and that of related deathbed experiences have been habitually connected in the history of parapsychology, background research into both subjects has been included in this chapter. The following chapters will specifically focus on the NDE proper, and the study of deathbed visions—though these are important in their own right—will be put off until the final chapter.

4.

Contemporary Research on the NDE

The contemporary era of scientific interest in the NDE dates from May 1971 when two physicians published a short paper in the *Canadian Medical Association Journal*. Simply titled 'Cardiac arrest remembered', the report concerned a 68-year-old man sent to the hospital complaining of pain in his left arm. Even though his cardiac functions tested within normal ranges, he suffered a coronary 10 hours later. He was immediately defibrillated and eventually made a full recovery. Later on he wrote a detailed report on his subjective experiences while nearly dying. He described being taken to the intensive care ward of the hospital in early evening, but didn't recall actually having the attack. He was apparently only partially projected since, upon making this observation, he separated from his body more fully.

'Almost instantly I saw myself leave my body,' he wrote, 'coming out through my head and shoulders (I did not see my lower limbs). The "body" leaving me was not exactly in vapour form, yet it seemed to expand very slightly once it was clear of me. It was somewhat transparent, for I could see my "other" body through it. Watching this I thought "So this is what happens when you die." '

The next thing the patient knew, he was travelling into space while sitting on some sort of small object. He felt very lonely. Down below he watched a pure white cloud moving to intersect with him, but the patient then apparently lost consciousness momentarily before he entered it. His subsequent sensations upon regaining consciousness were extremely pleasant.

'My next sensation was of floating in a bright, pale yellow light—a very delightful sensation,' he stated. 'Although I was not conscious of having any lower limbs, I felt something being torn off the scars of my right leg, as if a large piece of adhesive tape had been taken off. I thought "They have always said your body is made whole out here. I wonder if my scars are gone," but though I tried to I could not seem to locate my legs. I continued to float, enjoying the most beautiful tranquil sensation.'

The patient considered the experience ineffable but was soon brought back to reality by several sledgehammer-like blows to his side. These sensations were caused by the defibrillation (which electrically stimulates the body) and the patient 'came to' back in the body. He later told his physician that the floating sensations were so pleasant that, should he lapse again, he didn't want to be resuscitated.

Dr R. L. MacMillan and Dr K.W.G. Brown of the University of Toronto commented surprisingly little on the report when they published it. Remarking that it is rare for a person to remember the events surrounding cardiac failure, they merely called the patient's experience 'extremely interesting', suggesting that such experiences should be of comfort to cardiac patients and their relatives. They didn't consider whether such incidents represent objective events, and their total commentary consisted of barely six sentences! Despite their reluctance to speculate on their patient's out-of-body experience, however, the story was picked up by the press and was repeated in such publications as the *Los Angeles Times*. No one seemed to realize that such reports had been published by parapsychologists for years. The fact that the patient's experience was reported in a conventional medical journal was probably the reason for its dissemination.

The Moody revolution of 1975
The birth of widespread scientific interest in similar experiences dates from 1975, when an obscure Southern publisher issued a short book entitled *Life After Life*. It had been written by Dr Raymond Moody, a philosophy-teacher-turned-physician, and contained several NDE reports he had personally collected— primarily from people who had momentarily suffered clinical 'death'. The book caused a sensation and soon became a paperback best-seller.

What first sparked Dr Moody's interest in the NDE is obvious from the book. While still an undergraduate in college in 1965, he met a psychiatrist who had undergone a striking NDE some time earlier. While Dr Moody doesn't name the psychiatrist, it is plain that he is referring to Dr George Ritchie, who has since written extensively on the NDE he experienced in the military. (He nearly died shortly before entering medical school from pneumonia and tells the story in his little book *Return from Tomorrow*. This is the story he repeated to Raymond Moody, who was studying at the University of Virginia, where Dr Ritchie works.) This case probably represents the most complete account of an NDE ever placed on file. Dr Moody didn't know what to think of the story, however, and didn't even give it much thought at the time.

Some years later Dr Moody found himself teaching philosophy at a North Carolina college. While the subject of the soul and its immortality is certainly an important topic in philosophy, Dr Moody was nonetheless surprised when a student told him of his grandmother's pseudo-death during surgery. The report seemed identical to the incident Dr Richie had told him about years before. The coincidences between them were too remarkable for the instructor to dismiss, so he began discussing the survival issue in his classes. Though he usually refrained from specifically mentioning NDEs, many of his students started reporting them to him. By the time he entered medical school in 1972, Dr Moody had collected several such testimonies. 'What has amazed me since the beginning of my interest are the great similarities in the reports,' he comments in his book, 'despite the fact that they come from people of highly varied religious, social and educational backgrounds.'

Dr Moody eventually became more and more interested in these reports and began giving public talks on the subject. The result was that more reports flooded in. The philosopher-turned-medical-student ultimately amassed 150 cases which he broke down into three categories:

1. The reports of people revived from episodes of clinical or pseudo-death.
2. Similar stories from people reporting close calls with death during illness or from injuries.
3. Experiences of the dying themselves that they told to their friends and relatives, who reported them at second hand to Dr Moody.

It was from these reports that Dr Moody drafted the prototypical NDE which I summarized in Chapter 1.

Of course, there were serious problems with Dr Moody's book and case collection. It was not written in a scholarly way, though that was hardly a crucial criticism of the book to my mind. More annoying was the fact that Dr Moody didn't publish his cases in full, but reported 'sections' of them throughout his discussions on the subject. Nor was the method he employed to collect these cases very rigid.

Despite these formal criticisms of Dr Moody's seminal research, the sheer number of cases he published was certainly impressive. They consisted both of simple NDEs and otherworld journey/eschatological experiences which read like something from the Middle Ages:

(1)

It was about two years ago, and I had just turned nineteen. I was driv-ing a friend of mine home in my car, and as I got to this particular intersection down town, I stopped and looked both ways, but I didn't see a thing coming. I pulled on out into the interesection and as I did I heard my friend yell at the top of his voice. When I looked I saw a blinding light, the headlights of a car that was speeding towards us. I heard this awful sound—the side of the car being crushed in—and there was just an instant during which I seemed to be going through a darkness, an enclosed space. It was very quick. Then I was sort of floating about five feet above the street, about five yards away from the car, I'd say, and I heard the echo of the crash dying away. I saw people come running up and crowding around the car, and I saw my friend get out of the car, obviously in shock. I could see my own body in the wreckage among all those people, and could see them trying to get it out. My legs were all twisted and there was blood all over the place.

(2)

I had a heart attack, and I found myself in a black void, and I knew I had left my physical body behind. I knew I was dying, and I thought, 'God, I did the best I knew how at the time I did it. Please help me.' Immediately, I was moved out of that blackness, through a pale gray, and I just went on, gliding and moving swiftly, and in front of me, in the distance, I could see a gray mist, and I was rushing toward it. It seemed that I just couldn't get to it fast enough to satisfy me, and as I got closer to it I could see through it. Beyond the mist, I could see people, and their forms were just like they are on the earth, and I could also see something which one could take to be buildings. The whole thing was permeated with the most gorgeous light—a living, golden yellow glow, a pale color, not like the harsh color we know on earth.

As I approached more closely, I felt certain that I was going through that mist. It was such a wonderful, joyous feeling; there are just no words in human language to describe it. Yet, it wasn't my time to go through the mist, because instantly from the other side appeared my Uncle Carl, who had died many years earlier. He blocked my path, saying, 'Go back. Your work on earth has not been completed. Go back now.' I didn't want to go back, but I had no choice, and immediately I was back in my body. I felt that horrible pain in my chest, and I heard my little boy crying, 'God, bring my mommy back to me.'

More detailed reports of such otherworld journeys were included by Dr Moody in his subsequent book, *Reflections on Life After Life*, two years later.

But just *why* did Dr Moody's book *Life After Life* become such a long-term best-seller when it wasn't even brought out by a leading publisher? There were doubtless several interrelated reasons for the popularity and charm of the little book. The primary reason was probably pure chance.

The subject of death and dying has never been popular in our materialistic Western culture. We have been called a death-denying culture because the subject has been virtually taboo for years. A well-known British publisher once suggested that the study of death constituted the 'new' pornography, since it seemed to insult contemporary society's preoccupation with pleasure and personal self-indulgence. Remember, too, that because of the surge of medical discoveries by the 1930s, the terminally ill no longer died surrounded by their loved ones but were shunted off to hospitals where they were often avoided by both nurses and physicians. (Even today, fewer and fewer friends and relatives tend to visit terminally ill patients in the hospital. Society has successfully alienated itself from the dying, which conveniently helps people to segregate the dying experience from the rest of their lives.)

This sad situation began to change in the early 1960s when society underwent a radical transformation. Part of popular culture's modernization process included the so-called consciousness explosion or psychedelic revolution that burst on to the scene. For several sociological and cultural reasons, contemporary society—especially in the United States—again became interested in such subjects as psychic phenomena, parapsychology, holistic health, Eastern religions, and other forms of counter-cultures. Let me simply say that there was probably no single cause for this great consciousness explosion, which so permanently changed contemporary society. Some of it resulted from changes in the United States immigration laws which, for the first time, let many Oriental and Eastern spiritual teachers into the country. Their oftentimes simple and experientially oriented doctrines appealed to a spiritually bankrupt public whose interest in conventional religion had been dropping since the late 1950s. Psychedelic drugs had also been discovered by the public thanks to the popularization they received from such counter-culture figures as Dr Timothy Leary, who had recently been fired from his post at Harvard for promoting the use of such substances. There were also the harsh realities of the unpopular Vietnam War, which brought the horror of death and dying right into the homes of the populace through the nightly news.

It was during this time, too, that a Swiss-born psychiatrist working with the dying—Dr Elisabeth Kübler-Ross—first became known to the public. Dr Kübler-Ross had been counselling terminally ill patients for years. Based on approximately 200 interviews she had conducted in both Europe and the United States, in 1969 she published her celebrated book *On Death and Dying*. This book outlined the psychological stages of dying for the first time.[1] The book became a best-seller and it seemed that the subject of death had finally been forced from the closet. Society simply couldn't ignore the reality of death any longer, and the science of *thanatology*—the psychological study of death and dying—was officially born. So by the time Dr Moody came along with his research in 1975, the stage had been conveniently set for him. The general public had finally become open to learning about dying, death, and the possibility of permanent survival.

While the social and cultural factors outlined in the previous paragraphs can explain the backdrop to *Life After Life*'s popularity, there were other elements contributing to its fame. To begin

---

[1] Dr Kübler-Ross's stages of dying have not been universally accepted by psychologists. The Swiss-born physician was not the only clinician mapping out the process of dying during these years, and other researchers came to different conclusions. The widespread public acceptance of Kübler-Ross's work stemmed from the fact that she wrote a best-selling book, not because of the methods she employed before drawing her conclusions. Nobody working in thanatology, however, questions the importance of her seminal research nor the fierce devotion she gives to the dying, which continues today, 20 years later.

with, Dr Moody had by 1975 finished medical school and spoke with the prestige of a physician. He simply had the scientific credibility that other people publishing similar stories—such as religious writers and parapsychologists—sorely lacked. Everybody knows that you can believe what a doctor says! It didn't hurt either when Dr Kübler-Ross also revealed that she knew of similar cases from her own practice. The final reason for the book's popularity was probably the remarkably understated style in which it was written. Dr Moody didn't seem interested in proving anything by publishing his cases, especially survival of death. While his personal bias is clear from his comments and from the religious tone of the book's dedication, he didn't implicitly promote the survival interpretation in the text. He wisely let the cases speak for themselves in a quasi-objective sort of way. Though I am not trying to trivialize Dr Moody's work, his book tended to read like a highly sophisticated Ripley's 'Believe It or Not' column complete with popular-style knee-slap stories. The reader was left to interpret them anyway he or she wished.

Because the book became a best-seller, the scientific and psychological communities simply couldn't ignore it. But these communities were rather puzzled and annoyed by the book, for to their minds too many important and critical issues had not been raised.

Does every person experiencing clinical death undergo an NDE?

Are NDE cases really similar to each other, or did Dr Moody carefully choose or perhaps edit his cases to emphasize these common characteristics?

Were the people with whom Dr Moody spoke really close to biological death when their NDEs took place?

These were important problems complicating the study of the NDE and, luckily, they didn't take long to resolve. For in the wake of Life After Life's incredible success, several scientific researchers began to study the NDE for themselves, using more critical sampling methods and standards of evidence. Especially important is the pioneering research of three of these researchers: Dr Kenneth Ring, Dr Michael Sabom, and Dr Margot Grey—although her research in England wasn't published until some years after her colleagues' findings.

The research of Dr Kenneth Ring
Dr Kenneth Ring was a respected social psychologist at the

University of Connecticut, Storrs, when he first read *Life After Life* in 1977. Since he *was* a social scientist by training, his first reaction to Moody's work was to criticize its methodology. And because the physician's cases had not been collected through a random sample of people, Dr Ring had to ask himself several questions. Do NDEs commonly occur when a patient comes close to death, and do some elements of the Moody-type experience manifest more frequently than others? Does the cause of clinical death play any role in programming the characteristics of the NDE, or the incidence of the experience in general? Dr Ring also became interested in the religious background of people reporting NDEs.

So in order to study these issues, he and his staff decided to conduct an impartial, semi-random study.

The Connecticut researchers began by consulting with several local hospitals in order to find patients who had recovered from pseudo-death. Other individuals were contacted when they responded to newspaper ads, in which Dr Ring explained that he wished to interview people with similar close calls. Of course, this really wasn't a completely random sample, since several biasing factors could have led people to come forth or to co-operate in the study. Certainly those with interesting or meaningful stories to tell would be more likely to co-operate in such a survey. But at least Dr Ring's methodology was more sophisticated than Dr Moody's casual methods had been.

Because they used several different methods for finding promising cases, Dr Ring and his co-workers were able to contact 102 individuals reporting close calls with death. These people fell into one of three categories. Some had nearly died from medical complications. Several others had been involved in physical mishaps such as car accidents. The third category consisted of people who'd survived suicide attempts. Many of the people (36 per cent) were interviewed within twelve months of their experiences, while an additional 22 per cent were contacted within two years. The rest tapered off exponentially, with some respondents reporting experiences recalled from several years earlier. Dr Ring personally interviewed 74 of the informants, and each of the interviews followed a structured format—no matter who conducted it:

1. Demographic information concerning the respondent's sex,

race, education, religious background, and several other factors was taken.
2. The subject was then asked to describe his or her experience
    in his/her own words.
3. A series of specific questions were incorporated into the
    subsequent interview, to determine whether the respon-
    dent's experience confirmed or contradicted the prototypical
    NDE outlined by Raymond Moody in 1975.
4. A comparison between the respondent's pre- and post- ex-
    perience religious beliefs was made.

The demographic information collected by Dr Ring and his
staff was rather unexceptional and represented, by and large, a
typical middle-class population. The respondents were
predominantly white and roughly divided by sex (44 per cent
and 56 per cent respectively for male and female). They
displayed a range of ages, but tended to be Catholic or Protestant
with either some college or a high school education.

Dr Raymond Moody had written in 1977 that 'any investigator
who enters into this type of study sympathetically and diligently
will find there is ample case material'. Dr Ring found this claim
to be true since 48 per cent of his informants claimed NDEs
strongly resembling those previously published by his predecessor. These percipients were divided equally by sex. Dr Ring
found that his subjects typically experienced five characteristics
of the prototypical NDE: they became typically peaceful in the
face of death before leaving the body; they subsequently entered
some sort of darkness, but moments later perceived a light with
which they later merged. The Connecticut researcher refers to
these five features as the 'core' elements of the NDE. Dr Ring did
not, unfortunately, publish his respondents' narratives in full,
but offered piecemeal versions of them in his official reports. So
it is difficult to get a comprehensive 'picture' of the full NDE from
the reports themselves. This is the same problem that limited the
value of Dr Moody's 1975 study. Several of the extracts which Dr
Ring later published in his book *Life at Death* and his research
reports (see the references on p.246 at the end of the book) suggest, however, that his cases differed little from his predecessor's.

Before proceeding further, though, let me say that serious exceptions to Dr Ring's statistics could be made, since it isn't clear

to me that some of his respondents really underwent NDEs. He includes people who merely recounted feelings of bliss in the face of death in his inclusion criteria, while I would tend to exclude them. Since these individuals didn't report clear-cut out-of-body experiences, to say they had NDEs begs the definition. By my own calculations, based on a more stringent definition for the NDE (see p.15), roughly 20 per cent of Ring's respondents properly reported such experiences.

The following extracts represent some fairly typical examples of the cases Dr Ring and his associates collected. The first excerpt reprinted below came from a respondent injured in a car crash:

> At that time I viewed myself from the corner of my hospital room, looking down at my body which was very dark and gray. All the life looked like it was out of it. And my mother was sitting in a chair next to my bed looking very determined and strong in her faith. And my Italian girlfriend at the time was crying at the foot of my bed.

Notice that this case is similar to the following reported by a suicidal patient:

> I remember being up in the air looking down ... and seeing myself on the operating table with all the people around working on me. I can remember, what sticks out in my mind mostly, were the colors. Everything in that operating room was a very brilliant, bright color.

Dr Ring found a patient suffering from a near-fatal asthma attack who reported the famous 'tunnel' effect:

> I do remember thinking to myself that I was dying. And I felt I was floating through a tunnel ... When I say 'tunnel,' the only thing I can think of is—you know those sewer pipes, those big pipes they put in? It was round like that, but it was enormous. I couldn't really see the edges of it; I got the feeling that it was round. It was like a whitish color. I was just smack in the middle. My whole body, you know. I was lying on my back. I was just floating. And smoke or white lines or something were coming this way [toward her] and I was going the opposite way. [I felt] very peaceful, almost as if I were on a raft in the ocean, you know?

Entering the light and taking otherworld journeys comprised the experience of some of Ring's percipients. In the following case, the witness describes an NDE which resulted from complications during dental surgery:

> I took a trip to heaven. I saw the most beautiful lakes. Angels—they

were floating around like you see seagulls. Everything was white. The most beautiful flowers. Nobody on this earth ever saw the beautiful flowers that I saw there ... I don't believe there is a color on this earth that wasn't included in that color situation that I saw. Everything, everything. Of course, I was so impressed with the beauty of everything there that I couldn't pinpoint any one thing ... Everything was bright. The lakes were blue, light blue. Everything about the angels were pure white ... Everything about the whole thing was restful.

The truly remarkable aspect of Dr Ring's work was not, however, simply his case collection. By graphing out the characteristics of his respondents' NDEs, the psychologist made the following discovery:

The characteristics of the NDE do not seem to occur in random order. The NDE tends to unfold in several sequential stages. The more deeply the patient enters the NDE, the more stages he/she experiences.

For example, while 37 per cent of the psychologist's informants reported leaving the body, somewhat fewer experienced the tunnel effect on entering into a darkness. Only relatively few people experienced the bright light or embarked on an eschatological journey. Based on Dr Ring's chart of the sequential stages of the NDE, I have freely adopted Table IV, which illustrates this phenomenon.

So what exactly is Dr Ring's research revealing about the NDE?

It seems to me that he correctly demonstrated the basic soundness of Raymond Moody's original observations, but by using more scientific sampling procedures. That much certainly seems obvious, so there is little need to belabour the point. The real focus of Dr Ring's study, however, extends our understanding of the NDE by showing it to be a commonly reported experience. Whether you calculate the probability of having an NDE while clinically facing death at 48 per cent or 20 per cent makes little difference. NDEs obviously don't represent rare quirks of the death experience but probably something fundamental to it. The final importance of the Connecticut study is that Dr Ring showed that the NDE is a specific syndrome consisting of several predictable stages. He himself immediately understood the importance of the findings, for he writes in his book that 'most near-death experiences seem to unfold according to a *single pattern*, almost as though the prospect of death serves to release a stored, *common*

Table IV
Sequential Stages of the NDE from Data
Collected by Dr Kenneth Ring

Stage	Percentage of NDE informants reporting the features (Total N = 49)
1. Felt blissful sensations	60
2. Left the body	37
3. Entered a tunnel or darkness	23
4. Perceived a bright light	16
5. Entered the light	10

"program" of feelings, perceptions and experiences'.

These observations have a considerable bearing on the search to find explanations for the NDE. Some sceptics like to show that the phenomenology of the NDE (i.e. its core features) crop up now and then within other psychological contexts. We saw in Chapter 2 how Dr Stanislav Grof believes that typical NDE phenomenology occurs during psychedelic drug trips. This observation has led some sceptics to conclude that the NDE shouldn't be taken literally and is probably hallucinatory in nature. What they have not shown, however, is that the sequential stages of the NDE—so concisely mapped by Dr Ring and his co-workers—can be found within any other psychological context. It seems to be a concise, self-consistent experience usually linked to life-threatening situations. While this fact doesn't necessarily prove the objective reality of the NDE, it is clearly not a simple hallucination or delusion but something more complicated.

Even if the NDE cannot be explained by some reductionistic psychological model, psychological factors probably play some role in the experience. Dr Ring and his colleagues discovered this fact the more they examined their cases. In order to simplify matters for the reader, Dr Ring's primary discoveries will merely be summarized from his book *Life at Death*. The following findings are not codified in this order by Dr Ring, but are scattered throughout his book:

1. There was a marginal tendency for sickness-prone people to experience the deeper aspects of the NDE. Survivors of failed suicides or people involved in injuries reported them less frequently.
2. Women tended to have core NDE experiences in the face of illness while men had them more commonly during suicide attempts or accidents.
3. Suicide survivors rarely experienced the deepest aspects of the NDE, such as entering the blissful light.
4. The famous panoramic life-review is often reported by people involved in serious accidents, but it is surprisingly rare under other circumstances.
5. The percipient's religious background does not seem to correlate with experiencing the NDE in the face of death.

There is another finding that Dr Ring uncovered which deserves special comment. When he asked his 102 respondents whether they'd ever heard of the NDE, several had. But these people *reported them less frequently than the other respondents*. This finding aptly demonstrates that the NDE is probably not a product of the percipient's prior expectations.

It is extremely difficult to determine the exact meaning of these random findings, nor has Dr Ring been too concerned with using them to build an explanatory model for the NDE. The reason is that upon completing his first studies, Dr Ring's interest in the NDE began to change. Even in his 1977 publications he had noted that people become psychologically and spiritually transformed by their NDEs. Whatever the true nature of the experience, it struck Dr Ring that he should be studying these side effects more thoroughly. Nearly all of his subsequent research has focused on the transformational power of the NDE, which served as the subject for his book *Heading Toward Omega* in 1984.

The research of Dr Michael Sabom
While Dr Ring was busy exploring NDE reports in Connecticut, a supplemental study was being conducted down the coast in Florida. Dr Michael Sabom had just finished his first year in cardiology at the University of Florida when he discovered the NDE.

While professing himself to be only nominally religious, he and his family had joined a local Methodist church where they met Sarah Kreutziger. Ms Kreutziger was a psychiatric social worker recently enthralled by Raymond Moody's *Life After Life*, and she mentioned the book to Dr Sabom, who was participating in a Sunday school class. Dr Sabom's initial reaction was sceptical since he was highly critical of the unscientific way in which the cases had been collected.

'Being the only physician present that morning,' he would later write, 'I was asked for my opinion at the end of the class. The kindest thing I could find to say at the moment was "I don't believe it." '

Dr Sabom wasn't going to be let off the hook that easily, though! Ms Kreutziger had to make a presentation on the NDE in Gainsville, Florida, and she called Dr Sabom for some medical information. Their conversation finally encouraged the cardiologist to read Dr Moody's book for himself and to start making a survey of his own hospital patients. Since the social worker also served on staff at the University of Florida, they soon banded together. Finding perspective respondents wasn't too difficult since they had daily contact with seriously ill patients.

'Finding patients who had survived a medical crisis would be simple for both Sarah and me,' Dr Sabom explained in 1982. 'She had daily contact with patients in the kidney dialysis unit. Many of them had had more than one near-death encounter during their long course of kidney failure, which now required in-hospital dialysis. I, on the other hand, was caring for a variety of patients who had been resuscitated from cardiac arrest.'

It didn't take the cardiologist long to hit paydirt, for the third patient with whom he spoke reported a typical NDE. She was a middle-aged housewife with a history of sickness-related, life-threatening episodes. She was initially reluctant to speak with the physician, since she thought he might really be a psychiatrist! Her NDE report so resembled the type published by Moody that Dr Sabom's prior scepticism began to evaporate. Meanwhile, in the kidney dialysis unit, his enthusiastic colleague began turning up more promising NDE subjects and interviewing them. The success of these early studies led Dr Sabom to explore the NDE in considerably more depth. Fundamental to his research efforts were six issues that closely paralleled Kenneth Ring's concerns:

1.   Were people reporting NDEs really close to biological death?

2. Do such experiences follow a predictable pattern similar to that isolated by Raymond Moody?
3. Was the NDE truly a common by-product of close calls with death?
4. What educational, occupational, medical, social, or religious backgrounds/factors earmaked the person experiencing the NDE?
5. Did such factors influence the content of the reported NDE?
6. Do people fear death less upon recovering from an NDE, or is this common claim merely a general by-product of closeness to death?

These were certainly not easy questions to explore, and Dr Sabom (originally working in collaboration with Sarah Kreutziger) spent several years studying them. Their first case collection survey commenced in March 1976 and concluded 20 months later. Dr Sabom continued his research into the NDE when he relocated to the Veterans Administration Hospital in Atlanta, Georgia, in 1978.

Dr Sabom and Sarah Kreutziger published their first paper on the NDE in 1977, based on the results of their original studies in Florida. Working at two separate medical facilities, the careful researchers tracked down 100 survivors (71 males and 29 females) of life-threatening crises. Sixty-eight of them were discovered by Dr Sabom himself, while the others were referred to him by other people. He also diligently checked the patients' medical records to corroborate the information they offered. Each of the patients was personally interviewed by way of a format remarkably similar to Kenneth Ring's. Demographic data was first collected from the patient, and then he/she was asked to describe the NDE that was experienced—if such an episode had just been claimed. These patients were then asked if their experiences had changed their fear of dying. Dr Sabom also explored whether such experiences encouraged the patients to believe in personal survival.

It soon became clear to the two researchers that they were gradually replicating Moody's informal work. Sixty-one of the patients they interviewed reported clearly defined NDEs including the core feature of leaving the body. Simple NDEs made up 16 of Dr Sabom's cases, while 32 patients described other-world journeys to some foreign dimension. (These patients sometimes implied rather than specifically described separating from the body.) Thirteen of the percipients told of leaving the body and described a later eschatological episode—usually to a bucolic, pastoral setting.[2]

Some of these episodes represent relatively simple and uncomplicated events. Early on in his investigation, for example, Dr Sabom met a 50-year-old real estate broker who had been revived from cardiac failure. He was already hospitalized when the attack occurred.

> I don't remember anything for a while, and the next thing I remember I was hanging on the ceiling looking down on them working on my body. ... She [the nurse] put a needle in there and was shooting it into the IV ... Everything was there just like it always was there—the nightstand, the chair, everything I could think of ... It looked like he (the doctor) had one hand on my chest and he kept hitting it real hard. I could see the bed moving up and down ... It [the cardiac monitor] wasn't running at that time. The red light was on and there was a line across. Instead of running up and down like, there was just a line across. It seems that whatever they had done got the monitor running again. That's when I got back in bed.

For reasons that remain unclear, eschatological journeys figured more commonly in Dr Sabom's findings than in Dr Ring's. Sometimes the patient met people he knew to be dead. This feature is reported in the following account given by a 43-year-old man whose NDE took place when he suffered a postoperative coronary in the hospital:

> I came to some place and there were all my relatives, my grandmother, my grandfather, my father, my uncle who had recently committed suicide. They all came towards me and greeted me ... My grandparents were dressed ... all in white and they had a hood over their heads ... They looked better than the last time I saw them ... very, very happy ... I held hands with my grandmother ... It seems like I had just come up on them and they raised their heads up and they were all happy ... And all of a sudden they turned their backs on me and walked away and my grandmother looked over her shoulder and she said, 'We'll see you later, but not this time.'

Other former patients with whom Dr Sabom spoke reported

---

[2]It was Dr Sabom who decided to call these two types of the experience 'autoscopic' and 'transcendental' NDEs respectively. These two forms of the experience correlate with my (more semantically appropriate) simple and eschatological types.

beautiful landscapes. One of them explained that following his coronary he was transported to a beautiful otherworldly pasture:

> During this vision that I had, I couldn't see myself but I was standing on something high because down below me there was just the most beautiful, greenest pasture. There was just a small hill and then just flat meadow over to my right ... I was looking down on these cattle and sheep and on this shepherd, and they were in a meadow like, with cattle on the right and sheep on the left, and he was standing on just like a round knoll twenty or thirty feet high ... It was just like a beautiful sunshiny day ... The whole outline of it looked like a putting green on a well-kept golf course ... He had his back to me, but it was just like you see in the Bible. He had on this long robe and a cloth over his head with a band around it, and he was there holding something. I saw a staff, but I don't know ... I don't know specifically who it was ... Oh, I can see it now. It is just so stamped in my mind that it will never go away, I don't believe.

Like his colleagues in Connecticut, Dr Sabom wanted to explore the NDE in further depth, so he and Ms Kreutziger began looking into the demographic information they'd collected. Based on his interviews and the cases he collected both in Florida and later in Georgia, Dr Sabom concluded that between 27 and 42 per cent of near-death survivors undergo NDEs. This experience seems to be independent of the subject's educational or religious background, or any other demographic factor. The only significant effect Dr Sabom found in his data substantiated Dr Ring's previous finding—i.e. that people with prior knowledge of the NDE phenomenon experience it less frequently during clinical death than other patients. Dr Sabom was also interested in whether NDEs correlated with the length of time the patient was clinically dead. Since most of his patients were already hospitalized when their pseudo-deaths occurred, it was difficult for him to determine this. Most of the patients were resuscitated within moments of their cardiac failures, but by carefully looking at his informants' medical records, he found that more serious cardiac failures—during which the patient remains unconscious for more then 60 seconds—tended more commonly to induce NDEs.

On the basis of this significant discovery, Dr Sabom suggests that people closer to death more often undergo the experience. He also found that people who experience NDEs display a decreased fear of death upon recovery. This reduction in fear does not occur when people nearly die but *don't* leave the body.

If these findings are compared to those independently reported by Kenneth Ring, the parallels become obvious. The two sets of data substantiate each other magnificently. This is rather rare in parapsychology, where replication has been a severe long-standing problem. But there is an additional feature of Dr Sabom's work which deserves special comment, for in some respects it extended the scientific study of the NDE in entirely new directions.

The research of Dr Michael Sabom: Phase II

During the early years of his research, Dr Sabom became interested in the correct surgical observations made by his NDE informants. These cases suggested to him that NDErs really experience an objective separation of the mind from the body, during which they somehow perceive their environments.

Such a case was reported to the cardiologist by a 52-year-old nightwatchman with a history of cardiac problems. He entered the University of Florida's medical centre in November 1977 for cardiac catheterization and surgery. The poor man eventually underwent two NDEs when his heart failed, his second taking place in January 1978 during open-heart surgery. He later explained to Dr Sabom that this NDE occurred when he was first given anaesthesia. He blacked out from the drug, but soon regained consciousness and found himself floating two feet above his body. Such a unique perspective let him passively watch the physicians operating on him. The patient took particular interest in the surgery itself, especially when—on two occasions—one of the physicians stuck a syringe into his heart. The man also described the organ in considerable detail:

> They had all kinds of instruments stuck in that aperture. I think they're called clamps, clamped all over the place. I was amazed that I had thought there would be blood all over the place, but there really wasn't that much blood. Not that I expected it to be ... Somehow or another I was able to realize what was going on like I was looking from back behind my head. It's kind of scary in that I don't know why I should be able to do that. But I know what I saw. It's authentic, or I believe it is ... A lot of it was draped. I couldn't see my head too much but I could see from about my nipples down better ... I was out of my body ... [Sewing me up] they took some stitches inside me first before they did the outside. And then it was just like they sew you

up. The shorter doctor started down here and worked this way. The other doctor could have started in the middle and worked up. They had a lot of trouble right here, but the rest of it was pretty fast ... And the heart doesn't look like I thought it did. It's big. And this is after the doctor had taken little pieces of it off. It's not shaped like I thought it would be. My heart was shaped something like the continent of Africa, with it being larger up here and tapered down. Bean-shaped is another way you could describe it. Maybe mine is odd-shaped ... [The surface was] pinkish and yellow. I thought the yellow part was fat tissue or something. Yucky, kind of. One general area to the right or left was darker than the rest instead of all being the same color ... I could draw you a picture of the saw they used and the thing they used to separate the ribs with. It was always there and I can remember the details of that probably better than the other things. It was draped all around, but you could see the metal part of it. I think all they used that for was to keep it constantly open.

The nightwatchman also listened to the physicians discussing the surgery being contemplated. He overheard them talking of bypasses, a swollen vein they spotted and the need to twist his heart into a different position to better examine it. So detailed were the patient's observations that he even told Dr Sabom that the first physician wore patent-leather shoes, and the other had a blood clot under his fingernail.

Dr Sabom was most intrigued by this report, so he exhumed the patient's medical files from the hospital office and checked them out. To his surprise, the patient's out-of-body observations corresponded precisely with the surgical procedures recorded by his surgeons. Since the patient had suffered an aneurysm, part of his heart was discoloured just as he'd seen. The heart had been twisted during the operation, while a syringe had twice been inserted into it.

Even though many people have a basic understanding of simple surgical procedures, Dr Sabom felt that the nightwatchman's report was too detailed to be coincidental. Perhaps, the cardiologist figured, he really had seen the surgery performed on him. In Table V, I have listed several comparisons between the patient's testimony and the surgeon's report (both published in more complete form by Sabom in 1982).

It appeared to Dr Sabom that a new dimension to the NDE was opening up, since few previous researchers had recognized the importance of these curious cases. Relying on his own surgical training, Dr Sabom began to search for similar cases, hoping to

Table V
Patient and Physician Reports from a
Typical 'Veridical' NDE

Report by the patient	Report filed by surgeon
1. The patient saw his head covered and his body draped in layered sheets.	The patient was draped in several sheets to ensure a sterile environment.
2. He watched the physician use a saw on him.	In order to cut the sternum, a saw was employed.
3. He watched as his ribs were separated by a metal device which remained in place throughout the surgery.	A self-restraining retractor had to be used (as usual) to separate the patient's ribs.
4. Part of the heart was discoloured.	A ventricular aneurysm had to be dissected.
5. Part of the heart was cut and the organ twisted and examined.	The heart was turned upside down and the aneurysm removed.
6. The patient saw the physician inject something into his heart.	A needle and syringe were used to evacuate air from the heart's left ventricle.
7. Some stitching was performed inside the body before the chest was closed up.	Several subcutaneous sutures were made before the skin was closed.

find more evidence for the objective reality of the NDE. During the years between 1977 and 1982 he found six cases in which the patients correctly described their operations. These cases were later included in his book *Recollections of Death*, published in 1982.

A similar case came to Dr Sabom's attention from the medical centre at the University of Florida. This report was offered by a retired Air Force pilot. His NDE occurred in 1973 when he was hospitalized and recovering from a coronary. The patient was sleeping when the second attack took place, so he had little conscious recollection of it. When he regained consciousness, he found himself standing by his body and looking back at it. Medical personnel were rushing into the room to resuscitate him, and he watched while someone injected a liquid into him through his IV. Then they lifted his body from the bed to a plywood support, where the physician-in-attendance began pounding his heart in order to start it beating. Next the patient watched passively while the physician proceeded to place an oxygen tube in his (the patient's) nose. The former pilot even heard the typical hissing made by the pressure of the oxygen tank. The tube was later removed when a green face mask was placed over his nose and mouth. The mask, he explained further, was attached to a hose leading to the oxygen.

Probably the most extraordinary part of this patient's story concerns his defibrillation—the electrical shocks given the body to get the heart beating. But before discussing what the patient saw, let me explain *why* these observations are extremely important.

The problem with most of Sabom's surgical OBE reports is that some people, while supposedly comatose, retain some consciousness. In particular, they can retain their power to hear, which is why sensitive physicians carefully monitor their conversations while performing surgery. They don't want to say anything that might upset the patient! Since anaesthetized patients can sometimes hear, could the reports collected by Dr Sabom be the result of this phenomenon? Could his informants have translated what they heard (i.e. through the surgeon's discussions) into some sort of bizarre visual representation? This seems possible because during surgery physicians often discuss the procedures they are contemplating, especially in teaching hospitals. This is a problem we'll discuss in depth in Chapter 9, but it has a bearing on the following observations made by Sabom's patient.

The former pilot clearly saw the defibrillator used in his emergency resuscitation. He explained to Dr Sabom that the device had a meter consisting of two needles set under a square, clear frame. The nurse placed the first needle into a stationary position, while the second needle gradually and slowly moved up the scale. The patient especially noted that the needle rose higher and higher on the meter before he received each jolt. He also described the defibrillator itself, but that part of his report isn't as interesting or important as his earlier observations.

It seems that Dr Sabom was impressed with the description, for he states in *Recollections of Death*:

> From a general medical standpoint, this man's autoscopic report of his resuscitation accurately describes what would be expected during a CPR (Cardiac-Pulmonary Resuscitation) procedure performed by highly trained personnel in an intensive care unit setting. I was particularly fascinated by his description of a 'fixed' needle and a 'moving' needle on the face of the defibrillator as it was being charged with electricity. The movement of these two needles is not something he could have observed unless he had actually seen this instrument in use. These two needles are individually used (1) to preselect the amount of electricity to be delivered to the patient ('they moved the fixed needle and it stayed still') and (2) to indicate that the defibrillator is being charged to the preselected amount ('the moving needle seemed to come up rather slowly really. It didn't just pop up like an ammeter or a voltmeter or something registering'). This charging procedure is only performed immediately prior to defibrillation, since once charged, this machine poses a serious electrical hazard unless it is correctly discharged in a very specific manner. Moreover, the meters of the type described by this man are not found on more recent defibrillator models, but were in common use in 1973, at the time of his cardiac arrest.

It is obvious that these observations were completely visual. It is unlikely that they were 'cued' from what the physicians and/or nurses were discussing during the resuscitation. This was an emergency procedure and it is unlikely that the personnel would have talked about the defibrillator. The device is routinely used in hospitals and it is doubtful that the nurses needed to be instructed in its proper use.

Dr Sabom reports in his book that the patient listened closely to what the resuscitation team was saying. But the cardiologist still doesn't feel that he could have been familiar enough with the defibrillator to describe it properly:

> Had this man, from his training as an air force pilot, been exposed to CPR instruments and techniques which would have enabled him to give such an accurate, detailed account of his own resuscitation without having actually observed it from his autoscopic NDE? Throughout the interview, he used various medical terms ('lidocaine pushes,' 'defibrillator,' 'watt-seconds,' etc.) which might suggest that he possessed a rather sophisticated knowledge of medical jargon and

procedures. When asked about this, he explained that he had paid close attention to what was being said during his autoscopic NDE and could recall much of the words and conversation used by the doctors and nurses present ... Moreover, he flatly denied having ever seen this CPR procedure including the movement of the needles on the defibrillator, at any other time. The tone of this interview and of subsequent conversations I have had with this man have convinced me that he would have no reasons to lie about these statements. I feel this way partly because of his consistent downplaying of the significance of his own experience throughout our conversations.

The two reports I have quoted from Dr Sabom's book represent simple NDEs, which certainly don't have the complexities of eschatological NDEs with their rapturous journeys to the next world. Some people would probably prefer to believe that, while simple NDEs represent some sort of objective experience, other-world journeys remain subjective. But Dr Sabom has published cases where patients made interesting surgical observations and later described eschatological experiences within the *same* NDE. Such cases suggest that the otherworld journey could be just as objectively real as the NDE's more prosaic characteristics.

There is a final aspect of the Georgia-based cardiologist's research which is also important for us to examine. Dr Sabom eventually began to wonder to what extent the public understands cardiac procedures. *If* most people have some familiarity with them, it struck Dr Sabom that his test cases could be the result of this information. (Remember that most of Dr Sabom's informants were cardiac patients.) Perhaps while unconscious, for example, these individuals began to have hallucinations concerning their resuscitations and could have used their previous exposure to such information—perhaps from reading or from TV medical shows—to build up convincing portrayals of common CPR methods. While this theory didn't seem to explain the remarkable details his patients sometimes reported, Dr Sabom felt the possibility should be taken into consideration.

In order to implement this study, the cardiologist recruited several heart patients with a history of surgery, CPR experiences or other exposures to similar intervention procedures. Each of them was asked to envision a medical team resuscitating a patient and to describe the technique.

The results were more than revealing. Despite their expected

familiarity with standard cardiac procedures, every single
respondent severely misdescribed the intervention. This finding
stood in stark contrast to Dr Sabom's NDE survivors, who invariably described their resuscitations correctly. Based on this
short study, it is Dr Sabom's feeling that the medical observations
some percipients make during the NDE cannot be explained
normally.

The research of Dr Margot Grey

Most pioneering research into the NDE was conducted in the
United States, but that country had no franchise on the subject.
Dr Margot Grey's research has not gained the same public
recognition that Kenneth Ring's and Michael Sabom's received
when it was published. She did not publish her work until 1985,
by which time public interest in the NDE had begun to cool.

Dr Grey's interest in the NDE did not originally stem from Raymond Moody's *Life After Life*, so in this respect she differs from
her two confrères in the United States. She was first exposed to
the strange byways of the NDE in February 1976 when she experienced a personal journey. While travelling in India she
became seriously ill for three weeks. The cause of her high fever
was never conclusively diagnosed, but she felt she was near
death and longed to return to England. She had several out-of-
body episodes throughout this period, during which she passed
in and out of consciousness. She found that she could leave the
body by a simple effort of will. 'At the time this seemed entirely
natural and felt very pleasant and extremely freeing,' she later explained. 'I remember looking down at my body lying on the bed
and feeling completely unperturbed by the fact that I was going
to die in a strange country half a world away from home.'

During an early phase of her illness Dr Grey experienced leaving the body and floating in total darkness, as if projected into
outer space. Her first impression was that she'd died and later she
perceived herself floating down an endless tunnel. She could see
a pin point of light at the end, which grew brighter and brighter
as she travelled towards it—and she felt a sense of exultation
which finally broke into mystical sensations of joy.

Dr Grey survived her malady and eventually returned to Great
Britain. 'My mental energies seemed extended and refined by a
new consciousness,' she says in her book *Return from Death*, 'and
I determined to study the phenomenon that I had experienced in

order to try to discover what other people experience when apparently on the threshold of imminent death.' Since the research of Dr Kenneth Ring was receiving considerable public attention at the time, the British psychologist decided to replicate his work. Would a comparative British study of NDE cases, she wondered, procure similar data to that collected in the United States? Dr Grey didn't throw herself into the study of the NDE immediately, however. She waited until 1981, when she received an invitation from Kenneth Ring, with whom she had been consulting, to come to the United States. Public interest in the NDE was then booming, and the International Association for Near-Death Studies had organized headquarters at the University of Connecticut where Ring taught. Coming to the United States enabled Dr Grey to study hundreds of NDE cases filed with the organization, which soon proved to her that researchers such as Moody, Ring, and Sabom had not been mistaken in their observations. She interviewed several NDE witnesses in Connecticut before returning to England to begin her own studies.

Following on the leads suggested by Ring's survey, Dr Grey studied the NDE experiences of people suffering from life-threatening illnesses. She also examined the reports of suicide survivors and individuals nearly killed in serious mishaps. She found that the core features of the NDE were described by people from each of these groups, even though the suicide/mishap informants didn't seem to describe the later phases of the NDE—i.e. entering the light which heralds the eschatological journey. She explains in her book that 'suicide-related near-death experiences do not reach completion but tend to fade before the transcendental elements characteristic of the "core experience" make their appearance'. Of course, it is hard to tell from Dr Grey's book whether this was her subjective impression from her cases, or whether she tried to determine this fact objectively. Her research has never been systematic or rigid and she reports her cases in a somewhat informal manner. She also learned from her studies in the United States that the specific cause of pseudo-death had little influence on the content of the NDE. People who nearly died from different causes tended to report the same characteristic NDEs.

When Dr Grey returned to England, she had a clearer concept of the research she wanted to carry out. She began by asking several colleagues and other professionals to refer potential NDE witnesses to her. She never explained the type of case she was looking for, since she feared that her colleagues would be selective in the cases/people they sent to her. When she eventually met her informants, she took demographic information from them and then followed Ring's original interview format. Each percipient was asked to give a complete description of his/her experience. Dr Grey then tried to evaluate whether the experience paralleled or differed from the prototypical Moody-type experience. When this part of the interview had been completed, Dr Grey explored the long-term effects of the experience with her subject.

It took her eighteen months to collect the information she required, during which she spoke with 41 individuals with usable case histories. This case collection consisted of 32 investigations conducted in Great Britain, to which she added 9 cases from the United States. When she refined her cases further, she ended up with 38 cases in which characteristic NDEs were detailed. By breaking down the component features of the NDE described in these cases, Dr Grey found that they perfectly matched Ring's findings—with fewer and fewer people progressively describing the deeper aspects of the experience.

It is difficult, however, to make a precise statistical comparison between the relative characteristics of Dr Grey's and Dr Ring's cases. Ring had broken down the cases he investigated into five primary elements. The typical NDE patient (1) becomes blissful before (2) leaving the body. He/she may (3) enter a darkness or speed through a tunnel (4) towards a bright light, (5) into which he/she merges.

Dr Grey broke down the components of the NDE into 25 more specific characteristics. She took Ring's original five core elements and created subcategories within them. While Ring reported that 37 per cent of his NDE informants report leaving the body, for instance, Dr Grey broke down this characteristic into such categories as 'clear view of the body', 'suspended above the body', and so forth. But despite this problem, the parallels between the two findings are very striking. Table VI compares Dr Ring's original statistics with a representative sample of Dr Grey's findings.

Dr Grey extended her research beyond merely mapping out the features of the NDE. Like Dr Ring, she also became fascinated by the personal transformations reported by NDE survivors. These

Table VI
Representative Characteristics of the NDE

Component feature of the NDE	(N = 49) Kenneth Ring's cases	(N = 38) Margot Grey's cases*
1. Felt blissful sensations	60%	
Felt peace and euphoria		47%
Felt joy and happiness		29%
2. Left the body	37%	
Suspended above the body		32%
3. Entered the darkness (or experienced a tunnel)	23%	
Tunnel sensations		26%
Very rapid motion (in a darkness)		26%
4. Perceived a bright light	16%	
Distant point of light		21%
Saw a blinding light but eyes were not harmed		16%
5. Entered this light	10%	
Enveloped in light and love		39%
Travelled to a new and beautiful dimension		18%

*Some of the percentages seem disappropriate since Dr Grey's subjects sometimes reported more than a single feature per category.

people often return to life with enhanced spiritual and social values. Not uncommonly, they report suddenly developing psychic gifts.

But the British researcher also made a significant discovery that played little—if any—role in the research reported by her American colleagues. Dr Kenneth Ring and Dr Michael Sabom both found that their subjects reported rather pleasant experiences. While some of their witnesses had neutral feelings towards their experiences, everyone seemed to find it interesting and certainly not unpleasant. Dr Grey discovered, to the contrary, that several of her percipients reported nightmarish encounters with death—literal previews of hell itself. Such reports had been noted by other NDE researchers before 1981, and Raymond Moody mentioned the subject in the sequel to *Life After Life* that he published in 1977. These cases have been promoted by some Fundamentalist Christians in support of their religious beliefs. But the cases seemed to be extremely rare, so most scientific researchers preferred (in my opinion, biasedly) to ignore them. Dr Grey couldn't shove these cases aside, for they simply kept cropping up too often.

The subject of negative or hellish NDEs will be more fully discussed in Chapter 7.

So what did these three research projects prove? I think they uncovered some important facts about the NDE.

It has become clear that the original observations Raymond Moody made in 1975 were by and large correct—even if his research standards hadn't been too rigid or critical. Near-death experiences tend to be common by-products inherent to mankind since people from different cultural/social/religious backgrounds report the same type of experience. The patterns to which they conform obviously don't result from people tailoring their experiences to match those they'd read about or studied. Most people reporting their NDEs to researchers such as Ring Grey had never heard of Raymond Moody or his book. They tended to be intelligent individuals, eager to share their puzzling experiences with others, perhaps hoping that some light could be shed on them. Dr Grey eventually even confirmed that people knowledgeable about the NDE tend *not* to have them in life-threatening situations. This curious finding had been previously noted by both Ring and Sabom in their independent surveys. Obviously this finding is telling us something important about the NDE.

Prior knowledge is, in fact, the only demographic that influences the NDE. Even important psychological factors, such as belief in survival, don't seem to 'programme' a person to experience the NDE when threatened by imminent death.

Of course, none of these discoveries prove that the NDE is objectively real or represents the literal separation of the soul from the body. That would be extending the findings of Ring, Sabom, and Grey much too far. Their research primarily demonstrates that the NDE is an important and (at least) subjectively real experience that can't be easily dismissed by the scientific community.

But could some component of objective reality enter into the NDE? Certainly such a possibility is suggested by Dr Sabom's research. But we simply don't know whether many of his informants *didn't* see their surgical procedures correctly. Such cases —if they exist—would throw cold water on the importance of the cardiologist's veridical cases.

Despite the great progress of the research into the NDE between 1977 and 1983, the sceptics were vocal, too. Some of them felt that the scientific study of the NDE could be unfortunate for society, or that NDE researchers were glamorizing purely hallucinatory experiences. Some of these critics were debunkers in the worst sense of the word—i.e. curmudgeonly people annoyed by the fact that some folk have real spiritual or paranormal experiences. Other sceptics were more scholarly and educated. They rightly pointed out that there were problems with the research being reported, and felt that their position hadn't yet been heard. So let's see what these people have to say, in order to determine whether they have a sufficient case against the NDE.

5.

NDE Reports from Children

Could NDEs represent hallucinations people experience in the face of imminent death? Could such experiences result from the pie-in-the-sky religious indoctrinations we receive in childhood and through our collective cultural heritage?

This was the first theory the sceptics put forward to challenge the Moody revolution in 1975, and it is still being promoted today by some psychologists. While it sounds simplistic, this theoretical model for the NDE is both reasonable and eminently logical. No matter what religious sentiments any one of us entertains or respects, few people can ignore the influence of the Judaeo-Christian heritage in which most of us in the West were raised—complete with a belief in a heavenly realm filled with glorious music, flying angels, and gold-paved streets. Anyone who seeks to dispute the pervasive nature of this influence need only see Diane Keaton's wonderful little film *Heaven*, in which several people 'off the street' describe their visions of paradise. Their storybook descriptions reveal just how strongly our beliefs have been affected by our Western religious background.

The otherworldly realms contacted by people undergoing eschatological NDEs tend to mimic this familiar conceptualization, so it is understandable that the sceptics offhandedly dismiss the literal reality of the experience. It is also for this reason that cross-cultural studies of the NDE are sorely needed. If it could be shown that similar heavenly realms crop up in eschatological NDEs reported from different cultures, the sceptics' position would be significantly weakened. Few of these cross-cultural comparisons have been undertaken, however, and cultural influences do seem to contaminate NDE reports. The story of Er from Plato's *Republic* reported in Chapter 2, for example, reads very differently from the NDEs reported today. Whether or not NDEs represent a truly consistent cross-cultural phenomenon has simply not yet been determined.[1]

Despite this significant flaw in the evidence, there remain other lines of evidence inconsistent with the theory that NDEs represent culturally programmed hallucinations. Dr Glen O. Gabbard and Dr Stuart Twemlow—two veteran psychiatrists from Kansas —dispute this theoretical model in no uncertain terms in their book *With the Eyes of the Mind*. While they suggest that NDE reports from different cultures genuinely seem to resemble each other (a position they promote without citing much evidence), they approach the cultural/psychological hallucination model from a different perspective. 'Perhaps an even more compelling rebuttal', they continue, 'is contained in an examination of NDE reports from small children'.

Such a statement couldn't have been written before 1984, when the eminent psychiatrists' book was originally published. NDE reports contributed by children were conspicuously lacking when Dr Raymond Moody first brought the subject to widespread public attention. Nor did such chronicles play any role in the case collections subsequently undertaken by Sabom, Ring, Grey, and others. But it didn't take long before some researchers studying the NDE began focusing on such cases, in the hope that they would shed important light on the subject.

It is well known that small children don't have a concrete or sophisticated understanding of death and only come to recognize its nature later in life. Because it is such a murky concept to them, we wouldn't expect children to be culturally conditioned to have NDEs when faced with death. So if the NDEs reported by young children resemble those placed on record by more mature witnesses, perhaps we can reject the cultural expectancy model.

So just how do children conceptualize death?

The literature on how children envision death is vast, and the findings of several separate studies remain fairly consistent. Very young children between 3 and 5 years old conceive death to be some sort of journey, even though they have little understanding

---

[1]For a significant look at this lack of evidence, refer to Dorothy Ayers Counts's 'Near-death and out-of-body experiences in a Melanesian society', *Anabiosis*, 1983, 3, 115–36.

of its nature. This vague belief is complicated by the fact that this journey isn't perceived as a permanent one. After the child matures a bit and reaches 6 or 7 years old, he/she begins to understand the finality of death but still resists personalizing this information. Death to them is still something that happens to somebody else. It can take some children until they reach 12 or 13 years before they understand their own mortality. Certainly children under the age of 10 have little comprehension of death's greater implications, which is why parents should be careful when discussing the subject with them. Innocently telling young children that a deceased relative has taken a trip or was 'taken to heaven' by God can be extremely traumatic. Such euphemisms conjure up visions of desertion and punishments for children, who typically take such statements at face value.

In light of these conceptualizations, brilliantly outlined by Dr Maria Nagy in the 1940s, we shouldn't expect to see clear-cut eschatological NDEs reported by children less than 10 years old. Or at least their NDE reports should be contextually different from those reported by older persons, should the NDE really be some sort of culturally programmed hallucination. Young children simply don't have the conceptual skills to produce such elaborate hallucinations. But despite this fact, several researchers have found that children report NDEs fairly commonly.

The first case report

The first childhood NDE case was reported in the literature in the fall of 1983 by Dr Melvin Morse, a physician working at the Children's Orthopedic Hospital in Seattle, Washington. Dr Morse came across the case while treating a little girl in an emergency room in Idaho. The 7-year-old patient had nearly drowned in a public swimming pool only minutes before. Even though she was breathing by the time he treated her, she remained unconscious. The little patient finally regained consciousness three days later and was discharged from the hospital in a week. Luckily for the girl and her parents, no evidence of neurological damage was observed and the child was soon back in school. The first indication that she had undergone something resembling an NDE became obvious when Dr Morse examined her two weeks later. While he was talking with his patient, the girl suddenly recalled 'talking to the heavenly Father' during her previous trauma. She made this comment to the doctor rather openly, but seemed reluctant to say anything further.

The entire story of the NDE emerged more fully during a follow-up session, when the child explained how she recalled nearly drowning in the pool. 'I was dead,' she said. 'Then I was in a tunnel. It was dark and I was scared. I couldn't walk.'

The child wouldn't permit Dr Morse to tape-record her comments further, so he took written notes for the rest of the interview. The young girl explained that a lady named Elizabeth materialized by her side while the tunnel suddenly filled with light. Together they walked to heaven, which the child enjoyed immensely because of the brightness and the exquisite flowers she saw *en route*. The heavenly realm was guarded by a border which prevented her from looking into it directly, but at the periphery she met several deceased relatives and two other women. They were waiting to be reborn, they explained to the little girl (in pure Platonic tradition!).

Two other figures then appeared before her, whom she immediately took to be God and Jesus. They asked if she wouldn't prefer to return to earth. The little girl replied that she wouldn't. The kindly woman serving as her otherworldly guide then asked her if she wanted to see her mother once more. This suggestion was too much for the child, and she woke up in the hospital when she replied that she would.

The experience obviously made a strong impression on the child, for afterwards she often told her mother that she'd 'like to go back there' to the otherworld. She said further that 'it was nice'. It later turned out that while in the hospital, she had spontaneously asked the nurse about two mysterious friends—perhaps oblique references to the ladies she saw waiting to be reborn.

Dr Morse was disinclined to reject the importance of the child's testimony. When he reported the case in the October 1983 issue of the *American Journal of Diseases of Children*, he pointed to the strong similarities between his patient's story and those NDEs reported by adults. Phenomenology such as the out-of-body experience, sliding through a tunnel, reaching a border of some sort, and seeing spiritual guides and relatives represents core elements of the prototypical NDE.

But could this experience have been a fantasy or dream, perhaps based on the child's previous religious upbringing or Sunday school indoctrination? Dr Morse was interested in this possibility and explored it in some depth. It turned out that the girl came from a devout Mormon family and regularly went to church and Sunday school. She knew about heaven and the possibility of post-mortem survival, but Dr Morse didn't think that these simple beliefs could have programmed the content of her NDE. Neither are such experiences as coming to a border between the earth and the otherworld or journeying through a tunnel taught in Mormon eschatology.[2] The physician also rejected the theory that the girl's experience was an hallucinatory defence in the face of death. 'The findings of near-death experience in children', he comments in his report, 'must conflict with this reductionistic viewpoint because of their cognitive development level and perception of death.' Dr Morse also points out that 'in studies of children who are confronted with their own deaths, to my knowledge, this narcissistic retreat caused by the fear of death has not been described'.

Probably the most interesting component of the case is the child's assertion that she met people waiting to be reborn. This statement lends an obviously reincarnationist flavour to her narrative, which is markedly atypical of NDE reports in general. (The only similar case in the literature is the story of Er from Plato's *Republic* which was fully recounted in Chapter 2.) The reference is doubly fascinating since reincarnation is not a part of Mormon religious belief. While members of the denomination believe in the pre-existence of the soul, this belief refers to a form of disembodied existence preceding earthly life. It seems obvious that the child was not referring to such a phenomenon. Mormons also believe in the physical resurrection of the body, but they never refer to this phenomenon in terms of rebirth. It is just possible, however, that the young girl was referring to the Mormon belief that people can be baptized even after death. The process is usually undertaken by the person's surviving relatives, and this practice is sometimes called being 'born again'.

I was so puzzled by this report that I wrote to Dr Morse regarding this possibility in December 1984. I specifically asked him

---

[2] The NDE has, however, found its way into Mormon religious literature. A paper on 'The Mormon explanation of near-death experiences' by Craig R. Lundahl and Harold A. Widdison was published in the June 1983 issue of *Anabiosis—the Journal for Near Death Studies*. This information is not part of a typical Mormon child's religious education, however. It is, in fact, doubtful whether many Mormons even know of these cases in their historical literature.

if he could have misinterpreted what the little girl was saying. I received a lengthly and kind reply from him on 14 December. Dr Morse explained that, in response to my letter, he had reviewed both his tape and the subsequent notes of his talks with his patient. He was certain that she didn't speak of being 'born again'. Because of his own interest in the case, he had talked with the child's parents regarding their religious beliefs. While the couple subscribed to both pre-existence and continued post-mortem survival, they did not believe in reincarnation. Dr Morse concluded his letter by noting that, in his experience, most children recovering from life-threatening comas report out-of-body experiences.

The reincarnation issue raised by this child must remain an enigma. Since rebirth doctrines play no part in Mormon tradition, this component of the experience obviously wasn't culturally programmed. On the other hand, I think it's possible that the girl herself may have confused the Mormon belief in post-mortem baptism with reincarnation.

The case studies of Dr Glen O. Gabbard and Dr Stuart Twemlow
Since Dr Morse's patient was 7 years old when she reported her NDE, perhaps she was reaching the point when children first develop a reasonable concept of death. But what about even younger children—children too young to understand death's basic meaning? Dr Glen Gabbard (of the Menninger Foundation in Topeka, Kansas) and Dr Stuart Twemlow (of the University of Kansas School of Medicine) have been able to find and personally investigate two such cases. Both of the children were younger than 5 years old when the NDE-like episodes occurred. Because of their youth, neither child possessed the communication skills necessary to offer truly coherent descriptions of their encounters. But what they told their parents sounds strongly like prototypical NDE experiences. Both cases were later reported to the Kansas psychiatrists by the children's relatives.

The first case concerned a young boy they simply call Todd, who was 2½ years old when he bit into the cord of his mother's vacuum cleaner. She found him lying unconscious a few minutes later. At first she thought he was sleeping, but then she noticed that his skin had a bluish cast and that his breathing had stopped. She immediately called for an ambulance, which arrived seven minutes later. When he was admitted to a local hospital he was still not breathing and the situation looked hopeless. They boy's condition was touch and go for a considerable period of time before he finally began responding to treatment. According to the hospital records, the patient had been clinically dead for approximately 30 minutes, and it took several months for him to recover from the incident completely.

The child's parents first learned of Todd's otherworld journey when he returned home. While he was playing in the family living room one day, his mother casually asked him whether he recalled the mishap.

The child responded by saying that he 'went in a room with a very nice man and sat with him'. Some sort of bright light illuminated the room. When his mother pressed him further, Todd explained that the man 'asked me if I wanted to stay there or come back to you'.

The young boy could only say, in response, that he wanted to return to his mother. That concluded his description of his close call with death, and he went back to playing with his toys. Luckily, the mother took careful notes of the conversation, although she was probably not aware that her son's story seemed to represent a typical NDE. Since this conversation took place three years before Raymond Moody's work became known to the public, it is unlikely that the mother unconsciously tailored her report to conform to the typical NDE.

The second case investigated by the two Kansas psychiatrists concerned a slightly older child. Mike was 4 years old when he slipped into a public swimming pool. He was submerged for only a couple of minutes before being rescued by his mother, who was swimming nearby. The boy was stunned by his experience but seemed mysteriously euphoric when he recovered. When he finally regained his composure, he refused to leave the pool and kept talking of a long bridge with sparkling lights that he'd seen. The child compared the sight to Sleeping Beauty's Castle at Disneyland—so familiar to youngsters from the opening credits of the popular *Wonderful World of Disney* show. The boy also spoke of the golden lights and colours he had observed. Mike wasn't at all frightened by his close call with death and soon began telling everyone by the pool about his experience. His compulsion to speak of the occurrence lasted for several weeks, during which time his mysterious serenity was continuously noticeable.

Drs Gabbard and Twemlow have also collected a related childhood case, though this report is not evidential, for obvious reasons. It was told to them by a 29-year-old witness *recalling* a childhood episode. She testified that when she was 7, some life-threatening complications set in during a bout of mumps. While she was sick and crying in bed, she suddenly heard a celestial choir singing beautiful music. Then she remembered floating over her body and sensed invisible beings surrounding her. Next she floated right through the bedroom ceiling, and soon enjoyed the exhilarating feeling of floating down a dark tunnel illuminated by a tiny light at the end.

The witness's NDE turned into an otherworldly journey as it continued. She found herself in the presence of a bearded man dressed in a white robe who stood between the end of the tunnel and a beautiful realm beyond it. This realm was irresistibly alluring and the child asked the figure if she might enter it. The spiritual presence agreed to the request. The colours in this heavenly dimension, the woman later recalled, were breathtaking and she met several friendly people while walking through it. But the further she walked, the less friendly the people became, and she retraced her steps back to the entrance of the tunnel and complained to the robed figure about the situation. The being could only respond that it was time for her to return, a command with which she dutifully complied.

It is hard to base any firm conclusions on just three cases, but the Kansas psychiatrists feel that, if nothing else, these brief reports fully conform to the patterns of the prototypical NDE. When they are evaluated as a group, Drs Gabbard and Twemlow note several parallels between these NDEs reported by children and those collected by other researchers, among them Raymond Moody and Kenneth Ring. Table VII illustrates some of these comparisons for the reader.

Of course, these comparisons must be taken with a pinch of salt, since the most complete childhood NDE report the psychiatrists collected was really contributed by an adult. Even though she was recalling a personal experience, it is difficult to know whether she unconsciously revised her story to match other reports she'd read. But even if we discount her experience, we still have the reports of the other children to consider. They seem to be describing scattered components of the prototypical NDE, but in an obviously unsophisticated way.

Table VII
Comparisons between the Prototypical NDE and Childhood NDEs

Common components of the NDE	Components reported in childhood NDEs collected by Drs Gabbard and Twemlow (N = 3)
1. Witnesses commonly see a white light with which they merge.	All the children reported bright or twinkling lights during their NDEs.
2. People undergoing NDEs invariably report experiencing out-of-body episodes, and/or travelling through a tunnel.	A discrete out-of-body experience was described by one of the children years later, who also described a tunnel.
3. The percipients often see either their deceased relatives or spiritual guides in the otherworld.	Two of the children met loving figures who guided them through the gates of death.
4. Some people see a border separating the afterlife from earth.	One witness recalled seeing this border when describing her childhood NDE.
5. The witnesses are told either to return to earth or to make such a decision for themselves.	The children were either told to return home or asked whether they wished to see their mothers again.
6. The experiencers feel totally blissful during the encounter.	The parents sometimes noticed that their children were curiously serene because of their close calls.
7. Returning to the body is frequently noted.	Returning to the body is reported in one of the children's narratives.

The case collection of Nancy Evans Bush

Dr Gabbard and Dr Twemlow have not been the only researchers interested in the systematic study of childhood NDE reports. Another investigator has been Nancy Evans Bush, who has long been a guiding light for the International Association for Near-Death Studies (IANDS) in Storrs, Connecticut. She became interested in studying reports of childhood NDEs in the early 1980s and discovered several cases in her organization's extensive files. She eventually found 15 of these cases, even though most of them were reported retrospectively by the witnesses years later. Luckily, however, she also found two cases reported by parents of small children claiming NDEs. This total of 17 cases concerned children ranging from barely 12 months old (recalled later in life under hypnosis) to early adolescence. Despite this wide range, both the children and the retrospectively speaking witnesses invariably described classic NDEs.

The following case, for example, includes typical NDE components such as leaving the body and seeing a bright light. The NDE took place when the percipient fell down a flight of stairs.

> As I started to take the first step down, I flashed the beam of light up at the light bulb, curious to see if a burned-out bulb look 'burned.' I stepped out and fell into the darkness.
>
> The next thing I was aware of, was being up near the ceiling over the foot of the stairs. The light was dim and at first I saw nothing unusual. Then I saw myself lying, face down, on the cement, over to the side of the stairway. I was a little surprised, but not at all upset at seeing myself that way. I watched and saw that I didn't move at all. After a while, I said to myself, 'I guess I'm dead.' But I felt good! Better than I ever had. I realized I probably wouldn't be going back to my mother, but I wasn't afraid at all . . .
>
> I noticed the dim light growing slowly brighter. The source of light was not in the basement, but far behind and slightly above me. I looked over my shoulder into the most beautiful light imaginable. It seemed to be at the end of a long tunnel which was gradually getting brighter and brighter as more and more of the light entered it. It was yellow-white and brilliant, but not painful to look at even directly. As I turned to face the light with my full 'body,' I felt happier than I ever had before and have since.
>
> Then the light was gone. I felt groggy and sick, with a terrible headache. I only wanted my mother, and to stop my head from hurting.

The next case Ms Bush found in her Connecticut collection, like the previous one, also included the famous tunnel experience. In this case, reported below, the witness is describing an NDE he had when he was 10 years old. The episode resulted from a life-threatening illness of some sort.

> I don't remember the entrance, but in a little while I was in a dark tunnel. There was absolutely no sound, and all was black. I couldn't see to make my way through the tunnel, but I was being wafted along as a speck of dust, pitch black, but as I went along with neither sight nor sound, I felt at ease. I thought I was discovering a new cave.
>
> After a while the tunnel became square in section, and along I went and I became annoyed, and thought to myself that the journey was pointless and fruitless and I was wasting valuable time. Just when I was about to turn back in disgust (I was completely alone), I saw a tiny speck of light ahead. I went on and as I did the speck grew larger, and I thought it was well I hadn't turned back because I was going to discover something at last.
>
> At about 150 yards from the end, I saw plainly that there was brilliant white light out there beyond the square end of the tunnel. It interested me and I went on. All was yet quiet, and I went blissfully on, enjoying the journey at last.

These two reports suffer from the same potential problem that complicates Gabbard and Twemlow's third case. The sceptic could reasonably argue that the percipients tailored their stories to conform to the popular stereotype of the NDE. (Remember that these cases consisted of *memories* of possible NDEs, which could easily have been misrecalled over the years—especially in light of the publicity given to Moody-type NDEs by the popular press.) What is so extraordinary, however, is that both of those cases cited by the parents of NDE-reporting children followed the same classic pattern. These cases probably weren't distorted by memory problems, since the parents were not reporting purely personal experiences.

The first of these young mothers wrote to IANDS concerning her little son's NDE, which resulted from a swimming mishap. The incident had occurred during the summer of 1975 when the family was taking a lakeside vacation. The 3½-year-old disappeared while the family enjoyed themselves by the shore. He was found submerged in water 15 minutes later by a lifeguard. It took three weeks for the boy to recover fully from his close call, but luckily he didn't suffer any brain damage.

Seven years later, the boy suddenly started talking about the incident. His mother wrote to IANDS that:

Robin is eleven now, and about six months ago he shared something with me about the white light. I couldn't understand until I listened carefully.

. . . He said, 'A long time ago I was awake. Not asleep! I was going up in the air and saw you and Papy crying. Something came to me and said you have to go back. I felt good [to come back], but I liked all the people I saw.'

I asked Robin who he saw, and he said they were too bright, but 'One man held me and I felt so good I wanted to stay, but he said no.'

Just a few days ago, I reminded Robin of what he told me and he didn't remember and laughed at me. Maybe someday he will remember again.

A second childhood case Ms Bush studied was based on a phone conversation with the child's mother. The woman explained that her son had long been terrified of water, a situation exacerbated when he once fell into the pool of their apartment building. He was rushed to a local hospital and the situation looked grave, for the physicians treating him were convinced that the 4-year-old had suffered brain damage. They also believed that he would probably never remember his life-threatening experience.

Despite this serious prognosis, the boy recovered completely and soon exhibited a remarkable transformation. For some inexplicable reason his fear of water disappeared. It wasn't until a year later, though, that he began openly recalling his drowning experience. His mother told the IANDS staff:

One day he came to me and said, 'Sit down, I have to talk to you. Mother.' That's not a five-year-old. He never calls me 'Mother.'

He said, 'When I drowned, I didn't want to come back. I saw you, Josie and another lady working on me. I was sitting on the roof and I could see you.

'Then it got real dark and I walked down a tunnel. There was a bright light at the end, and a man was standing there.'

I asked him, 'Who was the man?'

He said, 'It was God. And I said I wanted to stay. But God said it wasn't my time yet and I had to come back. I put my hand out and God put his hand out and then God pulled his hand back. He didn't want me to stay.

'On the way back, I saw the devil. He said if I did what he wanted, I could have anything I want.'

I said, 'You know God is good and the devil is evil.'

He said, 'The devil said I could have anything I wanted, but I didn't want him bossing me around.'

I said, 'Mom and Dad wanted you back real bad, and God knew that. He let you come back to us.' And he said, 'When I fell in the water, I called and called for you, but you didn't hear me.'

Unlike many NDE reports, the final outcome of this little story isn't too comforting. The child eventually became very moody and started exhibiting behaviour problems in school. It never became clear if these problems related to his NDE, but his mother told Ms Bush that the child sometimes seemed obsessed with his previous experience. Nancy Bush has been personally sensitive to this growing problem, especially where children are concerned. She concludes her paper on childhood NDEs by writing that such reactions provide 'sufficient testimony to the need for thoughtful study of NDEs in children, with careful attention given to the aftereffects and the development of interventions that will support the children and their families as they work through integration of the experience'.

Evaluated as a large collection, it is obvious that the childhood cases recalled by Ms Bush's correspondents and informants clearly resemble the prototypical NDE. Working from the 17 reports she amassed, she found that the core characteristics of the NDE—previously graphed by Dr Kenneth Ring—showed up repeatedly in childhood cases. Table VIII is a table greatly simplifying the one published by Nancy Evans Bush, in which these features are statistically tabulated. Notice how the percentages replicate the findings of Dr Ring, with fewer percipients experiencing the deeper aspects of the NDE in a stage-like progression.

The potential contribution the study of childhood cases will make to our eventual understanding of the NDE isn't totally clear. Some researchers, such as Dr Glen Gabbard and Dr Melvin Morse, believe that childhood NDEs disprove several popularly proposed psychological models for the phenomenon. They specifically feel that such reports can't be explained as death-threat hallucinations, or the result of the children's religious up-bringing. Researchers such as Nancy Evans Bush, however, seem content to demonstrate that childhood NDEs differ little in content from those of adults. She feels that this fact demonstrates the subjectively real and stereotypical nature of such experiences, but hasn't yet commented on their ontological significance.

Table VIII
Components of the Prototypical NDE
in Nancy Bush's Childhood Cases
(N = 17)

Component feature	Percentage
1. Experienced a sense of well-being	53
2. Perceived some sort of light	65
3. Experienced leaving the body	41
4. Entered a darkness	41
5. Travelled through a tunnel	30
6. Encountered a spiritual presence	35
7. Saw some form of otherworldly realm	18
8. Encountered spirits of the dead	12
9. Instructed to return to earth	24

But do such experiences really *prove* that the NDE is a paranormal rather than a psychological phenomenon? There's hardly a consensus on this matter among researchers. Some students of the NDE readily believe that childhood NDEs help establish the literal reality of the NDE and the otherworld. But more circumspect researchers shy from drawing such far-reaching conclusions. Dr Gabbard and Dr Twemlow even found, for instance, that there might exist a psychodynamic process behind some features found in their cases. In their book *With the Eyes of the Mind*, they especially point to the 'being of light' so commonly cited by children reporting NDEs. They show that these figures could be internalized representations of the children's own parents. The researchers point out that these figures are more clearly defined in the reports of older children. This is the same way that children gradually perceive their parents while growing up, when the Oedipal conflict—so beloved of some psychiatrists —is fully resolved.

Of course, this conceptual model can't explain why *most* NDE percipients report similar spiritual guides, despite their chronological superiority to children. Nor do the Kansas psychiatrists promote their explanatory model dogmatically.

'We are not implying in this analysis', they write, 'that the being of light is definitively the internalized parent of the NDEer. That may or may not be the case. We are saying that whatever figure is perceived in the course of the near-death experience will be perceived through an individual filter or template of internalized objects, which is developmentally determined by the age of the child and the child's experience with significant objects in his or her environment.'

This is an elaborate way of saying that children perceive their experiences in childish ways, which is hardly an epoch-making observation!

Nor have the psychiatrists successfully shown how other characteristics of the NDE show evidence of such psycho-dynamic contamination.

Because so little research has been devoted to the study of childhood NDEs, it is impossible to predict what conceptual model for the experience they will support or disprove. But it is becoming clear that simple reductionistic models—especially beloved of the sceptics—can't readily explain them. Such experiences seem too inconsistent with the way children conceptualize (or fail to conceptualize) death. This fact doesn't prove that NDEs represent genuine otherworld journeys, however. If NDEs represent experiences genetically coded into the brain, for instance, there's no reason why children shouldn't experience them. This is a possibility to which we'll be returning in the next chapter, and it is probably the most serious counter-hypothesis to the possible 'reality' of the experience.

End note

After this book entered production, Raymond Moody personally published a selection of classical first-hand NDE reports contributed by children in his *The Light Beyond* (New York: Bantam, 1988). Dr Morse went on to publish other childhood cases in the *American Journal of Diseases of Children* in 1986 (Vol. 140, pp. 1110–1114).

6.

Experiencing Death Through Drugs?

'My mind left my body', the patient reported, 'and apparently went to what some describe as the second state. I felt I was in a huge, well-lit room, in front of a massive throne draped in lush velvet. I saw nothing else but felt the presence of higher intelligences tapping my mind of every experience and impression I had gathered. I begged to be released, to return to my body. It was terrifying. Finally, I blacked out and slowly came to in the recovery room.'

This type of experience is, of course, commonly reported by people who have had close encounters with death—ranging from suffering cardiac failure to freezing and to life-threatening falls. Contained within this narrative are several core elements of the classic NDE. The percipient cites an out-of-body experience to an otherworldly realm, contact with some type of spiritual intelligence, and a subsequent return to the body.

The account quoted above was not, however, contributed by somebody who experienced a close encounter with death. Nor was it published in a medical or psychology journal. The reporter wasn't even *threatened* by death, since he was in the hospital for routine surgery and was, in fact, describing a drug-induced hallucination. This hallucinatory experience had accompanied his emergence from a curious anaesthetic called ketamine, and his report was originally cited in a 1976 issue of *High Times* magazine. Ketamine is a general anaesthetic or analgesic (depending on the dose) often given to children or the elderly.

Or consider the following experience reported in a 14-year-old boy who thought he was dying:

I really thought I was dying. My mind left my body and went up into a corner of the bedroom. And I was watching myself as I stopped breathing. I kept telling myself from the corner of the room, 'Come on, start breathing. You can do it. Come on ... Just wake up. Wake up.' I was finally okay.

This young man was not really in any danger, though. His experience resulted from smoking phencyclidine, a close chemical relative to ketamine. It is better known on the street as PCP or 'angel dust'. It was originally developed as a general anaesthetic, but too many people had nearly psychotic reactions to it when it was first marketed, so it was soon withdrawn from medical use. Both ketamine and phencyclidine work similarly on the central nervous system. The drugs hyperstimulate the CNS until it is to shut down. When used during surgery, secondary drugs are employed to physically relax the patient, since the stimulating effect of these drugs can cause spontaneous motor movements.

NDEs, out-of-body experiences and drugs

People who report NDEs usually perceive their eschatological journeys while submerged in several internally deployed states of consciousness. Such individuals certainly aren't functioning in those states of mind common to everyday living. These inwardly focused states can also typically result from illnesses or mishaps that lead to life-threatening situations. More rarely they sometimes result from drugs commonly used in medical treatment. It isn't too surprising then that some sceptics have suggested that NDEs merely represent drug-induced or related hallucinations. This was, in fact, yet another conceptual model put forward to explain these euphoric out-of-body states when Raymond Moody's research became so popular in the 1970s.

The suggestion that NDEs might be nothing more than neurophysiological hallucinations, with roots lying more within the biochemistry of the brain than in the afterlife, received its most eloquent support in 1980, when Dr Ronald K. Siegel, a noted expert on both drugs and hallucinations, published a paper on the subject that year in the prestigious journal *American Psychologist*. Dr Siegel, who is also a psychopharmacologist at the University of California (Los Angeles), pointed out in his paper that most hallucinations, no matter what causes them, tend to include certain types of imagery—i.e. specific images so commonly reported that they have even been labelled 'hallucination constants' by psychologists. It was Dr Siegel's position that the core elements of the NDE represent little more than a peculiar constellation and expression of these constants. He specifically argued that such typical NDE components as the stereotypical 'tunnel', the 'city of lights', and the subjective 'reality' of the experience are often described by people taking hallucinogenic drugs. It therefore struck Dr Siegel that the NDE is probably little more than a highly structured hallucination.

It may seem that, in presenting this viewpoint, Dr Siegel is trying to simplistically dismiss the reality of the NDE. But this isn't really the case. He has, in fact, developed a careful neurophysiological model for hallucinations in general, and it was this model that he applied to the study of NDEs in 1980.

The possible process lying behind both NDEs and drug-related hallucinations has been of considerable interest to Dr Siegel, for as he explains in his *American Psychologist* paper:

> The remarkable similarity of imagery in life after death experiences and imagery in hallucinatory experiences invites inquiry about common mechanisms of action. The experiences can be considered a combination of simple and complex imagery. The simple imagery consists of tunnels, bright lights and colors, and geometric forms. As discussed above, they are probably caused by phosphenes, visual sensations arising from the discharge of neurons in structures of the eye. They also reflect the electrical excitation of organized groups of cells in the visual cortex of the brain.
>
> Most of the investigators undertaking to explain the complex imagery of people and places have described the visions as being the result of excitation of the central nervous system. As early as 1845 French psychiatrist Jacques Moreau maintained that hallucinations resulted from cerebral excitation that enabled thoughts and memories to become transformed into sensory impressions. Recent electrophysiological research has confirmed that hallucinations are directly related to states of excitation and arousal of the central nervous system, which are coupled with a functional disorganization of the part of the brain that regulates incoming stimuli. Behaviorally, the result is an impairment of perceptions normally based on external stimuli and a preoccupation with internal imagery.

But why would these false perceptions specifically structure themselves into the form of the NDE or the eschatological journey? Siegel believes that the components of the prototypical NDE are programmed by the setting from which the experience merges and by the subject's expectations. These psychological factors then interplay with certain biochemical changes in the brain that produce hallucinations, which result in an NDE:

The specific content of complex hallucinatory imagery is determined largely by set (expectations and attitudes) and setting (physical and psychological environments). For many dying and near-death experiences, the sets (fear of approaching death, changes in body and mental functioning, etc.) and settings (hospital wards, accident scenes, etc.) can influence specific eschatological thoughts and images.

I first met Dr Siegel in the summer of 1981 when the American Psychological Association held its convention in Los Angeles. It was a typically stifling California day and the temperature easily broke 100° Fahrenheit, but the weather didn't bother me. I had just returned from the East Coast, where the summer heat was coupled with unbearable humidity. Getting back to Los Angeles with its dry desert heat was delightful, and I didn't even take off my coat when rushing between the two hotels being used for the seminars. I had to keep on the move since the convention included not only a parapsychology symposium, but a special session on the NDE. Such well-known researchers as Dr Kenneth Ring, Dr Michael Sabom, and Dr Siegel were making presentations and it promised to be a symposium of special interest. Completing the program were Dr Bruce Greyson, a psychiatrist engrossed in those NDEs reported by suicide survivors, and Dr Robert Kastenbaum—the editor of *Omega—the Journal of Death and Dying*, who has written copiously and sceptically on the NDE. Dr Glen Gabbard also presented a paper.

Dr Siegel used the symposium to emphasize the relationships between NDEs, hallucinations, and psychedelic drug trips in particular. He presented several reports and drawings contributed by people undergoing LSD, mescaline, and ketamine experiences. Some of the drawings showed the percipients floating down tunnels, seeing eschatological landscapes, and so forth. It didn't take too much insight to see the obvious parallels between these drawings and Moody-type NDEs. Dr Siegel then turned to the experiences of people suffering from sleep apnea. This is a dangerous and sometimes fatal condition in which the patients stop breathing in their sleep. When revived from such episodes, these individuals sometimes describe typical out-of-body experiences—probably caused, suggested Dr Siegel, by a lack of oxygen to the brain. The UCLA psychologist clearly believes these experiences to be true hallucinations and not genuine releases of the soul from the body.

I was so intrigued by the resemblances between ketamine hallucinations and NDE reports that, later in the day, I asked Dr Siegel if I could try the drug. (He was studying its hallucinatory effects at UCLA at the time.)

'Sure,' he replied. 'What kind of operation would you like?'

It seemed that the study in which Dr Siegel was engaged only made use of people who needed surgery. The ketamine was used as their anaesthetic, and its hallucinatory effects were being studied secondarily. So my interest in this curious drug would have to remain scholarly and not experiential!

Most researchers interested in the NDE simply ignored Siegel's position and evidence when they were originally presented, even though out-of-body states *commonly* result from the ingestion of several known psychedelic substances. During the heyday of the psychedelic revolution back in the 1960s, for example, drug-induced OBEs were reported following the ingestion of such substances as LSD, mescaline, phencyclidine, methylenedioxy-amphetamine (the 'love' drug), hashish, marijuana, and nitrous oxide, and also from sniffing glue. (See Figure 2, which lists

Figure 2
Psychedelic Drugs Known to Induce OBEs and NDEs

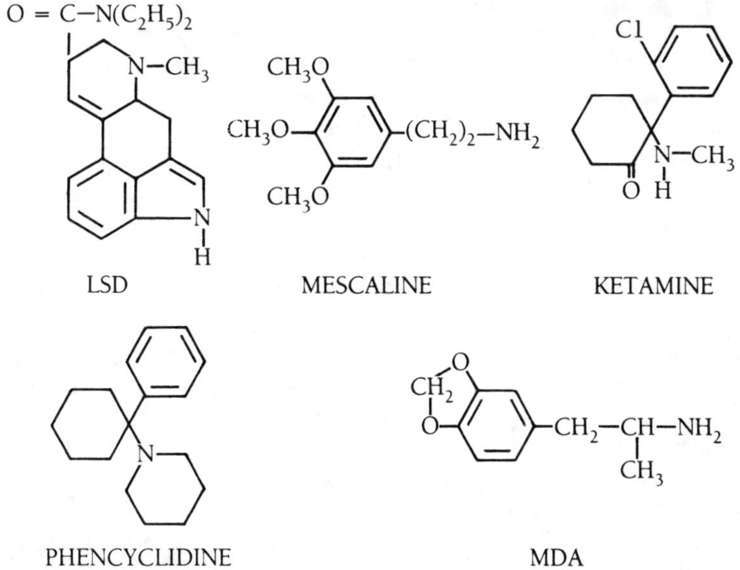

LSD

MESCALINE

KETAMINE

PHENCYCLIDINE

MDA

hallucinogens that specifically induce such experiences.) In fact, the shamans of many technologically unsophisticated cultures typically take hallucinogenic drugs in order to experience out-of-body states.

Rather impressive reports of out-of-body experiences can sometimes also result from certain physiological conditions that prompt hallucinatory episodes. For example, there was some interest in the use of hypercarbia (carbon dioxide build-up in the blood) for treating psychological problems back in the 1950s. Psychiatrists working with this procedure often elicited reports similar to NDEs and classic OBEs from their subjects. Researchers pioneering the study of experimentally induced hypercarbia at the University of Illinois, for example, collected several such accounts. The following is a typical OBE-like hallucination described by one of their subjects:

> I felt myself being separated; my soul drawing apart from the physical being, was drawn upward seemingly to leave the earth to go upward where it reached a greater spirit with whom there was a communion, producing a remarkable, new relaxation and deep security.

So Dr Siegel's 1980 paper and his 1981 report to the APA were not really saying anything original, but merely restating the fact that drug-induced hallucinations and the NDE share some suspiciously common ground.

Dr Siegel's reductionistic attempt to understand the NDE neurophysiologically was, however, a curious mixture of success and failure. The UCLA psychologist was certainly successful in showing that the NDE and more common forms of hallucinations share several similar features—enough, in certain respects, to regard the 'objective reality' of the NDE with suspicion. But he failed to make a strong case for his position in one important respect: he never demonstrated that the specific and predictable *sequence* of components that constitutes the NDE—i.e. its core elements—show up consistently during psychedelic drug trips. He only showed that several elements of the NDE, segregated and taken piecemeal, tend to appear randomly in *some* psychedelic trips. In other words, the building blocks of the NDE can be found in these cases, but not the highly structured NDE *syndrome* itself. It is for this reason that researchers studying the NDE had every right to reject Dr Siegel's model when it was first proposed, for his entire analysis of the NDE was terribly *post hoc* and contrived.

The primary problem with Dr Siegel's report was, perhaps, that he didn't delve into the literature on psychedelic drugs as deeply as he could have done. For had he explored it further, even more parallels to the NDE would have emerged in support of his theory. Entire sequences of imagery very typical of the pro-totypical NDE tend to emerge, for example, from the use of ketamine hydrochloride—a drug many recreational users believe can help you experience 'death' while still remaining very much alive! Some of these accounts read more impressively than those reported by Dr Siegel to the American Psychological Association, and it is rather surprising that he didn't stumble across them while conducting his literature survey.

Ketamine and the near-death experience

Ketamine was first synthesized in 1961 by Calvin Stevens at the Parke-Davis laboratories in Ann Arbor, Michigan, but it wasn't reported in the literature until 1965. It is chemically related to the better-known and notorious drug phencyclidine, and was developed when it became clear that phencyclidine caused violent reactions in some patients. Ketamine (available on prescription as Ketalar) is most often used intravenously or inter-muscularly as a general anaesthetic for patients unable to risk cardiovascular or respiratory depression during surgery. When taken in lower doses, it induces a short psychedelic 'trip' resembling that caused by LSD and was popularized by Marcia Moore and Howard Alltounian in their book *Journeys into the Bright World*. Similar mind-expanding and hallucinogenic episodes are sometimes reported by patients recovering from surgery in which ketamine is used. A report issued by Parke-Davis acknowledged that these 'emergence reactions' occurred in approximately 12 per cent of the patients receiving the drug.

But it is the curious and sometimes consistent nature of these hallucinations that has excited the interest of some researchers studying NDEs. Ketamine is classified as a dissociative anaesthetic since patients or users tell of being perceptually detached from their bodies and environment while under its in-fluence. The original Parke-Davis disclosure stated only that the drug induced psychological effects ranging from 'pleasant dream-like states' to 'vivid images, hallucinations, and emergent delirium'. But many experts on psychedelic drugs have specifically noted that these experiences resemble classic out-of-body experiences and NDEs. Dr Lester Grinspoon and James B. Bakalar—two experts on hallucinatory drugs at Harvard University—note in their encyclopaedic *Psychedelic Drugs Reconsidered* that ketamine hallucinations somewhat resemble those of LSD 'with a tendency towards a sense of disconnection from the surroundings' that may include 'floating, suspension in outer space, becoming a disembodied mind or soul, dying, and going to another world'. They also say that these reactions 'often seem so genuine that afterward users are not sure that they have not actually left their bodies'.

All this certainly sounds like the prototypical Moody-type NDE. In fact, the similarities between *some* NDEs and *some* ketamine 'trips' will be obvious to anyone willing to study the representative literature on both experiences.

The following account, for instance, was given by a woman who nearly died in childbirth. Her narrative has been condensed from the June 1983 issue of *Vital Signs*, the newsletter of the International Association for Near-Death Studies, which regularly publishes such testimonies.

> I found myself, quite suddenly, existing in a dark gray mist. I sensed that I had died. I had died and yet I still existed. A dazzling brightness infiltrated the mist and, ultimately, cradled me in a way that I cannot describe. The awareness of my physical body left me. I seemed to exist as consciousness only, pure and free-floating. My thoughts? I had none. But feelings my cup did, indeed, run over. Bliss ... rapture ... joy ... ecstasy, all of the above, and in such measure that it cannot be compared or understood. As the light continued to surround me and engulf me, my consciousness expanded and admitted more and more of what the light embraces: peace and unconditional love ...

The woman subsequently found herself in a pastoral world where she met a spiritual guide who counselled her. Then she found herself back in the hospital. Her doctor later told her that she had given him 'a very bad time' (i.e. come close to death) for a minute or two.

A vivid example of a ketamine-induced out-of-body experience, which closely resembles this NDE, was reported by an anonymous musician to Peter Stafford—a California writer on drugs and popular culture—who cites it in his *Psychedelics Encyclopedia*. The musician had taken ketamine (which can be injected, smoked, or dried and inhaled) while listening to some music. His absorption in the music, enhanced by the drug, led to his out-of-body experience.

> My perceptions were getting disoriented and when I closed my eyes
> a lot of information started to happen. Colors, patterns, cross-
> connections in sensory perceptions. Sounds and inner visions got
> confused.
>
> I got deeper and deeper into this state, until at one point the world
> disappeared. I was no longer in my body. I didn't have a body ...
>
> Then I reached a point at which I felt ready to die. It wasn't a ques-
> tion of choice, it was just a wave that carried me higher and higher,
> at the same time that I was having what in my normal state I would
> call a horror of death. It became obvious to me that it was not at all
> what I had anticipated death to be. Except, it was death, that
> something was dying.
>
> I reached a point at which I gave it all away. I just yielded, and then
> I entered a space in which there aren't any words. The words that
> have been used have been used a thousand times—starting with Bud-
> dha. I mean, at-one-with-the-universe, recognizing your Godhead—
> all those words I later used to explore what I have experienced.
>
> The feeling was that I was 'home' ... It was a bliss state of a kind I
> never experienced before.

The young musician wanted to prolong the state indefinitely, but
gradually found himself returning to his body. He didn't want to
return, but had little choice in the matter.

Leaving the body, 'transcending' death, journeying to a distant
space, entering into a oneness with the universe and then reluctantly returning to the body—these represent typical character-
characteristics of the NDE. Many ketamine users also describe
journeying through a void towards a new dimension of space.
This sensation can be linked to the reports of many NDE percipients who find themselves travelling down a tunnel and enjoying eschatological journeys.

For example, take the case reported by Dr R. L. MacMillan and
Dr K.W.G. Brown in the 22 May 1971 issue of the *Canadian
Medical Association Journal*. This report first brought scientific attention to the NDE, and it was a first-hand record of a 65-year-
old Canadian gentleman who had suffered cardiac failure. When
he was successfully revived by the staff at the University of
Toronto Medical Center, he told a strange story. As we saw in
Chapter 4, he remembered being taken to the hospital's intensive
care unit. He lost consciousness there, and then found himself
staring down at his own body. Next he was catapulted out into
space and floated in a bright light. He seemed only dimly or par-

tially cognizant of his body and revived back in his body when he felt powerful blows to it. Even the physicians were intrigued by their patient's perceptions and commented in their article that such experiences could be the basis for 'the concept of the soul leaving the body which is found in many religions'. They remained puzzled as to the specific meaning of the patient's experience and shied away from explaining it at all.

But was this patient's experience any more 'real' than the following ketamine hallucination? The report cited below was placed on file by Dr Robert Johnstone, an anaesthesiologist at the University of Pennsylvania, who reported his experience in a letter he wrote to *Anaesthesiology* in 1973.

Dr Johnstone was undergoing minor surgery for which he was given ketamine. His first perceptions upon receiving the drug were buzzing sounds in his ears. Then he lapsed into unconsciousness. This backout didn't last long, though. 'Gradually I realized my mind existed and I could think,' he recalled. 'I had no consciousness of existing in a body; I was mind suspended in space.' The doctor found himself floating in a void somewhere distant from the earth. 'I was not afraid,' he explained in his letter, 'I was more curious.' He then thought to himself that 'this is death. I am a soul, and I am going to wherever souls go.' Dr Johnstone eventually became confused by his experience and gradually became aware that he was back in his body.

What is so peculiar about ketamine, as I mentioned at the beginning of this chapter, is how commonly these NDE-type hallucinations are reported. Perhaps they result from the biological effects the drug exerts on the central nervous system. Ketamine seems to suppress those sections of the brain responsible for processing sensory information, while at the same time it stimulates the central nervous system. When unconsciousness doesn't result (or when the drug's effects wear off) the patient might easily experience being conscious but dissociated from his or her body and physical environment. Such a state, which resembles the effects of prolonged sensory deprivation, could well be experienced in the form of an out-of-body incident. The theory that ketamine represents a chemical analogue to sensory deprivation has been suggested by, among others, Dr Barbara Collier of Whipps Cross Hospital in London, who made a detailed study of ketamine effects in the early 1970s.

Dr Collier pointed out in her report that ketamine-related

hallucinations can manifest in many forms—including colour distortion, seeing figures standing by the patient's bed, floating faces, and so on. But the 'core' of the ketamine experience seems to be sensations typical of the out-of-body experience.

Dr Collier's first formal survey, for instance, entailed monitoring the reactions of 90 patients given ketamine before surgery. Twelve per cent of them reported hallucinations and sensations of 'floating' even when they emerged from the drug. Several of these patients later told Dr Collier that they had 'died' while separated from their bodies. One patient even reported that he had gone to heaven during his surgery, where he had confronted God. The patient believed himself reincarnated when he found himself back in the body! This experience burned itself into his memory, and he retained a perfect recollection of it even six months later.

More specific connections between ketamine hallucinations and the prototypical NDE became even more obvious when Dr Collier conducted a follow-up study. This survey entailed studying 11 further patients given ketamine for surgery. Ten patients reported that they had felt themselves floating away from the body when given the drug. Nine of them specifically experienced the mind *withdrawing* from the body. Three patients went on to relate how they looked back at their own physical bodies. Re-entering the body was also commonly reported. Two of the 11 patients also experienced leaving the recovery room while disembodied and flying out into space through a darkish void.

Possible differences between NDEs and ketamine hallucinations
While important parallels exist between the NDE and some ketamine hallucinations and/or emergence reactions, a few differences should be mentioned as well. These differences are important to keep in mind when specifically equating the NDE with ketamine hallucinations.

The first difference concerns the affective component typical of each type of experience. People undergoing NDEs tend to report a sense of peace and well-being while travelling out-of-body. Dr Kenneth Ring, for instance, found positive reactions to the experience present in 59 per cent of the 49 cases he recounted in his book *Life at Death* in 1980. (Positive reactions to out-of-body experiences in general tend to be just as high, if not higher.) On the other hand, people undergoing ketamine hallucinations—

especially if unprepared for what to expect—often report being frightened by their experiences. If you check back to the cases cited earlier, note that Dr Johnstone experienced an out-of-body ketamine 'trip' marked by extreme confusion. (Since ketamine essentially stimulates the central nervous system, such reactions may be physiological side-effects of the drug rather than true psychological components of ketamine hallucinations.) Recreational users, however, sometimes report typical sensations of ecstasy while enjoying the drug's influence. It's therefore possible that the anxiety experienced during some ketamine reactions results from the setting in which the drug is given. Coming out of surgery can cause uneasiness in itself! For example, the following account was placed on file by a physician familiar with ketamine and prepared for possible emergence reactions. His 'trip' reads just like a classic NDE accompanied by feelings of peace and love:

> I experienced my spirit coming out of my body and rising up. Immediately I had the thought, this is what it is like after one dies. It was a wonderful feeling and not the least bit fearful, as I had thought death to be.

It should be noted, however, that the qualitative differences between ketamine hallucinations and NDEs must be considered speculative. Very few statistics have been collected on the nature and specific phenomenology of ketamine hallucination; so even the minor differences noted here may not be representative of ketamine reactions in general. They could be the result of the incomplete information we currently possess on both the NDE and ketamine.

Explaining the parallels
The effects of ketamine are better known today than they were back in the 1960s. The drug is rarely used as a sole anaesthetic; other drugs are used in conjunction with it. These medications suppress the agitation the patient might have while recovering from surgery. They also prevent the patient from thrashing about while still unconscious. That the drug also has psychedelic properties is well known by street drug users, who often use it to precipitate LSD-like trips. Nor have the possible connections between the drug and NDEs and mystical states of consciousness gone unnoticed by the scientific community. Dr John Lilly—the

California-based dolphin expert who pioneered the study of sensory deprivation in the 1960s—believes that ketamine is literally a chemical road to the out-of-body experience. He experimented chronically with ketamine to the point of excess, a situation he describes in his disguised autobiography *The Scientist*. Dr Timothy Leary, the former pop guru of the psychedelic revolution, also typifies the ketamine 'trip' as a way of experimentally exploring the death experience in his book *Flashbacks*.

These enthusiastic endorsements have, however, been countered by Dr Ronald Siegel, who doesn't believe in romanticizing the effects of the drug. He considers such hallucinatory experiences as simple biochemical/neurophysiological reactions to the substance.

So which of these conceptual models is correct? What is the precise connection between ketamine and the NDE? To my mind, three possible theories can explain the close resemblances between some ketamine emergence hallucinations and the classic NDE:

(1) *Ketamine hallucinations demonstrate that the NDE is nothing more than a similar neurophysiologically induced experience.*

This model would correspond roughly to Dr Siegel's explanatory model for the NDE. He believes that the common components of the NDE can be found piecemeal in the literature on drug-induced hallucinations—especially those induced by LSD, mescaline, and ketamine. This fact suggests to him that NDEs constitute little more than hallucinatory by-products of brain chemistry. A related theory has been proposed by Lester Grinspoon and James B. Bakalar, who have suggested that the brain may synthesize a chemical similar to ketamine when severely stressed. When this chemical is reabsorbed by the brain, they suggest, the percipient may experience 'leaving' the body. But as I pointed out earlier, this type of theory cannot account for the predictable patterns of the NDE's phenomenology and the *inconsistency* of the ketamine trip. Remember that NDE-type hallucinations don't invariably emerge from ketamine use. Such imagery represents a subtype within a wide range of hallucinatory reactions to the drug.

(2) *Ketamine, because of its curious effects on the central nervous system, actually induces genuine out-of-body experiences.*

Many types of anaesthetics seem to induce OBEs, including nitrous oxide, ether, and even sodium pentothal. It may be that ketamine works on the body in such a way as to prompt the emergence of a real 'flight' of the soul. This theory is difficult to discount, especially if you happen to believe that NDEs and OBEs represent a genuine release of the 'soul' or consciousness from the body. But since ketamine is intensely psychedelic and hallucinogenic, it isn't too parsimonious to posit that these out-of-body sensations are 'genuine' while other types of ketamine-induced hallucinations (such as seeing human figures and floating faces) are delusional.

(3) *Ketamine-induced NDEs are actually pseudo-OBEs produced as a by-product of the hospital setting.*

It may well be that ketamine, in and by itself, doesn't really produce NDE hallucinations at all. While researching this chapter, I found relatively few cases of classic NDEs reported by people taking the drug in recreational settings. They seem to be almost exclusively reported by patients recovering in the hospital from surgery. Now this pattern could be a by-product of the high dosages needed to produce general anaesthesia. But perhaps the NDE-like hallucinations result from the hospital setting in which the drug is usually administered. We know that ketamine often induces in the patient some sense of disembodied existence. Now a patient coming out of surgery might naturally be concerned with death and whether he/she has survived his/her ordeal. The patient might then misinterpret these dissociative sensations and build up an elaborate fantasy based on them. Such a fantasy would be concerned with themes such as leaving the body, going to a heavenly realm, and other hallucinations typical of ketamine use. But it could be the patient's mind that is producing this imagery and not really the drug. Experts on ketamine have often remarked that the specific nature of the ketamine 'trip' can be influenced by the setting under which the drug is taken.

At the present time, these three theories are equally viable and they each offer self-consistent models for explaining the NDE. Earlier in this book I showed that reductionistic theories for the NDE are too simplistic to explain the experience. But the data summarized in this short chapter suggests that simplistic *paranormal* explanations for the NDE are similarly limited. The ultimate nature of the NDE may not be clear-cut, despite the efforts of some researchers to interpret it literally. It no longer seems very expedient to say that, by themselves, NDEs represent 'proof' of post-mortem survival. While ketamine-induced halluc-inations don't resemble the classic NDE in every respect, what parallels do exist between them cast doubt on most *simple* metaphysical explanations for it. The NDE seems to be an unbelievably complex phenomenon—a phenomenon perhaps combining psychological, neurophysiological, and paranormal features.

This possibility becomes even more obvious the more we ex-plore the NDE and realize that two forms of the experience exist. For while most people report blissful journeys to paradise, a few others recount truly nightmarish close calls with death in which they perceive hell.

These experiences have prompted some students of the NDE to suggest that it's not safe to die! This phenomenon will serve as the subject for the following chapter.

7.

The Problem of Negative NDEs

Is there a hell? Are some souls subject to eternal damnation after the death of the physical body?

These questions have been debated by theologians for centuries. Certainly many people throughout the world believe in an afterlife filled with unspeakable horrors—fire and brimstone being the least of them. The concept of eternal damnation is not uniquely Christian, either. The idea of 'hell' was first formalized in the teachings of Zoroaster in Persia around the time of Christ, and early Christianity adopted the theory of both hell and the devil from popular religious beliefs spawned by the prophet. Even certain schools of Buddhism, especially Amitabha Buddhism which is taught in Japan, teach the existence of hell. The Buddhist hell, in fact, is so fiendish that it makes its Christian counterpart sound like a fairy story.

Polls taken of the general public confirm the widespread belief in hell in the United States. These surveys indicate that roughly half the population believes in a traditional hell, though the percentages seem to be decreasing.

But is there any scientific evidence pointing towards the actual existence of hell?

Two years after the publication of *Life After Life*, Raymond Moody published some cases pointing to this possibility. Several of his witnesses encountered a 'realm of bewildered spirits', a place unlike the paradise visited by most otherworldy NDErs. It was described as a misty dimension, where its occupants wandered about in a state of extreme desolation.

The following description was published by Dr Moody in his *Reflections on Life After Life*:

These bewildered people? I don't know exactly where I saw them . . .
But as I was going by, there was this area that was dull—this is in contrast to all the brilliant light. The figures were more humanized than
the rest of them were, if you stop to think of it in that respect, but
neither were they in quite human form as we are.

What you would think of as their head was bent downward; they
had sad, depressed looks; they seemed to shuffle, as someone would
on a chain gang. I don't know why I say this because I don't
remember noticing feet. I don't know what they were, but they looked washed out, dull, gray. And they seemed to be forever shuffling
and moving around, not knowing where they were going, not knowing who to follow, or what to look for.

As I went by they didn't even raise their heads to see what was hap-
pening. They seemed to be thinking, 'Well, it's all over with. What
am I doing? What's it all about?' Just this absolute, crushed, hopeless
demeanor—not knowing what to do or where to go or who they were
or anything else.

They seemed to be forever moving, rather than just sitting, but in
no special direction. They would start straight, then veer to the left
and take a few steps and veer back to the right. And absolutely
nothing to do. Searching, but for what they were searching I don't
know.

Of course, this description is far from the traditional hell. But by
1978, one researcher was claiming that people *can* contact such
a realm during the NDE.

The findings of Dr Maurice Rawlings

Dr Maurice Rawlings is currently a clinical professor of medicine
at the University of Tennessee at Chattanooga. Among his other
positions, he is affiliated with the Chattanooga-based Heart
Association's Advanced Life Support Program and serves on the
teaching faculty of the American Heart Association. As you might
have guessed, his speciality is internal medicine and he is an
authority on cardio-pulmonary resuscitation. This latter speciality had led Dr Rawlings to the study of near-death encounters.

Dr Rawlings, however, doesn't share Raymond Moody's rather
idealized and poetic views about the afterlife. On the basis of his
own research, he believes in the literal existence of hell—and that
some people who have had NDEs have actually previewed it! He
presented his findings in his book *Beyond Death's Door*, which
has gone into many editions since its publication in 1978.

Dr Rawlings first came to this realization when one of his patients, a 48-year-old mail carrier, had a heart attack during a routine medical examination. The patient was undergoing a treadmill 'stress' test as part of a clinical EKG when he went into cardiac arrest. While Dr Rawlings was frantically trying to revive him, the mailman started screaming that he was in hell. 'Each time he regained heartbeat and respiration,' writes Rawlings, 'the patient screamed "I am in hell." ' As he continued working on his patient, Dr Rawlings could see the look of abject terror on the man's face. The patient kept complaining that he found himself slipping back into hell each time the doctor paused during the resuscitation attempt.

These visits to hell were not the end of the mailman's ordeal. Ultimately he experienced a more peaceful NDE during which he 'left his body', visited a paradise world, and met his deceased mother and step-mother. The Tennessee doctor was in for a surprise, though, when he subsequently interviewed his patient several days after recovery. While retaining complete memory of his blissful out-of-body experience, the mailman completely forgot about his several close encounters with hell.

This paradox has led Dr Rawlings to suggest that many people may experience hell while on the verge of death, but may forget about it because it is too psychologically shocking to recall. This, he believes, may explain the apparent rareness of such reports collected by other researchers. Nonetheless, encounters with hell may not be *that* rare, and Dr Rawlings has gone on to collect many additional rather terrifying NDE accounts from a diverse array of sources. He has included several of them in his recent book. Not everyone, however, seems to experience hell the same way. In other words, Dr Rawlings found that these reports do not seem to have the self-consistency that typifies the more common Moody-type NDE. Some experiences seem modelled after the popular Christian interpretations of hell, while other people appear to contact some sort of Dantean realm.

Thomas Welch, for example, described an NDE he personally underwent in his 1976 book *Oregon's Amazing Miracle*, which Dr Rawlings quotes with obvious relish. Welch had his NDE while working for a lumber company in Oregon. He was working on a trestle doing some logging work, but fell off and plunged into the river below. 'All I could remember is falling over the edge of the trestle,' he reported. 'The locomotive engineer watched me go all the way down into the water. The next thing I knew I was standing near a shoreline of a great ocean of fire. It happened to be what the Bible says it is in Revelations 21: 8.' It was a lake of fire and brimstone, and according to Welch it was 'the most awesome sight one could ever see this side of final judgment'. After the vision of the burning lake, Welch experienced a panoramic review of his entire life, and then a Christ-figure approached and conversed with him. Moments later he found himself back in his body, opening his eyes. He had been rescued by co-workers.

A very different nightmare NDE was reported to Dr Rawlings by another of his heart attack patients. Although she didn't see a lake of fire, her experience was no less horrifying:

I remember getting short of breath and then I must have blacked out. Then I saw that I was getting out of my body. The next thing I remember was entering this gloomy room where I saw in one of the windows this huge giant with a grotesque face that was watching me. Running around the windowsill were little imps or elves that seemed to be with the giant. The giant beckoned me to come with him. I didn't want to go, but I had to. Outside was darkness but I could hear people moaning all around me. I could feel things moving about my feet. As we moved on through this tunnel or cave, things were getting worse. I remember I was crying. Then, for some reason the giant turned me loose and sent me back. I felt I was being spared, I don't know why.

Then I remember finding myself back in the hospital bed. The doctor asked me if I had been taking drugs. My description must have sounded like the DTs. I told him I didn't have either of these habits and that the story was true. It has changed my whole life.

A similar surrealistic hell was experienced by yet another of Rawlings's patients, who suffered clinical death while being treated for high blood pressure in a hospital. At one point in her treatment, the patient lost consciousness and found herself travelling down a tunnel to a hideous cave. The rancid odour of decay enveloped the place and she saw half-human beings mocking one another. A Christ-like figure came to her aid soon afterwards. She then revived and found herself back in her hospital bed.

'There are a lot of other things that may have happened that I don't remember,' the patient admitted. 'Maybe I'm afraid to remember.'

It might be noted at this point that accounts such as those cited above may not be as anomalous as Dr Rawlings believes. Many people who have had spontaneous out-of-body experiences have found themselves wandering about in a misty, bleak world before returning to the body. The late Dr Robert Crookall was a retired British geologist who collected several hundred cases of classic spontaneous out-of-body experiences.[1] He found that while most people visit familiar earthly scenes during their disembodied travels, about 3 per cent report a world rather similar to the hell that some of Dr Rawlings's correspondents seem to be describing. A few of them also seem to be describing a world very similar to the realm of 'tortured souls' that Emanuel Swedenborg (1688–1772), the great Swedish philosopher and mystic, described in his book *Heaven and Hell*, which purports to be a report on his own visionary excursions into the realms of the afterlife.

People who survive suicide attempts quite often have hellish NDEs, reports Dr Rawlings. One 54-year-old housewife told him how she had descended into hell after over-dosing on Valium. She found herself going through a black hole. 'Then I saw a glowing red-hot spot getting bigger and bigger until I was able to stand up,' she reports. She then found herself in a place that was 'all red and hot and on fire'. She noted that 'the earth was like slimy mud that sank over my feet, and it was hard to move'. The heat was so intense that she could hardly move. She prayed, and awoke in a hospital room. She had been unconscious for two days.

But this unfortunate woman's experience isn't nearly as terrifying as a story told to Dr Rawlings by a medical colleague who had helped resuscitate a 14-year-old schoolgirl. The distraught girl had tried to kill herself with pills, and underwent cardiac arrest after being rushed to the hospital. During the only partially conscious moments of her initial recovery, she described how demons had been grabbing at her throughout her brush with the afterlife.

Criticism of the Rawlings effect
Dr Rawlings's research and case reports certainly make us stop

---

[1] These experiences were reported by people waking from sleep, who were sick with minor illnesses, and so forth. Dr Crookall's collection included several NDE reports, as I pointed out in Chapter 3.

and think. Could the patients whose accounts he cites really have experienced hell? Or can some other explanation be found to account for them? These questions are difficult to answer. One problem is that few mainline researchers studying the NDE seem very willing to confront Rawlings's research and claims. I realized this in 1978 when I attended a roundtable discussion on the NDE at the 21st annual convention of the Parapsychological Association, which was being held at Washington University in St Louis, Missouri. Dr Karlis Osis of the American Society for Psychical Research had organized the symposium, and several leading authorities on the NDE presented papers at the meeting. Among these participants were Dr Kenneth Ring, Dr Michael Sabom, and Dr Bruce Greyson. Most of them reported personal confirmations of Moody's original findings. None of these eminent researchers reported any data hinting that the NDE was anything but an encounter with paradise. And no one mentioned Dr Rawlings, though his work had recently been published and many newspapers were discussing his findings.

When the session was over I deliberately asked Dr Greyson, whom I had first met the day before, about the Rawlings work. He would only tell me that no one formally studying the NDE was coming up with data consistent with Rawlings's reports and that, in the view of some researchers, the Tennessee doctor was relying on improperly collected data. (I didn't quite follow this last point.)

Only one researcher has broken his conspicuous silence since Rawlings's work was published. Dr Michael Sabom blasted Rawlings and his book in a critique published in the November 1979 issue of *Anabiosis*, which was then the newsletter of the (soon to be) International Association for Near-Death Studies. Sabom's attack was not so much directed against Dr Rawlings's data as against the way the heart specialist had originally collected and presented it. Dr Sabom was particularly critical of the claim that hellish NDEs are rarely reported because most collectors of NDE cases are not actively involved in cardio-pulmonary resuscitation work. Dr Rawlings has long claimed that those using this type of medical procedure (such as himself) do confront hellish NDEs. Sabom, however, has pointed out that Rawlings has never presented any statistics to substantiate this claim. He has also criticized Dr Rawlings for relying on second-hand accounts, or cases collected by his colleagues, and has also pointed out that

Dr Rawlings does not explain in his book how long he waited after reviving his patients before taking down their NDE stories. Sabom believes that, after considerable time has elasped, revived patients may no longer have a very good memory of what happened to them during their crises.

Dr Sabom's contention, as he forthrightly states in *Anabiosis*, is that Rawlings's research is a 'curious combination of medical facts, religious opinions, and poorly documented near-death experiences', and that his research 'contributes little to the objective evaluation of the NDE'.

When I read Dr Sabom's review, I found that my own reactions were mixed. On the one hand, his points were well taken from a purely academic position. Dr Rawlings's level of reporting is not good, and he certainly did not adhere to the rules of proper data collection in compiling his reports. But on the other hand, Dr, Sabom's criticisms stuck me as rather inconsequential since they did not go to the core of the matter.

In my opinion, Dr Rawlings's data is certainly no more anecdotal than were Dr Moody's original accounts. In fact, Dr Sabom's several indictments could apply equally well to the cases in Moody's *Life After Life*! No matter how Dr Rawlings came to collect his data, the fact remains that negative or hellish NDEs have now been placed on record by obviously sincere witnesses. Dr Sabom's review struck me as an exercise in academic nitpicking merely to ensure that Dr Rawlings's uncomfortable findings could be facilely dismissed. My own opinion is that they can't be dismissed. Facts are facts, no matter how one comes by them. So any theory about the NDE must therefore explain both classic Moody-type NDEs and the type of cases Dr Rawlings has been collecting.

One of the few researchers who *have* attempted to explain Dr Rawlings's accounts psychologically has been myself. When I was invited to appraise current research on the NDE in 1979 for a popular magazine, I argued that 'these hellish experiences [may be] artifacts—hallucinations produced by the witnesses' minds as a reaction to the violent physical ordeals (such as chest pounding and electrical stimulation) which are part and parcel of normal resuscitation techniques'.

Most of Dr Rawlings's original cases were taken from the recollections of heart attack patients, many of whom experienced close encounters with hell during the very moments of their resuscitations. The possibly hallucinatory nature of the experience may be why, as Dr Rawlings has continually pointed out, patients who have this kind of NDE may forget them after recovery. Most nightmare-like NDEs occurring as a result of suicide attempts seem to result from drug overdoses, and these drugs might well produce hallucinations, perhaps coloured by the witnesses' own intense guilt feelings or their prior religious beliefs.

It is also possible that some of these cases were, in fact, dreams. There exists considerable literature on whether people—either sleeping or under general anaesthesia—can perceive while still 'unconscious'. These studies have a considerable bearing on the study of the NDE, though few researchers even broach the subject. Back in 1970, for example, a group of researchers from the University of Liverpool published a report on the experiences of patients under complete anaesthesia. They questioned 60 patients previously 'knocked out' by thiopentone sodium breathed through a face mask. When they were revived, close to half of them recalled dreaming and 5 per cent reported unpleasant dreams. It is the content of these dreams that's so interesting, for the researchers explain that the dreams 'did not involve people or places specifically, but were concerned with transcendental factors which the patient ... found extremely difficult to describe'. It is clear from earlier comments in the paper that these 'transcendental' factors related to some sort of spiritual or religious experience. The researchers further found, like Rawlings, that their patients soon forgot the dreams, which couldn't be remembered—and were even denied—only days later.

This fascinating study indicates that dream factors could represent an important aspect of the NDE experience, a possibility few NDE researchers have squarely faced.

Another objection to the Rawlings work was that the cases collected stemmed from his practice in Tennessee, a great stronghold of Christian Fundamentalist belief. Some researchers merely conjectured that Dr Rawlings's results were coloured by his subjects' religious backgrounds. This convenient theory was soon exploded, though, by the Gallup Organization, which undertook a survey of near-death experiences throughout the United States from 1980 to 1981. The pollsters found that 1 per cent of their respondents experienced negative or hellish NDEs, though the Gallup data is a bit perplexing, since the pollsters sometimes confused negative *reactions* to NDEs with genuinely nightmarish experiences. But a careful look at these cases revealed no geographic or religious factors consistent among the respondents.

Replication of Rawlings effect

Dr Greyson was not quite correct when he said that no one engaged in the study of the NDE was coming up with data similar to Dr Rawlings's. For soon after the Tennessee physician published his work, other researchers began reporting similar cases.

Dr Charles Garfield is one of America's leading authorities on the psychology of death. He is currently a psychologist at the Cancer Research Institute of the University of California School of Medicine in San Francisco. Speaking before the 85th Annual Convention of the American Psychological Association (held in San Francisco in 1977), he reported on his own research on the NDE. He stated that of the 25 patients whose NDEs he had personally studied, 'four reported lucid visions of a demonic or nightmarish nature'. Dr Garfield was able to interview these patients shortly after their brushes with death. In striking contrast to Rawlings, Garfield found that 'no significant changes in content were expressed by any of the patients in three interviews conducted at weekly intervals following the event'.

Dr Garfield's general conclusions seem to echo those of Dr Rawlings however. 'It appears that not everyone dies a blissful, accepting death', he argued. 'Almost as many of the dying patients I interviewed reported negative visions (encounters with demonic figures and so forth) as reported blissful experiences, while some reported both.'

Dr Rawlings's original work was published in 1978 and it has taken a decade to replicate it. New research recently published from England has not only confirmed the Tennessee physician's research, but even his suggestions about the rarity of such reports in the extant literature.

As I pointed out in Chapter 4, Dr Margot Grey began her personal romance with the NDE in 1976 when she fell ill with an undiagnosed disease and experienced a profound out-of-body experience. When she returned to England after consulting with experts on the NDE in the United States, she decided to undertake her own survey. It was not a truly random sample typical of the way Dr Michael Sabom, Dr Kenneth Ring, and others had conducted their research, since Dr Grey openly advertised for cases in the British press. But she wound up interviewing a large number of near-death survivors and, in general, replicated the work of her American colleagues. The majority of people with whom she spoke described the experience as peaceful and joyful, and spoke of out-of-body experiences, seeing the famous white light, beautiful landscapes, and so forth. But at the same time, she also began amassing Rawlings-type negative experiences, which she included in her excellent *Return from Death* published in 1985. They made a profound impression on her.

'From conversations with physicians who have recounted to me cases of NDEs reported to them by their patients following resuscitation from clinical death,' she reports in her book, 'and from my own research into the matter, I found evidence to support the claim that negative experiences are most likely to be obtained immediately after the event. This is due, so it seems, to the minimal time gap between the near-death episode itself and the procuring of the information pertaining to it.'

This particular finding is identical to the claim made by Dr Rawlings in 1978 and which was quickly denied by several other researchers.

What is so remarkable about Dr Grey's cases is that they sometimes conform to the same pattern typical of more classic NDEs. For example, compare the following two cases drawn from Dr Grey's study and note their conspicuous similarities:

(1)

I was working in the nursing home where I have a part-time job. I am a partially trained nurse. I had spent the day on the beach. It was a glorious hot day, but I am used to the heat having lived in Khartoum for about sixteen years. I was in the kitchen supervising the evening suppers, when I was overcome by the heat from the Aga cookers. I rushed outside the back door feeling faint and sick. I remember going down three or four steps. I don't remember falling, but the next thing that happened was that I had this experience. I found myself in a place surrounded by mist. I felt I was in hell. There was a big pit with vapour coming out and there were arms and hands coming out trying to grab mine . . . I was terrified that these hands were going to claw hold of me and pull me into the pit with them. As I lay there worrying what would happen next, an enormous lion bounded towards me from the other side and I let out a scream. I was not afraid of the lion, but I felt somehow he would unsettle me and push me into the dreadful pit. I remained in a state of semi-consciousness for about three days. I have never believed in hell, I feel God would never create such a place. But it was very hot down there and the vapour or steam was very hot. At the time I did not think very much about it, but in the intervening years I have realised both good and evil exist. The experience has transformed my life.

(2)

I went to St. Giles Hospital in London, to have an operation. Sometime while I was under the anaesthetic I became aware that I was hovering above my body looking down at myself on the operating table. I felt very frightened and began to panic. I wondered why I was no longer in my body and thought I must be dead. I next found myself in a very frightening place, which I am sure was hell. I was looking down into a large pit, which was full of swirling grey mist and there were all these hands and arms reaching up and trying to grab hold of me and drag me in there. There was a terrible wailing noise, full of desperation. Then suddenly I found myself rushing back through this dark tunnel and I found myself back in my body in the hospital bed. As I went back into my body it felt like an elastic cord, which had been stretched to its limit and then it let go. I sort of snapped back again and everything seemed to vibrate with the impact.

The conditions that led these subjects to the NDEs were not the same. The first woman's experience was a reaction to heat stroke, while the second subject nearly died during a routine hysterectomy. From the basis of these and similar experiences, Dr Grey believes that a typology for the nightmare NDE exists similar to the prototypical NDE characteristics first identified by Raymond Moody in 1975. (Remember that this pattern consistency was *not* originally obvious from Rawlings's research.) These special features of the negative NDE seem to create the following pattern:

Phase 1. The subject feels fear and feelings of panic instead of peace and joyfulness.

Phase 2. Just as with the more classic NDE, the subject experiences leaving the body.

Phase 3. Again similar to the classic NDE, the dying person enters into a dark region or void.

Phase 4. Instead of experiencing the presence of comforting religious figures, friendly deceased relatives, or a great white light, the subject is overwhelmed by a sense of foreboding and senses the presence of an evil force.

Phase 5. The subject finally enters a hellish environment, different from the beautiful and peaceful Elysium of the classic NDE.

What is so impressive is that Dr Grey also successfully replicated Dr Rawlings's findings revelant to the reporting of these special experiences. Most of the individuals Dr Grey met who experienced negative NDEs were reluctant to discuss their adventures, either with her or even with their own physicians. They also tended to forget or repress memories of the episodes upon recuperating from their sicknesses or life-threatening situations. This peculiar pattern did not puzzle Dr Grey, who feels that such experiences could be extremely threatening because they undermine the percipient's self-worth. NDE survivors may therefore naturally repress negative experiences from conscious recollection.

So is there scientific evidence pointing to the existence of hell? Like so many questions having to do with either religion or psychical research, this one, too, has no clear-cut answer. The rate at which these cases are reported is very variable, as Table IX indicates, so it is hard to draw definite conclusions from them.

To me, though, the biggest mystery is the way some NDE researchers play down the importance of these fascinating if frightening occurrences. I think Dr Grey's survey is representative. Based on her research, she states forthrightly in her book,

Table IX
Negative NDEs in Selected Collections

Study	Sample size	Percentage of negative NDEs reported
Garfield (1977)	22	18.0
Rawlings (1978)	33*	27.5
Ring (1980)	102	0
Gallup (1982)	225	1.0
Sabom (1982)	100	0
Grey (1985)	31	12.5

*Non-radom sample based on the reporter's collection plus cases drawn from other, earlier sources.

'I am obliged to conclude from the evidence I found that somehow it would seem that conscious awareness survives death.' Naturally the reader expects that Dr Grey would also posit the literal existence of some sort of hell. But when it comes to explaining negative NDEs—which represent experiences just as phenomenologically valid as classic NDEs—Dr Grey proposes a different opinion.

'I am inclined to feel that a more generalized archetypal interpretation is a possibility in cases of hell-like experiences,' she writes, 'where negative emotions have become trapped in the psyche and released during the near-death experience.'

This line of reasoning strikes me as totally uncircumspect and inconsistent, and Dr Grey offers her readers no evidence to support her opinion. People who suffer negative NDEs do not seem to be different psychologically from other near-death survivors. Nor does Dr Grey take into account the fact that hellish NDEs emerge from the same initial stages (such as leaving the body and entering the darkness) which earmark classic NDEs. Her line of reasoning is a desperate attempt to recognize and bolster the good within the NDE while decrying and rejecting the bad.

One thing seems certain, however: The debate over the issue of 'hell' will probably outlive its current proponents and detractors. The researches of Rawlings, Garfield, and Grey also indicate that the NDE is probably a much more complicated experience than many researchers had originally believed. Or maybe Swedenborg was right when he argued in the eighteenth century that there is no single plane of the afterlife, but that the otherworld is comprised of multiple levels, each differing from the others. It wouldn't be hard to believe, if such were the case, that different witnesses may simply be contacting different realms of the world beyond.

8.

Examining the Sceptic's Position

When this book is published, the scientific study of the NDE will be close to 15 years old. The official journal of the International Association for Near-Death Studies will be in its seventh volume, while over a dozen serious books on the subject will be in print. Certainly there has been no dearth of speculation over the explanation for NDEs, yet despite this large body of research and literature, several issues concerning the phenomenon remain unresolved.

So what do we know about the NDE for sure—if anything?

The subjective reality of the NDE
By the early 1980s, it was obvious that the NDE was a subjectively real experience, since the pattern of most NDE reports conformed to a precise, systematic, and sequential design. Because so many researchers independently confirmed this pattern, first outlined by Dr Kenneth Ring in 1979 and 1980, it didn't seem likely that it resulted from a reporting effect. In other words, it's unlikely that people deliberately tailored their experiences to conform to the type published by Raymond Moody in 1975. Many of the people Ring spoke with knew nothing of Raymond Moody or his book. Remember, too, that Ring, Sabom, and Margot Grey each found that people familiar with the NDE were less prone to undergo the experience than uninformed subjects.

Kenneth Ring and Margot Grey were not the only researchers who successfully replicated Ring's finding that the typical NDE comprises five sequential phases. The predictable content of the NDE has also been confirmed by two other researchers, both originally working in the early 1980s. The first of these projects was undertaken by James H. Lindley, Sethyn Bryan, and Bob

Conley of Evergreen State College in Olympia, Washington. Spurred on by the research of Kenneth Ring, they undertook their own case collection in the Pacific Northwest region of the United States by putting advertisements in the popular press. These notices asked people who'd faced death to contact them, and 35 people stepped forward in response, describing 55 close encounters with death. Another 14 people were contacted by word of mouth and completed the Evergreen collection. All the cases were the result of physical mishaps or illnesses, and the Washington researchers successfully identified each of Ring's five core elements of the NDE in their collection.

For example, the following comments were made by a previously ill hospital patient:

> My next awareness was floating in the air about five feet above the end of the hospital bed. I saw a body in the bed, it looked awful, a greenish-gray color ... it looked dead. Nurses and doctors were working on the body. A nurse was yelling a coded message over the intercom ... it dawned on me that maybe it was *my* dead body [lying] in the bed.

A cardiac patient described the tunnel he went through while out-of-body:

> I felt like I was going up at about a 45 or 50 degree angle ... at the end of the tunnel. I say tunnel but I don't mean a tunnel like a tunnel. It was kind of like a funnel.

Typical of the commonly reported eschatological journey, a 38-year-old woman experienced paradise when she nearly drowned:

> I was in a garden, right behind a bush but I could see everyone that was ahead of me. In the garden there was this one, big, large tree and there were children playing a game; there were seven children; and I saw a bunch of flowers, there was a butterfly and a deer next to me who I felt lick my face. At the time, I didn't understand that but I was more curious about what was going on beyond me. The children saw me and they beckoned me to come over. And I hesitated but when I finally decided to step over ... then I felt this heavy tug, like a vacuum and then I was forced out and the next thing I knew I was back in my own body.

While the Washington researchers were busy with their project in the Pacific Northwest, a similar investigation was underway down the coast in California. J. Timothy Green and Penelope Friedman were students at California State University, Northridge, when they initiated their survey. They too worked with a non-random sample of cases, which they collected by placing a simple advertisement in several Los Angeles papers. Their notice merely stated that 'psychological researchers [were] interested in interviewing persons who have been close to death or clinical death'. The two researchers used the following criteria for including cases in their study:

1. The respondent had to be not less than 18-years-old.
2. The person should have been close to death/clinical death as the result of sickness, accident, or unsuccessful suicide.
3. The subject should have recovered enough to be interviewed.
4. During the first phone contact, the person had to report 'having had an experience while unconscious'.

On the basis of these simple criteria, the California team interviewed 41 respondents (15 men and 26 women) who contributed 50 cases. The subjects ranged in chronological age from 18 to 67 years old. These subjects described such experiences as leaving the body, entering into a brilliant light, and sometimes emerging into a delightful paradise. For example, the following report was contributed by a subject with a ruptured ulcer:

> It was like I was in the corner of the room and looking back down on the room, and it was like looking through a yellow filter like you would use on a camera. The whole room was like a light yellow color. And there I was, laying on the bed and they had intravenous in me and there were two more nurses and a doctor and they were doing all of this stuff and the doctor was yelling at them that, you know, what were they trying to do, kill me, because they hadn't done anything before he got there and I just stayed up there in the corner looking down on this and then all of a sudden I was back.

The following report collected by the California researchers is doubly fascinating. The account was submitted by a suicide survivor, who apparently contacted both a hellish environment (typical of the reports collected by Rawlings and Grey) before contacting a paradisiacal realm. The subject told the interviewers:

> I was in a swamp ... and I just kept going and going and finally I got past this swamp and there was this beautiful white gate. It was so

beautiful, with beautiful flowers and the flowers were so tall ... and my grandmother had died about two years before then and she stood at the gate, at the opening, and she was beckoning me to come. When I saw my grandmother I was maybe twenty feet away from her and I fell on the ground, and I said 'Grandmother come and get me.' She called to me and said that she couldn't come get me, that I had to make it on my own ... and it seemed like forever, but it was just a short time ... and finally she told me to go back, that 'It isn't time for you,' and she kept telling me to go back. And I was begging her to help me because I didn't want to go back, I wanted to go into this beautiful kingdom that I had seen. It was so gorgeous. It was white, the whole place was white and it was like wrought iron and it looked like a beautiful kingdom. Then I woke up at the hospital and they had put me in the corridor and they were just waiting for me to die.

The obvious correspondences between the Ring studies, Grey's work, the Pacific Northwest project, and the California collection can be seen in their statistical breakdowns. Table X gives the comparative statistics from these four collections, which concern the NDE's core features. Note how closely they all match, with only one significant exception. Both the Olympia college and Northridge researchers found more people experiencing some sort of light than travelling through a tunnel or into a void. But this small difference doesn't change the fact that, in general, the stages of the NDE seem to be stable and even predictable.

Of course, those collections put together by the Washington and California researchers could have been contaminated. By the time their reports were collected, the phenomenology of the NDE was well known to the general public thanks to the popular media—which publicized such stories by way of TV shows such as *That's Incredible* and *In Search of* ... Similar stories were also reported in many books that the percipients could have read before stepping forward. But the fact that four different studies have shown similar findings is difficult to explain easily. So by 1980 it really did seem that Ring, Grey, and others were examining a 'real' experience, whether it be psychological, neuro-physiological, or paranormal in nature.

The 'reality' of the experience was further evidenced when Dorothy Ayers Counts in Canada published her cross-cultural research into the NDE in 1983. But for the first time it began to look as if the NDE was, in some respects, moulded by cultural influences.

Table X
Comparative Statistics on Stages of
the Prototypical NDE

Stage	Ring	Grey	Study Lindley/ Bryan and Conley	Green and Friedman
1. Peace, bliss, or sereneness in the face of death	60%	29–47%	74.5%	70%
2. Experiencing some sort of out-of-body state	37%	32%	70.9%	66%
3. Experiencing a dark void or entering a tunnel	23%	26%	38.2%	32%
4. Perceiving a light	16%	21%	56.4%	62%
5. Entered into the light	10%	10%	34.5%	18%

The problem of cultural contamination

Ms Counts was originally from the University of Waterloo, and she conducted her survey as part of her interest in the people of Papua New Guinea. She had been engaged in field work there since 1966, so in 1981 she returned to see if the locals reported NDEs as well. The Melanesian population of the country was converted to Christianity in the 1940s and 1950s, and younger generations have received formal educations. The cosmology of Christianity, however, is somewhat dissimilar to the deep-rooted cultural beliefs of the Melanesians. Ms Counts explains in her report, for instance, that the concept of a unitary human spirit or soul is inconsistent with their traditions, since the Melanesians differentiate between a person's 'spiritual essence' and 'shadow' —either of which is prone to leave the body during sickness. Melanesian teachings on the afterlife do not resemble Christian cosmology either, even though they have been occidentalized through the years. In contrast to such notions as 'being with God' or entering heaven, the Melanesians believe that the spirit or shadow remains close to the community where the deceased person lived. Neither do they clearly differentiate between living and dead, but see death in terms of a process rather than a specific event.

Even though these people believe in post-mortem survival, Ms Counts thought that their society was different enough from the West to make a survey of Papuan NDE reports interesting. So when she returned to Papua New Guinea, she began asking the locals if they knew of anyone who had 'returned to life' from death. Such a concept is not unfamiliar to the Melanesians and she published several such cases in her 1983 report.

One of her respondents was a young man known to his entire hamlet. The cause of his clinical death is not clear from the report, but his experience took place during a prolonged coma. It is clear that the townsfolk considered him dead, since they had prepared his grave before he revived. When he came out of his coma, the young man reported an eschatological voyage in which he met a fellow villager, whom he easily recognized. She was the wife of a local lay minister, and she had, in fact, died while the percipient was lying in a coma. She was delivering some food to a neighbouring town when she collapsed, and the young man had no way of knowing of her death. The following extract is a portion of his lengthy report to the Canadian researcher:

> The day I died I was very sick and was sleeping in my house. I died at noon [when the sun is high] and came back at six o'clock that afternoon [at dusk]. At the time I died there was a woman who hadn't died. She cooked food and distributed it. But when I died my spirit met hers on the road.
>
> When I died everything was dark, but I went through a field of flowers and when I came out everything was clear. I walked on along the road and came to a fork where there were two men standing, one on either road. Each of them told me to come that way. I didn't have time to think about it, so I followed one of them.
>
> The man took my hand and we entered a village. There we found a long ladder that led up into a house. We climbed the ladder but when we got to the top I heard a voice saying, 'It isn't time for you to come. Stay there, I'll send a group of people to take you back.' I heard his voice, but I couldn't see his face or his body.
>
> I walked around trying to see him, but I couldn't. But I saw the dead woman that I had met [earlier] on the road. I saw her leave me. I

wanted to call out, 'Hey, come back!' but I couldn't for this house turned in a circle. I couldn't see the man who talked to me [earlier], but I did see children lying [on platforms] over the doors and windows. As I was walking around, trying to see everything, they took hold of me and took me back down the steps. I wanted to go back to the house, but I couldn't because it turned and I realized that it was not on posts. It was just hanging there in the air, turning around as if it were on an axle. If I wanted to go to the door, the house would turn and there would be another part of the house where I was standing.

There were all kinds of things inside this house, and I wanted to see them all. There were some men working with steel, and some men building ships, and another group of men building cars. I was standing staring when this man said, 'It's not time for you to be here. Your time is yet to come. I'll send some people to take you back. You cannot stay. This woman you saw coming here, it was her time and she must stay. But you must go back.'

I was to come back, but there was no road for me to follow, so the voice said, 'Let him go down.' Then there was a beam of light and I walked along it. I walked down the steps, and when I turned to look there was nothing but forest. I stood there and thought, 'if they have started mourning for me, I won't go because the voice said "Stand there and listen. If there is no mourning and no dogs howling, you go back. But if there is mourning you come back." '

So I walked along the beam of light, through the forest and along a narrow path. I came back to my house and reentered my body and was alive again.

Several features of this case resemble those described by people reporting NDEs in the West. Experiences such as entering a darkness, travelling to a bucolic realm, and being ordered back to the body should be very familiar to the reader by now. But notice that this report is different in some respects from the prototypical NDE. The experience sounds more prosaic and focused on sights and sounds typically familiar to Melanesian life. So while some of the specific components of the NDE seem to be cross-cultural, the description of the experience seems to reflect cultural differences. Ms Counts failed to find any evidence that the Melanesians report out-of-body experiences or exhilaration during their NDEs.

Since the Canadian researcher worked with a small case collection, her work neither supported nor specifically disproved the proposition that NDEs are genuinely cross-cultural. While certain features of the NDE tended to crop up in Counts's Melanesian cases, some predictable features of the core NDE were not components of her cases. Table XI highlights both the similarities and the differences between Western and Melanesian NDE reports.

Table XI
Cross-Cultural Components of the Prototypical NDE

Common features of the NDE	Features reported by Melansians
1. Leaving the body and looking back from a disembodied perspective	Not reported
2. Feelings of bliss or exhilaration during the experience	Not reported
3. Projected down a tunnel or into darkness	One subject reported moving through a darkness, but most of the percipients merely walked on a path to the next world
4. Met and conversed with spirit guides or deceased relatives	Commonly reported
5. Received into a bucolic paradise realm	Commonly reported
6. Ordered to return to their bodies by a guide or internally perceived voice	Commonly reported

Because of the discrepancies between her findings and Western cases, Ms Counts is sceptical that her data support the theory that the NDE really entails the release of the soul. She suggests that such experiences may be special hallucinations (called hypnagogic images) which typically occur when a person is fluttering between waking and sleeping. She concludes in her report:

Clearly, near-death and other types of visionary experiences are widespread cross-cultural phenomena that share some basic features. Also, clearly, the way in which people interpret these experiences is influenced by the expectations that they have learned from the cosmological and philosophical teachings of their particular culture. The culturally structured nature of these experiences is consistent with the explanation that out-of-body and near-death experiences are the result of a psychological state known as hypnagogic sleep. The Kaliai data presented here suggest that this, rather than an objectively experienced 'life after death,' is the most reasonable explanation for the phenomena. This is, however, only a small sample of cross-cultural data and, as I indicated earlier, no profound conclusions can be drawn from it. Obviously there is a need for researchers to collect cross-cultural data so that it will be possible to begin to separate the culturally derived content of these experiences from the content that is shared by people regardless of their heritage.

Based on the present status of our research, it seems likely that the NDE is subjectively real but not completely consistent in different cultures. Undoubtedly, much more research should be directed towards studying the NDE in non-Western societies. But showing that the NDE is subjectively real doesn't mean that it is objectively real.

The sceptic's position
Since the inception of NDE research in the 1970s, two different types of criticism have been levelled against the NDE. The first is that Moody-type NDEs really don't exist and have been unintentionally manufactured by some researchers, probably by selectively reporting their cases. The information and studies reported earlier in this chapter and book have basically disproved this criticism. But even if the NDE is a subjectively real experience, is it really the release of the soul from the body—the sort of flight that might occur when a person is dying?

Several objections have been raised to this simple interpretation of the NDE, and we'll focus on them for the rest of this chapter.

One important critic of the NDE has been Dr James E. Alcock, a psychologist from York University in Toronto, who is a total sceptic regarding the paranormal. His detailed and critical look at the NDE was published in 1979 in *The Skeptical Inquirer*, a periodical expressly devoted to debunking the paranormal and other borderline subjects. Dr Alcock begins his paper by urging us to take a more scientific approach to the subject. Simply because obvious causes of hallucination can't explain the NDE, he points out, doesn't mean the experience is necessarily paranormal. Nor does Dr Alcock feel that NDE researchers have exhausted every possible psychological, neurological, and pharmacological explanation for the experience. The Canadian psychologist also suggests that NDE witnesses could be unreliable. Many of the percipients placed their stories on record years after they occurred, when several sources of distortion could have significantly interfered with memory retrieval. So perhaps people describing past NDEs are systematically misrecalling them, which could explain the similarities between the various reports. People relating their experiences may be moulding their memories to match similar cases they've read or heard. Dr Alcock also supports the position independently posited by Dr Ronald Siegel—i.e. since NDE stories resemble psychedelic drug and so-called mystical experiences, it is doubtful that 'leaving the body' really represents the flight of the soul.

Dr Alcock goes on to emphasize the discrepancies between the researches of Dr Raymond Moody and the deathbed research of Dr Karlis Osis and his colleagues, which was summarized in Chapter 3. (If you recall, Dr Osis was interested in studying cases in which the dying person saw deceased friends and relatives at his/her bedside.) If both types of experiences are real, why do some people leave the body when facing death while others see peaceful visions?

In the light of these criticisms and problems with the NDE, Dr Alcock believes that conventional psychology *can* explain the experience. He suggests that the NDE is best understood when placed within a spectrum of related experiences, such as mystical or peak experiences, out-of-body excursions, hypnagogic imagery, and hallucinations in general. While many people believe such experiences to be paranormal, it is unlikely that there is anything supernatural about them. Such experiences, argues Dr Alcock, probably represent curious but normal experiences people chronically misrepresent. Blissful peak experiences, in which the individual feels himself merging with the universe, may be simple psychological or neurophysiological experiences, while OBEs probably represent misperceptions which emerge from the hypnagogic state between waking and sleeping. (Since out-of-body experiences typically occur when the witness is falling asleep, Dr Alcock sees little reason to believe in their objective reality.)

In short, Dr Alcock believes that the NDE shouldn't be considered a unique human experience, since it has so many characteristics in common with other psychological phenomena. Any explanation for the NDE should be capable of explaining the rest of these experiences. So what could this far-ranging explanation be?

In order to explain the NDE, Dr Alcock follows Ronald Siegel in turning to the study of hallucinations. Following up clues independently unearthed by his colleague, the Canadian psychologist shows that some of the features of the NDE resemble drug-induced hallucinations, such as seeing tunnels, reliving experiences from the past, the preponderance of religious imagery, and so forth. Dr Alcock believes that NDEs result from hallucinatory episodes which the percipient, based on his/her prior expectations, subsequently structures (i.e. remembers) into the specific form of the 'core' NDE. (Since the patient usually feels that he/she is dying, for instance, tunnel sensations or bucolic scenes would be *interpreted* in the form of an eschatological journey.) Sometimes this moulding process occurs years later, when the patient comes to grips with the experience and elaborates it to match stories reported by other witnesses.

Looking back at Dr Alcock's criticisms today, close to a decade later, it is clear that the Canadian psychologist has given us some excellent food for thought. Some of his criticism no longer seems pertinent, though, since research subsequent to 1979 has demonstrated the objective similarity between independent NDE reports. Nor can memory faults explain the consistency of these stories. Scientists interested in the NDE have collected similar accounts from people soon after their resuscitations, and even from people unfamiliar with Dr Moody's research.

Both of these findings significantly weaken Dr Alcock's position, but they certainly do not completely undermine his explanatory model. Since there is considerable evidence that NDEs, peak experiences, some hallucinatory experiences, and out-of-body states share common ground, perhaps Dr Alcock is correct in suggesting that any explanation for the NDE should explain these features. The specific role that suggestion plays in the perception of the NDE also needs to be more carefully evaluated, especially since cross-cultural studies of the phenomenon indicate that such distortions commonly occur. But on the other hand, I don't think we should be obsessed with finding a general explanatory model for NDEs and (possibly related) hallucinatory experiences, for there is an important flaw in Dr Alcock's reasoning that we must take into consideration.

It seems to me that Dr Alcock and Ronald Siegel overlook the fact that any two categories of human experience will probably share some sort of common ground, just by pure coincidence. For example, let's take a look at the 'experience' of looking at my pen, with which I'm writing this sentence, and a carrot. Both happen to be orange and correspond in general shape, but it would be ridiculous to posit that my pen *is* a carrot. But this is exactly the line of reasoning employed by both Alcock and Siegel. They have stressed the similarities between NDEs and hallucinations but have overlooked the differences. We should be evaluating the similarities *and* the differences between NDEs and other (possibly related) radical psychological experiences. Do these similarities represent genuine common ground between NDEs and other psychological experiences, or is their similarity swallowed by the differences?

One of the problems with Dr Alcock's paper is that NDE research conducted since 1979 has invalidated several of his critical points and suggestions. Although an interesting approach to the NDE, his article is, simply stated, dated. But just as research on the NDE has become more sophisticated, so have the critics. Some of them have important things to say and their writings should be carefully examined.

Dr Robert Kastenbaum has been interested in the psychology of death for many years and has written several books on the subject. Originally the editor of *Omega—the Journal of Death and Dying*, Dr Kastenbaum is currently the director of the Adult Development and Aging Program at Arizona State University. Unlike his colleague in Canada, he is not a public opponent of parapsychology, and even opened the pages of *Omega* to the subject in 1974. So his scepticism regarding the NDE is not based on any dislike for the paranormal. While some of his points resemble those published in 1979 by Dr Alcock, Dr Kastenbaum has delved into the study of the NDE more deeply and with greater insight.

The psychologist first began writing on the NDE in 1977 when he contributed a popular article on the subject to *Human Behavior* magazine. Dr Kastenbaum explained that he objected to the romantic tone of much NDE research on both moral and psychological grounds. One of his chief criticisms was that by glorifying the NDE, researchers such as Dr Moody and others could be encouraging people to commit suicide—i.e. to explore the experience and the future life. This may sound like unfounded and wild speculation, but there is a precedent for his concern, since something of the sort happened in the 1950s when Morey Bernstein's *The Search for Bridey Murphy* was a best-seller in America. This book reported on several sessions in which a Pueblo, Colorado, housewife was hypotically regressed to her 'past life' in Ireland. The case popularized the then unfamiliar and strange concept of reincarnation, and some unbalanced people purportedly killed themselves upon reading the book, hoping to escape life's miseries by seeking a future incarnation on earth. Dr Kastenbaum was probably concerned that popular belief in the NDE might spark off similar rash behaviour. Fortunately, however, the psychologist's concern was premature and no such incidents were reported in the wake of Moody's success. On the contrary, there is even some evidence that people can control their self-destructive urges by reading about the NDE. Realizing that death does not terminate conscious life can convince suicidal invididuals that such behaviour won't relieve their problems. One psychologist in California even gives his suicidal patients NDE reports to read and has achieved significant success with this form of therapy.

Of course, moral objections to the popularization of the NDE must remain secondary to the sceptic's position. Dr Kastenbaum realizes this point, so the focus of his *Human Behavior* contribution is geared towards more pressing issues. His primary criticism was that NDEs don't seem to be invariably reported by people resuscitated from death. Only some people report classic NDEs, while most others experience little or nothing in the face of life-threatening situations. People who consciously recollect life-threatening crises tend to report an entire range of curious perceptions, of which the NDE is only a single example. Dr Kastenbaum points out that most people typically retain consciousness but don't report leaving the body. Nor do NDEs—when they *do* transpire—necessarily conform to the Moody prototype.

'The existence of other types of reports from the dead-or-almost-dead frontier does not of itself discredit the kinds of accounts that made up the current wave of interest [in NDEs],' Dr

Kastenbaum suggests, 'but they do make it difficult to accept the implication, drawn by some, that the process of dying-unto-death is usually a joyous one.'

He was probably referring to the fact that some people experience hellish and nightmarish NDEs. This finding had recently been made by Dr Charles Garfield, whose paper on the subject (cited in Chapter 7) Dr Kastenbaum later published in his anthology *Between Life and Death*.

Dr Kastenbaum's piece in *Human Behavior* was a generally circumspect reply to the popular success of Raymond Moody's *Life After Life*, but it wasn't his last word on the subject. He has kept abreast of contemporary NDE research and his thinking has similarly evolved. The psychologist returned to the study of the NDE in 1984 when his book *Is There Life after Death?* was issued. This interesting book is structured in the style of a debate in which Dr Kastenbaum argues both sides of the survival question. The entire first section of the book is devoted to research on the NDE and its implications. During the course of this prolonged discussion, he points out several problems with taking the NDE literally, some of which repeat points he originally raised in 1977:

1. Not everyone reports NDEs in the face of clinical death; only a subgroup of patients experience them. If the NDE were an objectively real experience, everybody should have them.
2. When NDEs are reported, the stories don't necessarily conform to the Moody-style prototype. Some people have contradictory and unpleasant experiences (of the sort summarized in the previous chapter).
3. NDEs do not merely happen when a person experiences pseudo-death, but resemble drug-induced hallucinations and peak experiences. They also resemble out-of-body experiences which generally take place when the percipient is in good health. So NDEs probably emerge from the state of consciousness experienced by the subject right before dying, not necessarily from death itself.
4. Since out-of-body experiences resemble NDEs so closely, the NDE is probably a specific type of out-of-body experience, which could be a perfectly normal psychological phenomenon.

5. Research has shown that people reporting NDEs sometimes only *perceive* themselves close to death and probably experience NDEs only because they mistakenly believe their situations are life-threatening. If NDEs really occur in the face of death, they should only occur when the patient faces mortal *physiological* danger.

6. Since former patients reporting NDEs have survived their ordeals, it is improper to say they were really 'dead' in the first place.

7. Since people report their NDEs retrospectively, it is impossible objectively to determine whether their experiences correspond to clinical death. The hospital patient reporting an NDE upon recovering from temporary cardiac failure, for example, is merely *assuming* his experience corresponds to the crisis.

8. People facing life-threatening situations often become depersonalized, which is a curious shift of perceptual awareness during which they become psychologically detached from their environment. Such people may perceive either their surroundings or themselves as momentarily unreal. This type of experience is a psychological defence in the face of a traumatic situation, easily explainable psychologically. NDEs resemble some forms of depersonalization and probably represent examples of the phenomenon.

9. NDE reports conform to cultural patterns and expectations and don't appear to be truly cross-cultural.

Because of these factors, Dr Kastenbaum does not feel that the NDE is objectively real or that it points to permanent survival. He believes that it is probably a psychologically useful fantasy. When we face a life-threatening situation, he says, our first response is to escape from it. When escape is obviously impossible, we can only respond by changing our psychological, rather than physical, behaviour. We simply can't run from cardiac failure the same way we can run from a speeding car, so we respond internally (perhaps by changing the brain's chemistry) to perceive the situation in a less serious light. The end product of this process is the NDE. According to Dr Kastenbaum:

> We recover and perhaps become survivors with NDEs to share. This happens if our bodies have sufficient self-healing potential and the stress and damage do not continue too long. Or we die. Despite ac-

tivation of the internal adaptive system, the circumstances of our illness or injury are too massive, too excessive for recovery. Even when death is the outcome, however, the brain hormones still perform a valuable function. They comfort. They lull. They throw open, for the last time, the gates that hold back our reservoir of individual, cultural and racial fantasies. Out come these images, arranging themselves to please. Arranging themselves to tell us one final bedtime story.

Dr Kastenbaum believes that this explanatory model for the NDE is more scientific and parsimonious than metaphysical or paranormal conceptualizations. He points specifically to the fact that the neurosciences have even found the chemical basis for some NDE phenomenology. The brain can secrete endorphins and enkephalins—chemicals that produce euphoria—during periods of stress or elevated emotions, which seem to be a prerequisite for the NDE. Perhaps, suggests Kastenbaum, these chemicals produce the typical bliss which NDEs commonly sport. Perhaps future researchers will uncover more leads towards understanding the experience.

'The core NDE is a fascinating episode involving physiology, psychodynamics and cultural heritage,' writes Dr Kastenbaum in his *Is There Life after Death?*, 'all in the service of helping us to survive a threat to life or to end our existence with a comforting dream?' He ends with the piquant remark, 'If you insist on making more than this of the NDE, then you are insisting on fantasy.'

Do the criticisms and suggestions of psychologists such as Dr Kastenbaum explain the NDE better than paranormal or metaphysical conceptual models?

Sceptics of the NDE have offered a sometimes insightful look at several problems confronting the phenomenon and its interpretation, but this doesn't mean that their arguments are either correct or even cogent. The criticisms of sceptics such as Dr Kastenbaum can be grouped into three categories: some of them seem to be correct, some of them are probably incorrect, while the rest tend to be irrelevant to the study of the NDE. So before exploring the NDE in greater depth, Dr Kastenbaum's criticisms should be re-examined, in order that the real problems facing the paranormal (survivalistic) interpretation of the experience will be more obvious.

Not everyone has an NDE in the face of clinical death

This point is certainly obvious from the polls and interviews published by Kenneth Ring, Michael Sabom, Margot Grey and several other researchers. Their surveys indicate that roughly 20–60 per cent of any given sample of near-death survivors report NDEs. Now this statistic may be telling us relatively little. The fact that some people don't have or don't recall NDEs upon reviving from clinical death has little bearing on those who do. Some individuals simply may not have come close enough to death to experience the soul's release.

Of course, this is a somewhat weak line of reasoning, since some people have NDEs when they merely *perceive* themselves to be dying. So there must be several psychological, biological, and neurophysiological reasons why some people experience NDEs and others don't. Though interesting, these co-factors may have little bearing on the specific nature of the NDE. If the soul can genuinely leave the body, such a process could easily produce or be the product of physical/neurophysiological events within the organism. Possibly the NDE takes place only when several co-factors work in conjunction, which may not be present in the face of every life-threatening situation for every person.

There is also a second problem with the 'not everyone has NDEs' criticism. Because some individuals don't recall NDEs doesn't mean they haven't experienced them. Many people block block upsetting psychological experiences from their memory, which is the precise process behind some phobias. It is also possible that the recollection of an NDE is complicated by the problem of state specific memory, an interesting phenomenon well known in psychology. Psychologists have long realized that learning can be a function of a subject's state of mind. People can learn information while in specific states of mind, such as while hypnotized, but can only recall it when returned to the same state. Remember that old saying, 'If you lose your car keys while drunk, get drunk again and you'll remember where you put them'? There is some psychological truth in this principle, which possibly explains why some people simply cannot remember NDEs when they have been resuscitated. A person experiencing a life-threatening situation is not exactly in a normal state of consciousness. He/she may either plunge into an inwardly focused and introspective state or become hyperalert to his/her surroundings. Strange experiences taking place in such states may not be easily recalled when the patient recovers.

The phenomenon of state specific memory may sound far-fetched but there is considerable scientific evidence for its existence. There is also some direct evidence that this phenomenon interplays with the NDE. As we saw in Chapter 7, some of Rawlings's patients didn't recall their negative NDEs upon recovery, even though they had described them to the physician earlier. Other people (as Nancy Bush found in her study of the NDE in children) only recall NDEs while reliving their crisis situations under hypnosis. Though these experiences could be confabulations caused by either explicit or implicit hypnotic suggestion, perhaps these memories could only emerge when the subject entered into a special state of consciousness.

The NDE is not necessarily a self-consistent experience

This fact should be obvious from the published studies, even though the issue wasn't apparent in 1975 when Raymond Moody published his first work. We now know that the prototypical NDE is a genuine phenomenon—a point currently supported by considerable evidence collected by researchers in several different countries. The sceptic is correct, however, in pointing out that the self-consistency of the NDE has little bearing on its objective reality. (People in different cultures report surprisingly similar forms of psychotic hallucinations, for example, but that doesn't mean such hallucinations are objectively real.) Nor is the NDE perfectly self-consistent even when we look at prototypical cases. Some sceptics like to point out that NDE reports differ from each other in sometimes important ways. Some individuals report leaving the body while other percipients find themselves instantaneously projected to the otherworld. Some witnesses report tunnels or voids while many others never make such observations. Some people see their deceased relatives living in the otherworld, while other terminal patients experience them by their bedsides. Why, asks the sceptic, should there be so much inconsistency within even Moody-type NDEs?

I don't think that any partisan of the NDE claims that everyone has the exact same experience, a point originally made by Moody himself in 1975. Some of the discrepancies between NDE reports may result from problems of memory, since different witnesses may simply recollect different parts of their experiences. Remember that memory is essentially a highly variable and subjective process and not a photographic record of a person's past experiences. Or perhaps the NDE is an experience which simply occurs in different ways. Some percipients—for reasons we havn't deciphered—may skip some phases of the NDE during the soul's flight.

The real crux of the self-consistency issue, though, is that some people have NDEs radically different from the prototypical form. Dr Kastenbaum especially points to nightmarish encounters. Since these types of NDE obviously represent psychological or subjective experiences, he believes, NDEs in general probably lack any objective reality.

There are two possible responses to this line of reasoning. Probably the most obvious is that people respond to life-threatening crises on many levels. It is possible that, for some unknown psychological or purely biochemical reason, some people experience vivid hallucinations when near death. Religious backgrounds or fears of dying may translate into highly unpleasant subjective experiences such as the hellish encounters recorded by Rawlings and Margot Grey. But just because some people have unpleasant visions/hallucinations in the presence of death doesn't mean that other types of NDE are similarly subjective. Another response to the inconsistency within the NDE is to take a Swedenborgian approach to the subject. Emanuel Swedenborg was an eighteenth-century Swedish scientist, theologian, and mystic. Based on his personal visions and out-of-body experiences, he believed that several distinct 'planes' exist in the otherworld. Each dimension has its individual cartography and differs from the others. Swedenborg's multiple worlds concept of the Great Beyond has had a long history in religious thought, and even the ancient Jews popularly believed in multiple heavens. If this belief is, in fact, cosmologically true, then it isn't surprising that NDE percipients sometimes contact different otherworld levels while having their experiences. Our own earthly terrain changes from place to place—from forests to deserts to streams— so why shouldn't the afterlife? Since the multiple worlds concept of the Beyond is so pervasive in religious thinking, perhaps these beliefs (and NDE reports) point to a literal truth. So while the problem of nightmarish NDEs proves that the phenomenon is more complicated than the early NDE researchers believed, such experiences have little bearing on the nature of the prototypical NDE.

NDEs do not necessarily emerge from life-threatening experiences

This finding is probably the most important issue raised by the sceptics, for if prototypical NDEs take place when the percipient isn't really facing death, obviously the experience isn't the simple release of the soul in response to the crisis.

Ever since the turn of the century, some researchers interested in the paranormal have known that NDEs emerge from a range of circumstances. Certainly they commonly surface from clinical death, but they also take place under less stessful circumstances. Take the experience of J.W. Skilton (summarized in Chapter 3) which F.W.H. Myers included in his *Human Personality and Its Survival of Bodily Death*. Skilton was unloading timber from a boxcar when he had a classic NDE complete with spiritual guides, leaving the body, encountering deceased relatives, and so forth. Similar reports have been placed on file more recently. Before continuing any further, let's examine one of these cases.

The following case was reported in 1950 by the well-known historical writer William O. Stevens, who was fascinated by the paranormal and wrote several books on the subject. He originally received the following case from a reader, Miss Iris Valerie Yeoman, who explained to Stevens that, since childhood, she had suffered from an intense fear of death. She was even afraid to sleep, scared that she wouldn't wake up in the morning. This obsession played an important role in her life until she reached 18. One night she was lying in bed when she felt herself dying, even though she wasn't sick. She couldn't explain her feelings, but suddenly saw several deceased relatives standing by her bed-side. What followed was a typical NDE:

A curious sensation began at my feet. Almost like a tight glove being pulled from a finger. This pulling sensation travelled up my body until it reached my shoulders, and throat. Then came a second of blank unconsciousness, and I found myself standing beside the bed looking down at the body on the bed. Had I actually lived inside that? To my surprise I found that I still had hands, and feet, and a body, for I had always regarded the soul as a something without shape and void. In those days I had read no Spiritualistic books on after death conditions, and to find, that though I was 'dead' I still had form, was new to me. I looked with pity, not unmixed with contempt at those who were mourning me. Then suddenly, on the blank wall, on the side of the room farthest from the door, appeared an opening, like a tunnel, and at the far end a light. The power that had drawn my body from me, drew me irresistibly towards this passageway, which as I moved nearer to it seemed to lead steeply upwards. Without any exertion on my part, I was drawn up the passage and soon found myself standing at the top, on the summit of a hill covered with the greenest grass I had ever seen. I glanced round. The country was un-dulating, and beautiful. Wooded scenery gave way to a glint of water, here and there. There was no sun visible, but the light had a wonder-ful and unusual quality.

Beside me I found a very tall veiled figure. I could not see the face, but I knew that he was a trusted friend. I knew, too, that he was smil-ing at me, when he spoke. 'Look back at the way you have come,' he said. I looked down the passage. My body still lay upon the bed. My friends were still grieving for me. Then I was told to shift my atten-tion, and immediately I found that I could see the entire world as clearly as I had observed the details of my room. The earth was shrouded in clouds of depression, fear, and pain, my heart swelled with pity. I held out my arms, and cried to my friends, and to the world. 'Look up. Look up. Can't you see that I am alive, and well, and happy? Far more alive than I ever was on earth. There is no death. Death is Life.' Then I woke, and the old terror had passed for ever.

There really isn't much evidence that Miss Yeoman was close to death physically, and her unusual experience seemed to be some sort of response to her overwhelming fear of ego-loss. Despite these facts, notice that her experience contains several elements of the core NDE—i.e. seeing deceased relatives, spiritual guides, leaving the body, travelling through a tunnel, and enter-ing the otherworldly realms. Since relatively little was known about the NDE when this case was published, it's difficult to believe that the witness cribbed it. Certainly this case shows that classic NDEs do not only emerge from closeness to death but may be sparked by other factors.

The fact that many NDErs were never really close to death has also been demonstrated by some recent research reported by Dr Bruce Greyson, a psychiatrist currently posted at the University of Connecticut in Farmington. Dr Greyson has been particularly interested in NDEs reported by suicide survivors and originally collected 30 such cases. Each participant in the study was asked to complete an interview in which extensive demographic infor-mation was compiled. Dr Greyson's subjects were predominant-ly Caucasian, their mean age was 28.9 years, but only 30 per cent of them considered themselves particularly religious. The really important data emerged from the study when Dr Greyson examined his subjects' medical records. He found no correlation between the seriousness of their suicide attempts and the intensity of the resulting NDEs. Characteristic experiences such as seeing a bright light and entering a void were reported by those patients least endangered by their unsuccessful suicide attempts.

Dr Greyson's studies suggest that the *perceived* imminence of death catalyses NDEs more commonly than direct physical threats.

Similar findings have recently been reported by Emily Williams Cook, Dr Ian Stevenson, and Dr Nicholas MacLean of the University of Virginia. Speaking before the 1986 conference of the Society for Psychical Research in Cambridge, they reported on 40 NDE cases acquired by the school's Division of Parapsychology. By checking their informants' medical histories, they found that less than 50 per cent were physiologically endangered when they experienced their NDEs. Most of them merely perceived themselves to be facing the Grim Reaper. So again it appears that the perceived threat of death prompts NDEs more commonly than biological danger. Such findings have an important bearing on any explanation proposed for the NDE.

What conclusions can be drawn from the Greyson and University of Virginia studies is not conclusively known. It could be that people extremely close to death don't commonly *recall* NDEs. Perhaps their mental states were too impaired when the incidents occurred, but that doesn't necessarily mean they didn't undergo them.

NDEs seem to be nothing more than common out-of-body experiences which have no specific relationship to death

The fact that even typical NDEs don't necessarily emerge from genuinely life-threatening biological circumstances is important to remember. NDEs begin to look more and more like out-of-body experiences—i.e. common episodes where people momentarily feel that their consciousness is detached from the body. The following example, for instance, is from my own file on the subject.

> During the summer of 1965 I was a student attending classes every day. It was extremely hot that August and after classes ended at 1:00 in the afternoon, I could hardly wait to get home, flop on my bed, and take a nap. This was a ritual to which I adhered almost every day. One day, however, turned out to be different. I came home as usual,

kicked off my shoes, turned on the radio, and lay down on my back patiently waiting for sleep to overcome me. Then it happened. I began to feel oddly chilly and started to tremble. I flipped over onto my side, realizing at the same moment that my whole body was pulsating and that I was almost paralyzed. I concentrated on these sensations and soon afterward blacked out for a moment. An instant later I found myself floating in the air and, in another instant, I was standing at the foot of the bed staring at myself. I made an abrupt about-face (I didn't walk around, I merely willed myself to turn) and tried to walk towards the door to my room, which led to a hallway. I felt as though I were gliding through jelly as I moved, and I lost balance for a moment and almost fell over. Everything was blurred by a cloudy hue that enveloped a whitish form, which I perceived as my body. A moment later I found myself awakening on my bed. But I also realized that I had never really been asleep!

Sometimes the experience can be frightening, but this is a relatively rare reaction. The following case is also drawn from my own collection of NDE reports:

...In 1966 and prior to the arrival of our first child (March 1967) I began to have very vivid experiences and could only describe them to my husband as 'my nightmare thing,' except that it was not a dream. I would be lying in bed, just before going to sleep, and a strange feeling would come over me. My eyes would go to tunnel vision and I would feel like some huge suction was pulling on me. Then suddenly I would be plastered against the ceiling and could see my body lying in bed. I wanted back in that body more than anything else, but something pulled on me and would take me into the hallway. I would struggle with every ounce of energy I could muster against this. Then when fear would reach its peak, I would be 'lowered' back into my body.

Judging by polls conducted in the United States, England, Iceland, and Australia, these fascinating experiences seem to be relatively common. They can occur under a wide range of circumstances. Some people have them when falling asleep or when they sit to meditate; other percipients claim to experience them when they are sick or knocked unconscious by accident, or can deliberately induce them. If NDEs represent some specific subcategory of the out-of-body experience, the key to explaining them could rest with developing conceptual models for the latter. For by explaining the out-of-body experience (OBE), we might be explaining the NDE as well. One of the problems with the work of Ring, Sabom, and others is, in fact, that they have rarely interpreted the NDE within the framework of the OBE.

Parapsychologists have been studying the out-of-body experience for a good many years, and the results of these experiments will be reported in Chapter 10. For the moment, the precise interrelationships between the OBE and the NDE will be deferred. But before concluding this discussion, let's turn back to Dr Kastenbaum and the way in which he uses this interrelationship to criticize the NDE.

The problem with Dr Kastenbaum's contention that NDEs merely represent out-of-body experiences is that the criticism really says nothing; it is merely an exercise in circular reasoning. Saying that the NDE is really an OBE is only reclassifying the experience, not explaining it. Dr Kastenbaum is merely explaining one mystery by invoking yet another one. He also bases his line of reasoning on an important premise: that OBEs merely represent psychological experiences and little more. While it is true that OBEs tend to be commonly reported by the public, there is no proof that they can be explained psychologically. I personally feel that a great deal of experimental evidence suggests that the OBE is a paranormal experience, perhaps the literal separation of consciousness from the body. If this theory for the OBE is correct, then equating the NDE with the OBE supports the survivalist implications of the former. For if the out-of-body experience represents the temporary release of consciousness from the body, the NDE would probably entail its permanent release and survival. We will return to this important issue in Chapters 9 and 10.

Since the people reporting NDEs were successfully resuscitated, they weren't really dead to begin with, nor should we assume that their experiences temporally coincided with pseudo-death

This point has been repeated endlessly ever since the NDE first came to public attention. Since the people reporting NDEs were successfully revived from their life-threatening crises, can we really say they were genuinely 'dead'? Perhaps NDEs have no bearing on the 'real' experience of death at all.

This argument may be more semantic than practical, and it would be easier to evaluate if the criteria for death were better established in conventional medicine. Science and medicine have battled with the issue of identifying the specific 'moment' of death for years, and still seem to be struggling with the problem. The issue has become more complicated with the development of sophisticated life-support systems which can keep the body functioning sometimes indefinitely. Current medical thinking is that death is a process more than a discrete event, since there is no simple biological factor that specifically signifies biological death. Defining the moment of death is so problematic, in fact, that entire books have been written on the subject. Before proceeding further with our discussion of the NDE, let's explore these issues in a little more depth.

Continued loss of consciousness is certainly a life-threatening situation when it results from a patient's medical problems. A patient will die in such a state unless some sort of intervention is implemented. If these procedures fail, the patient enters a state of brain death in which the brain's self-regulation ceases.

The concept of brain death is crucial to any understanding of biological death and is linked to what's called intracranial homeostasis by physicians—i.e. those biological factors upon which the brain relies to function properly, including the self-regulation of oxygen flow, sugar, blood, and the elimination of waste. The internal pressure within the skull must also be constantly monitored and stabilized. When any of these factors is disrupted, the brain can cease operations and the patient becomes irreversibly brain dead if the organ's tissue significantly decays. But even if the patient enters brain death, the body can be kept functioning by machines. Irreversible coma results when the brain's homeostasis is blocked for a prolonged period of time, and it is usually during this period that a person is eventually pronounced dead.

The problem with defining the precise moment of death is that, because of the development of better and better resuscitation procedures, people can be revived from longer and longer comas.

Trying to establish firm biological criteria for death became so complicated that specific guidelines were not finally codified until 1968. That year the World Medical Assembly stated that brain death was proper evidence for biological death in general. The upshot of this pronouncement was that death became something which had to be diagnosed, not merely observed. Brain death is currently diagnosed when the patient has entered into an unresponsive coma, cannot breathe spontaneously, exhibits no brainstem reflexes, and no electrical output can be recorded from the brain. The days when the lack of a heartbeat signified death are gone forever. Even with these criteria, however, physicians still sometimes find it difficult to diagnose brain death, and a patient's brain functions will have to be tested repeatedly over several hours before death is proclaimed. But even these neurophysiological criteria have been challenged by some physicians.

These medical issues are central to the problem of whether people reporting NDEs were really dead or not. The sceptics who say that they were never objectively dead base their criticisms on the 'discrete' event model of death. Since this model has no support from within the medical community, the entire foundation of this criticism is extremely weak. The best we can say is that death represents a process and that NDEs sometimes occur from within its context.

If we consider brain death synonymous with biological death, there exists some impressive evidence linking NDE reports to this complicated biological state. Probably the most readily observable biological concomitant of brain death would be a 'flat' EEG when the brain no longer generates electrical impulses. The brain's electrical activity can be monitored by an electroencephalograph, which registers these impulses through electrodes and records them on a moving chart. When the brain ceases to function, the lines on the EEG Chart stop recording any rhythmic patterns and become flat. Needless to say, a flat EEG isn't exactly a promising sign for the patient! Currently, there is some limited evidence that patients experience NDEs during such episodes of temporary (but reversible) brain death. Some of the first evidence received considerable publicity in 1979 when the official newsletter of the Association for the Scientific Study of Near-Death Phenomena (the precursor to IANDS) carried a story on the work of Dr Fred Schoonmaker.

Dr Schoonmaker was chief cardiologist at St Luke's Hospital in Denver when the story was published. Completely unknown to most NDE researchers, he had been quietly studying reports of the phenomenon since 1961, having collected some 1,400 cases. Most of these were taken from hospital patients recovering from serious illnesses. The reports were usually recorded from the patients soon after the NDEs occurred: Dr Schoonmaker found that 60 per cent of the patients he interviewed reported NDEs then, while another 18 per cent acknowledged them later on. More interesting, however, is the physiological data Dr Schoonmaker collected on his cases. Several of his reports came from people who were undergoing surgery or other interventions when their NDEs took place. Because these patients were being monitored, Dr Schoonmaker was able to amass information concerning such factors as their blood oxygen levels. EEGs had also been routinely taken for some patients. The physician found no evidence that lack of oxygen to the brain (which could feasibly produce hallucinations) could explain the NDE. Even more significant were 55 cases in which patients with temporarily flat EEGs reported invariably pleasant NDEs.

These cases could help prove that NDEs are genuinely related to imminent death and don't emerge simply from states of consciousness linked to life-threatening situations. Dr Schoonmaker's 55 patients probably exhibited little biologically determined consciousness by the time brain death ensued. For this reason it is unfortunate that, despite the upsurge of scientific interest in the NDE, the Denver-based cardiologist has never published his findings. He stated in 1979 that he planned on writing a book on his research, but it has never been published. So at the present time it is impossible for other researchers to evaluate his claims critically. The fact that Dr Schoonmaker has not published his data is a terrible loss to NDE research. We don't even know whether his cases resemble those collected by Moody, Ring, Sabom, and others, although the cardiologist claims that they do.

The NDE is merely a unique form of depersonalization, a phenomenon well-known to psychology

Depersonalization is a common psychological phenomenon in which a person perceives himself to be 'unreal' or perceives his body as a foreign object. Such experiences can occur when an individual is depressed or under stress, and it is commonly reported by some epileptics. It is often typified by a flat feeling in which the person becomes indifferent or emotionally neutral towards his body or himself.

Several examples of this curious phenomenon have been placed on record, and explanations for it range from cognitive (perceptual) models to neurophysiological speculations. The following two examples of depersonalization have been taken from Carney Landis's encyclopedic *Varieties of Psychopathologi-*

cal Experience. The first case was reported by a hospital patient suffering from recurrent psychotic episodes. The second report was a spontaneous experience contributed by a British teenager.

(1)

I feel as though I'm not alive—as though my body is an empty, lifeless shell. I seem to be standing apart from the rest of the world, as though I'm not really here. Is there something wrong with my ears? I hear you clearly, yet your voice sounds far away—distant and unreal. Whatever has deadened my feelings has deadened my hearing, too. It's the same with my eyes. I see but I don't feel. I taste but it means nothing to me. I'll eat anything you put before me. We had walnut cake which I normally adore—but it might have been a piece of dry bread. I eat, not for pleasure, but only to live. Perfume doesn't smell pleasant any longer. I'd have no preference for the smell of these roses over the smell of the cabbage cooking.

(2)

The most unusual occasion when this occurs is when I am out of doors. The last time was within the last month or so. I was in Nottingham with a friend and suddenly as we were walking along, I seemed to be completely apart from myself. I felt that I was somewhere above looking down on the scene of which I was a part and yet not a part. I was walking and talking, as though automatically. I couldn't feel any movement and yet I knew that I was walking.

Everything appeared to be of little importance any more. The experience on this occasion lasted for at least five minutes, but time as far as I remember passed as usual. We crossed the road, and although my legs moved with the motion, I felt that my brain had gone somewhere else and from there was just watching me.

I was completely unable to tell whether I myself was still present or whether I was the part which had gone. In short there were two different beings, the one watching the other.

The experience disappeared as suddenly as it had come and once again I felt complete.

Note that the second percipient specifically reports an out-of-body-like episode so typical of NDEs in general. Depersonalization is also often accompanied by incidents of derealization, in which the person perceives similar unreality in his physical environment.

But does depersonalization explain the NDE?

I don't think so. Depersonalization is really not an explanation for anything, but merely a category or label for a wide range of unusual experiences. So the sceptic who equates NDEs with depersonalization is merely reclassifying the experience. Who is to say, for instance, that the British teenager's experience just cited wasn't a genuine OBE? Maybe her consciousness really did temporarily leave the body. (This may sound like a strange claim, but in Chapters 9 and 10 we'll be examining a considerable amount of evidence supporting it.)

Reclassifying even classic NDEs by calling them episodes of depersonalization has had a long history in NDE studies, beginning with the work of Dr Russell Noyes, Jr. (of the University of Iowa) and Roy Kletti. Back in the early 1970s, these two researchers became interested in the subjective experiences of people facing sudden danger, such as serious falls, car crashes, and so forth. Since the concept of the prototypical NDE wasn't known then, they merely labelled such experiences depersonalization. By 1979 they had collected 114 cases of depersonalization in the face of danger and charted out their characteristics. Table XII gives part of their statistical breakdowns, based on a selection of 59 cases in which the percipients believed they were facing imminent death. Note that many characteristics of these episodes (marked by asterisks) resemble features common to the NDE. In the same paper from which these data are drawn, Noyes and Kletti compare their cases to 26 additional reports in which the precursory crises weren't perceived as life-threatening. These individuals tended to report the same types of experiences, but not as commonly.

The cases and statistical data collected by Russell Noyes and Roy Kletti are extremely interesting, since most of their reports emerged only from *perceived* dangers. Few of their informants were in any genuine or immediate biological danger of dying. A person swerving on the freeway, for example, certainly perceives himself to be in extreme danger, but the experience presents little internal biological threat. Such a person is nowhere close to biological death, physiologically speaking, unless he/she crashes into another vehicle!

But while reading through the reports collected by Kletti and Noyes, the critical reader will notice something strange. Relatively few of their respondents reported experiences that really sound like NDEs. Their seminal paper on danger-related depersonalization, for example, included five cases and was published in a 1976 issue of *Psychiatry*. Their first case concerned a racing

Table XII
Subjective Experiences in the Face of Extreme Danger
(from a study by Noyes and Kletti)

Feature	Percentage reported (N = 59)
Altered sense of time	80
Unusually vivid thinking	71
Increased speed of thoughts	69
Sense of detachment from the experience	67
Feelings of derealization	67
Movements performed automatically	64
Lack of emotion	54
Detachment from body*	54
Sharpened vision or hearing	49
Flashbacks of previous memories*	47
Enhanced cosmic understanding*	43
Saw colours or visions	41
Sense of harmony or unity with the world	39
Felt controlled by external force	37
Surrounding objects seen as small or distant	36
Saw vivid mental images*	36
Heard voices, music, or other sounds*	25

*indicates features common to the NDE.

enthusiast involved in a crash, who felt a sense of unreality during the episode. The second case was contributed by a female student depersonalized when her car swerved. She described the experience in terms of a blissful, mystical, or peak experience, but reported nothing resembling an OBE or a heavenly visit. Similar cosmic thoughts were experienced by a climber when he fell, nor did either of the two remaining cases published by

Noyes and Kletti resemble prototypical NDEs. Only one of their respondents mentioned an out-of-body sensation, in fact. (Their car crash victim reported a typical OBE while his car sped out of control.)

Despite their impressive collection and statistics, it soon becomes apparent that Noyes and Kletti based their depersonalization model for the NDE on cases barely resembling the phenomenon. Few of their published cases include examples of out-of-body experiences, tunnels, dark voids, or eschatological visions. While it is true that 54 per cent of their percipients reported being 'detached' from their bodies, it is not clear what criteria they used to make this determination. (Were their informants describing, for example, physical detachment or merely some form of psychological detachment?) Certainly classic, discrete OBEs don't show up commonly in their published cases.

It seems to me that since the early 1970s, other critical researchers have merely mimicked the Noyes and Kletti classification error, probably not realizing that their (Noyes/Kletti) early studies probably have little bearing on the NDE.

The fact that NDEs probably don't represent episodes of depersonalization has been recently emphasized by Dr Glen Gabbard and his colleagues in Kansas. Dr Gabbard, Dr Stuart Twemlow, and Dr Fowler Jones began studying the out-of-body experience in the 1970s. While conducting their survey, they extracted several cases of depersonalization from the psychiatric literature on the experience and broke down their characteristics, which were then compared with the phenomenology of the typical OBE. In stark contrast to the findings of Noyes and Kletti, the Kansas researchers found few similarities between the two experiences. People suffering from episodes of depersonalization rarely experience out-of-body incidents. They find the entire experience unpleasant and often think the sensation is pathological. Such emotional reactions don't bother the person undergoing an OBE, which is usually pleasant and even 'holy' to

[1]Remember that these findings represent generalizations, since both depersonalization and out-of-body experiences are variable phenomena. Individual cases can be found in the literature which counter the several patterns Gabbard *et al.* found in their survey. For more information on their cases and statistics, the reader should consult *With the Eyes of the Mind* by Glen O. Gabbard and Stuart W. Twemlow.

some people.[1] Dr Gabbard and his colleagues have harshly criticized equating NDEs with depersonalization as the latter is usually conceptualized in psychiatry.

NDEs conform to cultural stereotypes and expectations

At the present time, not enough systematic research has been conducted on the way NDEs occur in different cultures. Some proponents of the NDE point to the research of Karlis Osis and Erlendur Haraldsson, suggesting that their studies demonstrate the cross-cultural consistency of the NDE. These researchers, however, were really studying deathbed visions and were not concerned with the NDE, so their findings (which have not gone unchallenged even by some parapsychologists) have no bearing on the prototypical experience.

It seems likely that the NDE is a universal experience, since even the ancient Greeks reported them. The issue is not really whether it is a cross-cultural phenomenon, however, but to what extent such reports resemble or differ from each other. Some preliminary evidence shows that cultural influences probably do play a role in the NDE. The famous case of Er from Plato's *Republic* reads differently from those NDEs reported today, while the cases collected from Papua New Guinea by Dorothy Ayers Counts were obviously complicated by cultural factors. The percipient in one of her cases, for instance, journeyed to the other-world where the dead were busy building boats. Instead of interacting with a spirit guide, the witness was ordered back to earth by one of the boat builders! So it is beginning to look as if the NDE is some sort of archetypal experience which is perceived slightly differently from place to place, from culture to culture. Such a finding may have a crucial bearing on the explanation for the experience.

In conclusion, then, have the sceptics made a cogent case for believing the NDE is either an hallucination or a delusion? Neither of these possibilities seems likely. Most of the popular criticisms levelled by Dr Kastenbaum and others, though thoughtful, have been based on limited case studies, errors in logic, or errors in semantics—i.e. by sometimes erroneously reclassifying the experience into more familiar terminology.

But despite these problems with the sceptics' position, some of their insights can't be totally ignored. Whatever its nature, the

NDE is beginning to look like a more complicated phenomenon than it appeared to be in 1975. Two findings in particular should prevent us from supporting simplistic metaphysical explanations for the NDE. It is unlikely that NDEs emerge specifically from biological closeness to death; more regularly they seem to emerge from *perceived* threats to life. While some NDEs obviously take place concomitantly with clinical death, these cases cannot undermine the importance of those NDEs reported from much less serious conditions. It also seems obvious that cultural factors influence the specific way the prototypical NDE is experienced.

It is rather curious, however, that few of the sceptics or debunkers ever cite the research of Dr Michael Sabom. As we saw in Chapter 4, the Georgia physician has identified and corroborated a specific and revealing feature of the NDE—namely that people reporting them sometimes 'see' things beyond their (sensory) capabilities. Only one contemporary (and benign) critic has taken up the challenge these cases present. Dr Bruce Greyson, who considers himself theoretically neutral when it comes to explaining the NDE, has suggested that they could be psychological episodes during which the percipient uses extrasensory perception to reinforce the experience. He doesn't personally promote this viewpoint, but suggests it to show that paranormal features don't necessarily prove the objective reality of the NDE. The paranormal components of the NDE are important enough, however, to serve as the subject for the next chapter.

9.

Paranormal Aspects of the NDE

The following report was published in 1968 by Celia Green, the director of the Institute of Psychophysical Research in Oxford. She and her colleagues were collecting reports of out-of-body experiences when they found the case.

The percipient was having an operation for peritonitis but developed pneumonia while still hospitalized. She was lying in an L-shaped ward when she underwent the NDE.

> One morning I felt myself floating upwards, and found I was looking down on the rest of the patients. I could see myself; propped up against pillows, very white and ill. I saw the sister and nurse rush to my bed with oxygen. Then everything went blank. The next I remember; was opening my eyes to see the sister bending over me.
>
> I told her what had happened; but at first she thought I was rambling. Then I said, 'There is a big woman sitting up in bed with her head wrapped in bandages; and she is knitting something with blue wool. She has a very red face.' This certainly shook her; as apparently; the lady concerned had a mastoid operation and was just as I described.
>
> She was not allowed out of bed; and of course I hadn't been up at all. After several other details; such as the time by the clock on the wall (which had broken down) I convinced her that at least something strange had happened to me.

Because the Oxford researchers only catalogued their cases and didn't investigate them, this case must remain uncorroborated. Nobody can prove that it really happened, since the nurse wasn't contacted or interviewed.

Despite this problem, the case is representative of the legend and lore of both NDEs and the out-of-body experience. People undergoing these episodes commonly claim they saw or experienced people, places, or conversations beyond their sensory

capabilities. Probably the most common claim is when the percipients correctly report what took place during the surgery they
had undergone. In Chapter 4 we saw that Dr Michael Sabom built
his case for the reality of the NDE on such reports.

Claims of similar paranormal factors crop up repeatedly in
NDE cases. The following, for instance, was collected by Celia
Green. It was contributed by a gentleman whose wife underwent
an NDE when she nearly drowned.

> [My wife] was having a bath and I was in the sitting-room reading. Ap-
> parently she was lying in the bath face downwards when she went to
> sleep. She said that she left her body and came into the sitting-room
> and tapped me on the shoulder. I have no knowledge of this, but cer-
> tainly I went to the bathroom and found her lying face down in the
> water, her body quite mottled. I dragged her out and applied artificial
> respiration and she came to almost immediately. She has stated that
> she watched all my actions.

Note, however, that little effort was made to substantiate the
paranormal components of the NDE. There is no indication that
the reporter ever determined whether his wife's observations
were correct. Her claim was taken at face value.

This lack of formal corroboration is a perennial problem with
such reports. Too often the 'veridical' (from the Latin *veritas*,
meaning truth) elements of the NDE slide by with little comment. The researchers merely assume that the observations were
correct and that the percipients really 'saw' or 'heard' beyond
their sensory capabilities while out-of-body. Since seriously ill or
nearly dead people usually lose consciousness and close their
eyes, their reports often seem inexplicable and impressive.

Taking veridical cases so literally might not be wise, though,
for a little story recounted by Dr Susan Blackmore shows the
limitations of taking NDE/OBE reports so uncritically. Dr
Blackmore is currently a psychologist with the University of
Bristol's Brain and Perception Laboratory. She is an expert on the
out-of-body experience, even though she remains extremely
sceptical of the paranormal. She explains in her delightful book
The Adventures of a Parapsychologist that she once personally investigated a typical 'veridical' OBE report in the 1970s. She was
sent the case by Dr Karlis Osis of the American Society for
Psychical Research. The informant was a Canadian architect,
who during his OBE crossed the ocean to London. While visiting
the city, he followed a cobblestoned street bordering three-storey

houses set behind distinctive railings. The experience was so vivid that he even memorized the route he covered by the river Thames. When he returned to his body, he located the scene of the OBE on a map and claimed that he later contacted a British colleague and described the OBE; whereupon the other man checked the site in the Fulham district of London and 'proceeded to describe the character of the street, the buildings, the style, the building setbacks and entrance yards—all exactly as I had seen them'.

Dr Blackmore was impressed by the case and eagerly journeyed there with her husband to corroborate the story, but her findings didn't agree with the enthusiastic report from Canada. She explains that she located the street with ease, but the rest of the investigation fell flat.

'We found it [the street] easily enough, but what a disappointment!' she writes in her book. 'We searched and searched, walked most of the streets of Fulham, and found nothing like it. We pored over maps of London to find any other street that might lie in similar bends by the river, but when we tried we met with no more success.'

Dr Blackmore next checked whether the percipient possibly projected back into the past. She and her husband examined historical maps of the district, but failed to find any evidence that the street described by the percipient ever existed.

This little case should serve as an object lesson for OBE researchers and students of the subject. Never should the paranormal or the 'veridical' features of the experience be taken literally. Such claims should be investigated and independently corroborated by the researcher with critical detachment. The collapse rate for paranormal claims is extremely high in parapsychology, a fact any seasoned researcher will readily acknowledge!

But if the NDE represents the objective flight of consciousness from the body, should we expect these paranormal features to crop up repeatedly? The possibility is certainly logical. Most people report that their sensory capacities were not diminished during their experiences, and that their floating selves saw, heard, and sometimes smelled with ease. These claims seem rather curious, since there is little reason to believe that the soul or out-of-body self comes complete with ethereal eyes and ears! But the fact remains that, whatever their nature, people having OBEs and

NDEs somehow vividly experience the physical world (or a representation of it) and it is the researcher's responsibility to look into such claims. The assumption is often made that the partisans of the NDE point out that individuals having the experience often perceive themselves in some sort of etheric duplicate of the physical body. This perception is not, however, an invariable feature of the experience, since some percipients become totally disembodied during the NDE. They tend to experience themselves as balls of light or pinpoints of consciousness with no bodily encasement. The method by which these percipients experience their environment remains extremely problematic.

Operating-room NDEs reconsidered
Probably the most impressive study of the NDE's paranormal features was made by Dr Michael Sabom in the 1970s. In Chapter 4 we saw how the Georgia-based cardiologist became fascinated by the reports of surgical patients. Sometimes they correctly described complicated procedures and equipment, or repeated conversations the physicians held in the room. These were the cases that finally broke down Dr Sabom's reluctance to study the NDE. His painstaking research into his respondents' medical histories and their surgeons' reports is commendable. But is there any problem with these cases that compromises their importance?

One colleague of mine has suggested that Dr Sabom's cases might only be superficially impressive. The setting for these remarks was a conference on the paranormal held in Denver in November 1983. I had been asked to speak on the evidence for survival and I focused on NDE research in general, and promoted Dr Sabom's investigations in particular. During a round-table discussion later in the day, a fellow parapsychologist made the following point: since Dr Sabom never reported whether some surgical NDE percipients misdescribed their operations, the few veridical cases in his collection could be misleading. We simply have no inkling as to whether these cases were exceptions (coincidences?) within a large collection of less impressive reports. My response to this criticism emphasized the extreme detail found in Sabom's best cases. The patients contributed such precise and exact observations that each case, taken separately, corroborates the paranormal features of the NDE.

In order to refresh the reader's memory, let's take a look at a typical veridical NDE reported by Dr Sabom in 1982 in his *Recollections of Death*. Towards the middle of his book, the cardiologist presents six 'test' cases where paranormal observations were reported by coronary patients. Dr Sabom investigated each of them personally. One of the reports was contributed by a 62-year-old retired mechanic, who was interviewed a year after his experience occurred. The mechanic explained to the physician that his NDE took place while the doctors were trying to resuscitate him after a serious coronary:

When they got me to the hospital they took me in there ... pulled my clothes off me and put me upon the table. That's when I really had the heart attack ... Then all of a sudden it seemed like I moved up. I got up. The room seemed like it was in a glow. I don't know where the light was coming from. I was looking down and they were working on me. Just like getting up out of the bed, just about. I was above myself looking down. They were working on me trying to bring me back. 'Cause I didn't realize at first that it was my body, I didn't think I was dead. It was an unusual feeling. I could see them working on me and then I realized it was me they were working on. I felt no pain whatsoever and it was a most peaceful feeling. Death is nothing to be afraid of. I didn't feel nothing. They gave me a shot in the groin. Dr. B came up and decided to put one in my left—well, not in my armpit, but on my side. Then he changed his mind and went to the other side, next to the heart ... I saw them trying to bring me back with those pads. They put something on those pads, it looked like a lubricant, and rubbed them together and put them on my body, and then it jumped. But I couldn't feel it, even at that time. They brought it back and then hit it again when it went right out again.

When the patient recovered he described the resuscitation procedure to the physician, especially how the doctor changed the location for the injection. The surgeon was surprised by his account and told him that, during the resuscitation, he (the patient) was legally dead and couldn't have seen the treatment. Even though obviously befuddled by the story, the doctor corroborated the patient's observations before leaving the room.

'I felt like I was alive,' the former patient emphasized during his talk with Dr Sabom. 'It was just as though I was standing there talking to you. I could hear them [the doctors] and see them working on me and hear them talking and giving them [the nurses] orders and directions. It seemed like I was alone above my body and seeing everything that was going on.'

Dr Sabom interviewed the witness in depth and extracted considerable information concerning the defibrillation procedure, the injections he received, where the nurses were standing in the room, and so forth. Later the cardiologist examined the hospital records, where the procedures used to save the percipient were recorded by the physician handling the case. Each of the patient's observations had been correct but for a few inconsequential errors. The needle placed in his groin, for example, hadn't been for an injection but to extract blood, while the syringe had been inserted into his left (not right) side. Dr Sabom emphasizes in his book, however, that the lab slip could have been wrong, or the patient simply confused left and right while disembodied. Dr Sabom later spoke with the patient's wife, and she testified that her husband originally reported the NDE to her upon regaining consciousness. She said that his story always stayed the same.

As should be obvious from Chapter 4, this case is typical of several included by Dr Sabom in his *Recollections of Death*. But just how impressive is it?

The problem with surgical or emergency-room NDE reports is that the researchers studying them work from a false premise. When presenting them to prove the objective reality of the NDE, they merely assume that the patients, being unconscious, had no sensory capabilities. Since patients knocked out by drugs or otherwise comatose typically close their eyes, it seems obvious that they can't see or hear anything. But there is growing evidence that unconscious/comatose people do not totally lose consciousness and can hear, register, and remember transactions carried out in their presence. So could these so-called veridical surgical NDEs be the result of this phenomenon? This issue is a problem, called 'sensory cuing' in psychology, that hasn't been addressed by NDE researchers. Dr Sabom briefly mentions it in his book, but spends little time considering it or evaluating his cases in its light. So for the next few pages let's explore the problem. We will be concerned primarily with two related issues:

1. What do unconscious anaesthetized/comatose patients experience during surgery?
2. Are their perceptions clear enough to explain the veridical features of surgical NDEs?

Sensory cuing and the NDE

Since most people rendered unconscious close their eyes, there is no question of their picking up optical cues. But when a person loses consciousness, his/her capacity to hear is the last sensory channel to cease functioning and it is this phenomenon that could seriously complicate research on surgical or emergency-room NDEs.

To properly understand the problem of sensory cuing and its relationship to the NDE, a second phenomenon well-known to psychology must also be explained. *Synaesthesia* is a curious phenomenon in which information from one sensory channel is transcribed and experienced in a second mode. Such transcriptions sound bizarre, but people occasionally report 'hearing' colours or 'seeing' music. Synaesthesial experiences are commonly reported by psychedelic drug users, but they can be experienced in other states of consciousness as well. I once had the experience while in college studying music. It was late at night and I had completed a busy and exhausting day. I was literally too tired to sleep, so I turned on the radio in my living-room and sat on the couch. Soon the sounds of a Mozart piano sonata filled the the room, but suddenly my perceptions began to change. I realized that I wasn't really hearing the music, but could feel it. Each individual note and chord registered on my skin. I could feel each mallet stroke from the keyboard literally striking my limbs until the experience became unbearable. Finally I had to turn off the music and recuperate from the episode. I turned the radio back on some time later that night, but the unusual perceptions were not repeated.

Everyone reading this book can experience a form of synaesthesia for themselves. If you happen to be an opera lover, put on a recording, sit back, and close your eyes. Notice how scenes from the opera enter your mind while you listen to the music. Soon you will probably be visualizing the scenes while the singing continues. Your auditory perceptions are being simultaneously translated into visual images. Something of the same sort might occur during surgical procedures when the patient unconsciously visualizes the operation being performed. Since the patient's consciousness is clouded either by drugs or brain dysfunction, he/she could easily confuse such visualizations with reality. Or the information received from cuing could be transcribed neurologically by synaesthesia into visual representtions.[1]

The fact that surgical patients can hear while seemingly unconscious has been known for years. The 4 October 1959 issue of the *British Medical Journal* published an editorial on the subject, which prompted a doctor from St Bartholomew's Hospital in London to contribute his personal experience. In the issue of 5 December the physician wrote:

A few weeks ago, during a caesarean section for which the mother had a general anaesthetic—thiopentone, suxamethonium chloride, intubation, nitrous oxide, oxygen, tubocurarine and pethidine—I encountered an unusually long umbilical cord. The following day the patient said: 'I remember you saying something during my operation.' I asked her what it was, and she replied: 'You said, "My God, what a long cord."' And I had. But she had no complaint of pain, and if she was awake so was her baby, because he cried instantly. The cord measured 84 cm.

Many surgeons will be familiar with such reports and stories. Since 1959, however, considerable experimental research has been conducted into the sensory capabilities of 'unconscious' patients. The results of these studies have been mixed, but they indicate that surgical patients still perceive their surroundings.

One such experimental report was published in the *British Journal of Anaesthesia* in 1970 by D.D. Brice, R.R. Hetherington, and J.E. Utting from the University of Liverpool. They played a specially prepared tape for each of their 'unconscious' surgical patients. Eight different tapes were employed for the experiment, which featured such sounds as piano music, birdsong, church bells, and so forth. The tapes were prepared to be easily differentiated and each patient was subjected to a single recording. Sometimes it was replayed several times during the surgery. When the patients regained consciousness they were interviewed and asked to recall dreams or unusual perceptions they experienced. During these sessions, the patients were told that recordings had been played for them, and 12 subjects felt they would recognize the tapes if reexposed to the sounds. Each subject then heard the target recording, but it was played in the same

[1]The precise cause and neurophysiological mechanism for synaesthesia is unknown, but some researchers feel that out-of-body experiences could represent a special form of the phenomenon. For more information on this conceptual model, see Harvey J. Irwin's *Flight of Mind* (Metuchen, N J: Scarecrow Press, 1985).

session along with a control tape—i.e. a recording used for the experiment which the subject had *not* heard. The subjects failed to pick out the correct sounds to a statistically significant degree.

The research of Brice, Hetherington, and Utting did show, however, that patients commonly dream during surgery. These dreams often concerned cosmic themes and conversations with God. Sometimes the subject felt that death's mystery or Nature's secrets had been revealed to them, but they found it difficult to communicate their experiences to the physicians.

These surgically related dream episodes may be significant, since they imply that the subjects either experienced an NDE or something similar to it. Or possibly the cerebrations of unconscious surgical patients gravitate to such themes. Could such dreams set the stage for hallucinations that resemble NDEs? Could NDEs be little more than cosmic dreams catalysed by the drugs administered for surgery, or by the surgical setting itself? These issues are important and should be further explored by researchers studying the NDE.

Despite the failure of their research, the Liverpool surgeons cite three similar studies in their paper that showed positive findings. These early studies were confirmed in 1983 when Dr Keith Millar and Dr Neal Watkinson published their experimental study of surgical recall. Both researchers served in the Department of Psychiatry at the University Hospital and Medical School in Nottingham. Their experiment employed the services of 53 female subjects facing either gynaecological or upper abdominal surgery.

When each subject was rendered unconscious for the operation, the following instructions were read to her: 'This is very important; the surgeon wants you to remember some words. It is important for you to do so.' Special lists of words were then dictated to the unconscious patient. When the list was completed, it was repeated with the instructions: 'I'll repeat the words because you need to know them.'

This experiment was designed to make the recall more emotionally meaningful for the subjects. The problem with the previous Liverpool research was that little reason existed for the patients to recall the words. The researchers in Nottingham circumvented this problem by emphasizing the importance of remembering the instructions. This sort of task experimentally mimicked the situation people really confront in surgery, since they might be especially vigilant and register information important to them, perhaps spoken by the doctor.

When each patient recovered from the operation, she was interviewed and listened to a tape-recorded series of 40 words. Only 10 'target' words were included in the tape with the rest serving as the controls. The subjects successfully identified the targets better than chance, which supports the surgery recall theory.

The research of Drs Millar and Watkinson demonstrates that 'unconscious' surgical patients register information specially presented to them. But note that, in this study, the finding was merely a statistical one. None of the patients had any conscious memory of previously hearing the words, and simply found the target words 'familiar' upon presentation. Only one report so far placed in the literature on surgical recall suggests that systematic observations can be made during chemoanaesthesia. In 1963, Dr John T. Brunn—himself a physician—reported on his personal experience to a meeting of the American Society for Clinical Hypnosis. Dr Brunn explained that he was given sodium pentothal for dental surgery. Prior to the operation he gave himself hypnotic suggestions to recall the procedures used. Not only did these suggestions work, but he even recalled the conversations spoken in the room by his oral surgeon and the nurses. These surprising moments of lucidity were, however, interspersed with episodes of disorientation. More recent research has suggested that people in a coma retain similar levels of consciousness.

So what can we conclude from these reports and experimental findings?[2]

Dr Brunn's report suggests that people have the capacity to register their surgical experiences either through hearing or through other cuing sources. While the research of the Nottingham and Liverpool physicians shows that this perception is usually limited in scope, the *potential* for such recall could be limitless. Because he was so highly motivated to remember his experience, Dr Brunn's recollections were probably unusually detailed, but the implications of his report are staggering. If it is possible for 'unconscious' patients to hear, many of the surgical observations reported by NDE percipients lose their value. The sceptic couldn't be faulted for suggesting that surgical and

[2]For a comprehensive bibliography of scientific papers on surgical consciousness, see Arthur Cherkin and Phyllis Harroun's paper 'Anesthesia and memory processes' in *Anaesthesiology*, 1971, *34*, 469–74.

emergency-room NDEs result when the patients pick up verbal cues, convert them into visual representations, interweave them with dreams (especially dreams focusing on cosmic/ metaphysical topics), or transcribe them by synaesthesia. The result of such a process could be a subjectively convincing experience in which the patient 'sees' his surgery or resuscitation from a disembodied perspective. Dream factors may subsequently cause the patient to 'experience' an eschatological journey.

Each aspect of this synaesthesia/hallucination model for the NDE can be supported by evidence easily found in the literature on surgical consciousness. But while the sceptic can't be faulted for making these suggestions, that doesn't mean he/she is necessarily correct. What NDE researchers need to undertake is a critical re-evaluation of Dr Sabom's surgical and coronary NDE cases. If each and every statement offered by these patients can be explained by sensory cuing, the case for the objective reality of the NDE begins to collapse. But if some cases surmount the cuing theory, the objective reality of the NDE would seem likely.

Let's take a critical look again at Dr Sabom's Florida patient, for example, whose report was quoted earlier in this chapter (see p. 180). The mechanic suffered a coronary which resulted in an NDE. Table XIII breaks down each segment of the patient's report, for which comments on sensory cuing are provided.

The breakdowns in Table XIII indicate that, generally, the patient's observations can be explained on the sensory cuing hypothesis. What sounds impressive and paranormal in the case evaporates when we critically evaluate it. Only the patient's description of the defibrillator pads isn't easily explained by cuing, since the sounds of the pads rubbed together with lubricant probably wouldn't translate easily into an optical representation. But he could have seen the procedure on a TV documentary or medical series. Since there is no record of the spoken comments during resuscitation, it is doubly difficult to reject cuing sources for the experience.

If we take each of Dr Sabom's best cases from his *Recollections of Death*, similar sources of sensory cuing become obvious to the reader. For example, Table XIV is derived from Dr Sabom's second coronary case. The patient was a 60-year-old housewife who suffered a coronary while hospitalized for back strain.

The two case examples in Tables XIII and XIV reveal how easily

Table XIII
NDEs vs. Sensory Cuing: A Case Examination

Observation	Cuing source
1. The patient saw the physician working on him	Easily perceived by cuing.
2. A syringe was inserted into his groin.	Patient could have felt needle stick.
3. He saw the physician approach him to give an injection into his side, but moved to the other side.	The patient could have heard the doctor's footsteps or voice, and then heard him move to the other side. The physician may have explained to the other members of the resuscitation team why he was changing the site of the injection. Since the needle was inserted in both places (as the patient explained later to Sabom), he probably felt the sticks, which cued him.
4. He saw the defibrillation pads.	Unless the patient was familiar with resuscitation procedures from TV shows and so forth, it is doubtful if this information was cued.
5. He saw lubicant placed on the pads, which were rubbed together.	This perception is hard to explain by cuing, since the procedure probably would not be verbally described by the resuscitation team.
6. The patient saw his body jolt when defibrillated.	Easily explained by tactile cuing.

cuing can explain the NDE's supposedly paranormal features. Unless researchers can find cases that surmount this problem, the sceptics have the right to remain unconvinced by the evidence.

Table XIV
NDEs vs. Sensory Cuing: A Second Case Examination

Observation	Cuing source
1. The patient saw several physicians and nurses rushing into the room.	She could easily have heard the commotion.
2. She saw the physicians using an IV.	She could have felt the IV needle inserted.
3. She saw them punching her chest.	She would have felt the punches.
4. She saw other people packing up her belongings (since she was to be taken to Intensive Care) from her bedside table.	While more difficult to explain, the nurses could have been verbally instructed (by the physician) to pack her belongings, or the patient could have heard her toiletries jiggled or a closet opened and closed.
5. The patient saw the physician lift her eyelids.	She could have felt the procedure.
6. She saw the physician feel her wrist for a pulse.	She could have felt the procedure.
7. She saw an equipment cart in the room and a 'breathing machine'.	She could have heard the equipment when it was wheeled in.
8. She saw a cone-shaped device placed over her face.	She could easily have felt the pressure while breathing in the oxygen.

Can the sensory cuing problem be overcome?

Since sensory cuing is a contaminating factor in NDE research, we should look for cases too complicated to be explained by synaesthesia. Two sorts of cases could counter the sensory cuing hypothesis:

1. Cases in which the patient's surgical observations could not have resulted from oral or tactile cuing.
2. Cases in which the patient correctly observed scenes outside the operating room.

While the evidence isn't strong, I think a few cases meeting these criteria have been documented.

An excellent example of the first case type has been published by Dr Sabom himself in his *Recollections of Death*. This particular report was discussed earlier, in Chapter 4 (see p. 91), but let's re-examine it. The patient was a retired Air Force pilot who suffered a coronary while recuperating from his first heart failure. Upon leaving the body, he watched with detachment while he was being resuscitated. Later he gave a precise report on his observations to the Georgia cardiologist. Some of the pilot's descriptions concerned the placement of an oxygen mask over his nose. Before the doctors positioned it he heard the typical hissing sound made by pressure from the oxygen tank. The patient also noted that the mask was green.

This specific observation is particularly interesting. Although nowhere in his report does Dr Sabom state that the observation was correct, it probably was. Doctors and nurses attempting to rescue people from death really wouldn't stop to discuss the oxygen mask's colour! Nor would the patient have known the shade unless he'd seen similar masks in the hospital. Since the patient was recovering from an earlier coronary, however, prior familiarity with the hospital's equipment is certainly possible.

But what is more provocative is the former pilot's description of the defibrillator. During his interview with Dr Sabom, the patient described the machine. 'I remember it had a meter on the face,' he recalled. 'I assume it read voltage, or current, or watt-seconds, or whatever they program the thing for. It was square and had two needles in there, one fixed and one which moved.'

The patient soon became fascinated by the gauge and described it in considerable detail. He recalled that the second needle 'seemed to come up rather slowly, really. It didn't just pop up like an ammeter or a voltmeter or something registering.' Later he explained that the fixed needle moved each time a jolt was given, but it never passed the second indicator. He further reported (correctly) how the machine was discharged—i.e by pressing a special button located on top of the device.

Dr Sabom subsequently checked the patient's records and found that the defibrillator used to resuscitate him contained two needles, used to calibrate and charge the shock, set in a panel. Since the machine was in standard use, it's difficult to believe that the physician co-ordinating the procedure barked orders to the other physicians/nurses on its use. So the observations offered by the ex-pilot couldn't have been based on oral cues or tactile sensations. Every shred of evidence supports the fact that he *watched* the procedure. Since the patient was presumably unconscious with his eyes closed, his story suggests he really did 'leave his body' during the resuscitation attempt. Even if he had opened his eyes momentarily, glimpsing the machine can't explain his obviously prolonged observation of its functions.

A second case published in Sabom's collection also includes a possible extrasensory factor, and this report exemplifies the second criterion outlined earlier in this section. The patient was a retired labourer interviewed by Sabom in 1977, a year after the percipient's coronary. The story is very similar to many emergency-room NDE reports. He initially suffered spasms before suddenly leaving the body.

> As I was going, I could see my body lying there as I looked back with no remorse ... I saw the whole show, and I didn't know who it was at first, and then I looked real close and it was me and I thought: Oh, man, what is this? And I didn't feel no different than I do now. I was looking from up, down ... I was going up slowly, like floating in a dark, or semi-dark corridor like. They were working the hell out of me. They were crawling on top of me with their knees. Actually, they cracked my pelvic bone on the right side and that's right where I saw the knee as I was going up.

Some sort of lapse occurred in the patient's recall or experience, since he didn't remember being defibrillated. But he did recall the intracardial injection he received:

> I saw them stick the needle in there almost in the center of the chest but on the left side ... They just plunged it in and gave me whatever that fluid was ... I could see things very clear, very vivid ... They put that needle in me and nothing happened so they started crawling all over me again, beating on my chest. I had three fractured ribs on the left side ... And I kept thinking: What is this? What's happening? And I kept going up and up and up ...

The patient's next observations focused on the hallway outside the room, where he saw his wife, eldest son, and daughter coming to visit. 'There was no way, being out, that I could have seen anybody,' the labourer told Dr Sabom.

The report looked impressive, so Dr Sabom decided to talk with the patient's wife. It turned out that she hadn't planned to visit her husband that day, but her eldest son and daughter dropped by unexpectedly. Since they had no competing plans, they decided to visit the patient and were walking down the corridor when they saw considerable commotion up ahead. It didn't take them long to realize the cause. According to the information she gave the cardiologist, she and her children were still several rooms down the corridor when the resuscitation took place. When she finally saw her husband wheeled from the room (to be transferred to the intensive care unit), his face was pointed in the opposite direction from the family. Nor did the trolley pass by them during the emergency. The patient was still disoriented the following day, but reported the NDE and his observations to his family, to their extreme consternation.

'Even if he had just been laying there in the hall without the heart attack or anything,' explained the patient's wife, 'he couldn't have recognized us from the distance.'

Even more impressive is the fact that the couple had six children, and different children came for each visit, but the patient saw the correct visitors on this special occasion. Could he have heard the family chatting down the hallway, cuing him to their presence? This theory seems unlikely since the family remained in the corridor during the NDE. Since there was considerable commotion in the room during the resuscitation, the noise probably masked any sounds from the hallway. So here again the evidence conflicts with the sensory cuing hypothesis.

Probably the best 'distant observation' NDE case in the literature, however, wasn't collected by Dr Sabom but was reported in 1984. This extraordinary case was investigated by Kimberly Clark, a social worker at Harborview Medical Center in Seattle, Washington. Her first encounter with the strange byways of the NDE represents an extremely well-documented example of a veridical NDE.

Ms Clark's case involved a migrant worker named Maria who suffered a coronary while visiting friends in Seattle. Ms Clark was called into the case because of the patient's social and financial problems. Since she was in otherwise good health, the patient was easily resuscitated and the social worker interviewed her later that day. It struck Ms Clark that Maria was upset, not because of the coronary, but because of her near-death experience. She explained that during the resuscitation, she floated to the ceiling and watched the physicians working on her. Ms Clark wasn't impressed by the story. She thought that Maria probably heard the emergency team in her room and imagined the rest. 'I reasoned that she could hear everything that was going on,' she says in her report, 'and while I do not think she was consciously making this up, I thought it might have been a confabulation.'

The patient proceeded to explain that her NDE didn't stop in the hospital. She became distracted and soon found herself floating outside and over the emergency-room driveway. Next she floated up to the third-floor ledge where she spotted a tennis shoe. Maria was literally obsessed with the tennis shoe, and asked the social worker to check her story and retrieve the object. She was so bothered by her NDE that Ms Clark decided to humour her and explore the ledge. The result of the little expedition was singularly impressive:

> With mixed emotions, I went outside and looked up at the ledge but could not see much at all. I went up to the third floor and began going in and out of patients' rooms and looking out their windows, which were so narrow that I had to press my face to the screen just to see the ledge at all. Finally, I found a room where I pressed my face to the glass and looked down and saw the tennis shoe! My vantage point was very different from what Maria's had to have been for her to notice that the little toe had worn a place in the shoe and that the lace was stuck under the heel and other details about the side of the shoe not visible to me. The only way she would have had such a perspective was if she had been floating right outside and at very close range to the tennis shoe. I retrieved the shoe and brought it back to Maria; it was very concrete evidence for me.

Certainly neither sensory cuing nor any other psychological factor can explain this case, and hopefully more reports of this calibre will enter the literature in the future. So while we should be sceptical of paranormal claims, it seems likely that some extrasensory factor interplays with the NDE. The three cases outlined in this section indicate that the NDE's psychic connection can't be completely dismissed by the sceptic. Nor can any combination of hallucination, expectancy set, sensory cuing, or errors in memory explain such experiences. Some other factor obviously programmes the NDE in part.

The veridical aspects of the NDE represent important components of the experience, for they suggest that the experience is objectively real. But the role such factors play in the experience is extremely complicated, so two further psychic aspects need to be examined.

The first of these mysteries became obvious by 1980 from the early cases collected by NDE researchers. In Chapter 1 we saw how Rick Bradshaw, while crushed between two cars, was shown his future during his NDE. Mr Bradshaw's claim matched the story I originally heard from the biker in my neighbourhood bar. God told the biker's friend when his paralysis would lift, and the prediction was precisely fulfilled. Such cases have come to be called precognitive NDEs, and the commonality of these cases was later confirmed in 1985 by Dr Margot Grey.

The importance of tackling precognitive NDE cases was first stressed by Dr Ring in 1982 when he published his paper 'Precognitive and prophetic visions in near-death experiences' in *Anabiosis—the Journal for Near-Death Studies*. Dr Ring broke down his cases into two categories: (1) precognitive cases in which the percipient was given personal information regarding his future, and (2) prophetic cases in which he/she saw apocalyptic visions of the earth's future.

From the specific standpoint of parapsychology, the precognitive NDE cases tend to be more interesting. Because of their far-reaching nature, apocalyptic visions cannot be evaluated scientifically, but simple precognitive experiences certainly can. Well-documented NDEs which contain precognitive elements can't be easily explained as delusions. The problem with these 'flash forward' cases, however, is that they rarely get documented. The evidence behind them is usually based solely on the percipient's claim. For instance, the precognitive information has seldom been placed in writing before it came to pass, or even been told to a second witness, such as a friend or relative. Sometimes the precognition is 'remembered' only when the target event takes place. Such cases are weak, since it is possible that they result from some sort of confabulation.

From my own reading of the literature, however, one incident published by Kenneth Ring surmounts these problems. The case was originally collected by Raymond Moody, but more information on it was published by Dr Ring several years later.

The subject had her eschatological NDE in 1971 when her heart and lungs failed during surgery. During her otherworld journey she met several spiritual guides, who revealed her future. She was simultaneously shown a picture of Raymond Moody and told that she would eventually meet him to reveal her story! Remember that this incident took place four years before *Life After Life* was published, long before Raymond Moody became famous.

The upshot of the NDE came in 1973 when Belle (the name she is given in the Ring report) was living in Charlottesville, Virginia. Some time that year Raymond Moody and his family moved to that city and occupied a house on Belle's street. Even though they lived so close to each other, they never met, although Belle glimpsed Moody jogging down the street occasionally. She paid little attention to him, and did not recognize him as the man whose picture she had seen in her NDE. Belle finally met Dr Moody formally in 1975. The precipitating event took place at Halloween. Belle felt poorly and didn't plan to take part in the festivities that evening, but she instructed her husband to distribute candy to the trick-or-treaters while she rested in the house. Her husband couldn't resist calling her to the door, however, when a cleverly dressed boy rang the doorbell. Belle grumbled her way to the door and asked the child's name. The young man—whose mother was standing by him—replied, 'I'm Raymond Avery Moody, the third.' Hearing the name brought the precognitive NDE back to Belle's mind. She immediately turned to the boy's mother and said, 'I need to talk to your husband.'

Mrs Moody was surprised by the remark and asked, 'Oh, did you have one of these experiences Raymond is writing about?'

The question made little sense to Belle, and she asked Mrs Moody what she meant. The upshot of the encounter was that Belle finally met Dr Moody and told him her story, which the psychiatrist placed in his *Reflections on Life After Life*. The prediction given her in her NDE was thus fulfilled, and the events were witnessed by her husband and Dr Moody's wife.

Very few cases of precognitive NDEs are this concise and well-documented. Premonitory NDEs tend to be vague, and the percipients sometimes merely 'feel' they know what the future holds. The exact purpose or role such premonitions play in the NDE is totally mysterious, unfortunately, and they contribute little to our understanding of the NDE phenomenon.

The other significant factor implicated in the NDE concerns the 'coming back' syndrome reported by NDE percipients. Most interviewers find NDE survivors claiming that their experiences transformed them. Upon facing and triumphing over death, these fortunate people find earthly life different and more rewarding. Often they become less concerned with the material rewards of living—such as financial security and collecting physical possessions—and concern themselves with developing better interpersonal relationships, become more involved in their church, report better insight into other people, and so forth. The transformational aspects of the NDE tend to be so significant that entire books have been written on the pheno-menon. Books such as Dr Kenneth Ring's *Heading Towards Omega*, Dr Charles P. Flynn's *After the Beyond* and P.M.H. Atwater's *Coming Back* focus on the ways NDEs permanently change the percipient's life. Considerable research has even proved that these transformations result specifically from the NDE itself, not from the life-threatening situations that produced it. This finding has been documented by studying the subsequent lives of NDE survivors and other people who came close to death but who never reported any unusual experiences. Coming close to death, in other words, doesn't change people's lives *unless* an NDE takes place.[3]

The following extracts are taken from Ring's *Heading Toward Omega*. Both were contributed by NDE survivors trying to describe the changes in their lives prompted by their experiences.

(1)

My joy comes from another's smile. I also notice that I reach out and touch people more ... I seem to make people feel better. I know this—that when there's a family problem, everyone turns to me ... I have more insight into other people [now] ... It's very difficult for me to lose my temper anymore. I can see the pain in other people's eyes. That's why they hurt other people because they really don't understand ... The most important thing that we have are our relationships with other people ... It all comes down to caring and

---

[3]The only exception to this finding, rarely noted by NDE researchers, concerns failed suicides. People who live through serious suicide attempts sometimes see great cosmic significance in their survival. Sometimes their lives are totally transformed by their close calls.

compassion and love for your fellow man ... Love is the answer. It's the answer to everything.

(2)

Although this event occurred a long time ago, it marked a very crucial point in my life. I began a new chapter; a chapter which was to continue for the rest of my life. This moment and the following minutes and hours changed my life entirely. I was transformed from a man who was lost and wandering aimlessly, with no goal in life other than a desire for material wealth, to someone who had a deep motivation, a purpose in life, a definite direction, and an over-powering conviction that there would be a reward at the end of life similar to the pot of gold at the end of the rainbow ... The changes in my life were completely positive. My interest in material wealth and greed for possessions were replaced by a thirst for spiritual understanding and a passionate desire to see world conditions improve.

Nor is it rare for NDE survivors to report frequent psychic experiences in the wake of their recoveries. Some percipients even claim they have become psychic upon returning to the world.

Some statistical data bearing on this subject was published by Kenneth Ring in 1984 in his *Heading Toward Omega*. He spoke with several NDE survivors and found that, upon recovery, they began reporting waking ESP experiences, frequent out-of-body experiences, encounters with ghosts, and other psychic experiences. They told Dr Ring that such experiences were more common in their lives now than before their NDEs.

Of course, it isn't possible to know if these people were experiencing real psychic encounters or merely deluded themselves into thinking they were. But whatever the case, the pattern Dr Ring found in his data has been widely confirmed. While the Connecticut psychologist was collecting his evidence, for example, Dr Richard L. Kohr of the Pennsylvania Department of Education was engaged in a similar project. Dr Kohr conducted his research while surveying over 500 members of the Association for Research and Enlightenment—a large organization in the United States devoted to the legacy and teachings of Edgar Cayce (1877–1945), a seer famous for his clairvoyance. The study was designed to determine what type of people were members of the ARE, but Dr Kohr used it to study the NDE. Some of the items on the survey form explored the respondents' metaphysical beliefs, including their feelings on death. Other questions specifically asked them to specify whether they'd ever had psychic experiences, and if so, what kind. Based on the replies to the survey, Dr Kohr isolated a subgroup of ARE members who claimed NDE experiences. He found that people reporting NDEs more commonly reported day-to-day psychic experiences than the other respondents. It is not clear, however, whether these experiences specifically followed the NDEs or not.

While Dr Margot Grey offers no detailed statistics in her book, she found that people recovering from NDEs commonly reported psychic encounters. Some of her percipients reported that they had even developed healing powers.

If these reports and claims represent genuine psychic fallout from the NDE, what does it mean? Some writers on the NDE claim that such psychic fallout proves the objective reality of the experience. If NDEs were purely hallucinatory, why would people become psychic in response to them? Believers in the literal reality of the NDE suggest that the experience is a powerful psychic occurrence that enables psychic skills to develop—i.e it is a spiritual catalyst of our inner psychic potential. Such a theory sounds reasonable enough and is consistent with a literalist interpretation of the NDE. My own feeling, however, is that a simpler solution to this curious psi connection could be posited.

Considerable laboratory evidence collected since 1950 has shown that people who believe in extrasensory perception score better on statistical ESP tests than disbelievers. The original discovery of this data was reported by Dr Gertrude Schmeidler, a psychologist at the City College of New York, in her book *ESP and Personality Patterns* (which she wrote with R.A. McConnell, a biophysicist at the University of Pittsburgh). The book reports on several experiments in which believers and sceptics were compared on simple ESP tests, such as guessing geometric symbols printed on cards. She found that the believers repeatedly outscored the sceptics. Experimental parapsychologists call this interesting phenomenon the 'sheep–goat' effect, which has been replicated several times by independent researchers. Some of them believe, in fact, that the sheep–goat effect is experimental parapsychology's most stable finding. The cause of the phenomenon isn't too difficult to understand.

Believers in psychic phenomena are probably more psychologically open to extrasensory perception than the sceptics, so they are probably highly motivated to perform well on laboratory tests. People sceptical of (or hostile to) the paranormal are more likely to 'bar' such experiences from entering their minds. Since extrasensory perception works through the unconscious levels of the mind, it is feasible that the sceptic erects blockades to keep such information from entering consciousness, or changes the information so that it is incorrect when it surfaces. (Oftentimes, for instance, the sceptics will score significantly below chance expectation—i.e as though their conscious minds were being fed incorrect information.)

The theory that we can subconsciously block threatening information from entering consciousness is well known in cognitive psychology, and considerable experimental evidence has confirmed the effect. (The phenomenon is called 'perceptual defence' in psychology.)

The fact that NDE survivors report being transformed by the experience isn't surprising. It's difficult not to be transformed by any powerful experience, whether it is psychological, paranormal, or even psychopathological in nature. My feeling is that people recovering from NDEs probably *do* start having psychic experience more commonly in their daily lives, or perhaps merely start noticing them for the first time. But I don't believe these experiences rise from the specific nature of the NDE itself. NDE survivors may be psychologically programmed by their experiences to be more open to psychic information, while their barriers to psi become minimal. Dr Ring's reports could be merely some sort of super-sheep/goat effect emerging from the NDE. Many survivors might be saying to themselves, 'If this can happen to me, what other strange phenomena are possible?' or something to that effect.

NDE survivors probably became super-believers in the paranormal, which significantly opens them to extrasensory influences and the development of psychic skills. So while the excellent research of Kenneth Ring, Margot Grey, and Richard L. Kohr is telling us something important about the power of belief, it probably has little bearing on the NDE itself.

10.

The Ecstasy of Experience—
Explaining Simple NDEs

The NDE represents a two-sided mystery for both science and psychology. Whatever the experience's primary nature, somehow the out-of-body experience is integral to it. But the NDE is more than a simple out-of-body experience, since it contains visionary and culturally programmed components. So when we propose explanatory models for the NDE, we have to address both these sides of its complicated phenomenology.

The fact that the NDE is composed of an out-of-body experience plus some sort of X-factor was statistically demonstrated by Dr Glen Gabbard and his colleagues in Kansas in 1981 when they systematically compared the two experiences. In order to base their evaluations on a large collection of cases, the psychiatrists worked with 339 OBE reports they received in response to an interview Dr Stuart W. Twemlow gave to the popular press. Since these cases were submitted voluntarily, the Kansas team's collection can't be considered a random sample of out-of-body reports; but the sheer size of their collection was sufficient for studying the experiential features of the experience. Since several of their informants reported OBEs linked to life-threatening situations, these cases represented an NDE subgroup within the data. The researchers compared these 34 cases with the less dramatic out-of-body experiences sent to them and found that most of the features generally linked to the classic NDE were less commonly reported during non-life-threatening out-of-body states. Those percipients chronicling traditional NDEs more consistently reported the following perceptions:

1. They frequently heard unusual noises (such as buzzing or rushing sounds) during the early stages of the experience.

2. Travelling down through a tunnel was commonly reported.
3. Encountering spiritual beings while out-of-body seemed par-
    ticularly widespread during life-threatening OBE journeys.
4. Brilliant lights were commonly perceived or reported.

Aside from the purely phenomenological components of the
experience, those percipients reporting typical NDEs had more
lasting psychological reactions to their out-of-body experiences.
They more commonly believed that there was a purpose behind
their experiences and that the encounter was primarily a
religious or spiritual phenomenon. Compared to those subjects
reporting spontaneous out-of-body experiences from less critical
settings, the NDE relaters claimed consistent lasting benefits and
life changes from their experiences.

So it would seem that the NDE is a more powerful spiritual and
psychological experience than simple out-of-body experiences.
Whether this finding is due to the experience itself or specifically
to its connection with death is, however, unclear.

Because the NDE closely resembles an elaborate form of out-of-
body experience, it might not be proper to build a conceptual
model encompassing both simple NDEs and eschatological
journeys. Perhpas these incidents represent discrete but related
syndromes, a possibility few previous writers on the NDE have
ever considered. For the rest of this chapter, I will try to build an
explanatory model for simple NDEs before tackling the larger
problem of eschatological NDEs/otherworld journeys.

Simple NDEs and the out-of-body connection

Looking back to Chapters 1 and 4, it should be obvious that simple NDEs represent relatively uncomplicated phenomenological
experiences. Many of Dr Michael Sabom's coronary and
emergency-room NDE reports would fall into this category. The
percipient usually reported undergoing a life-threatening trauma
before suddenly finding him/herself floating from the body,
often watching a resuscitation team trying to save him or her. Little else heappens during the experience, which terminates when
the percipient finds himself reluctantly returning to the body.

The following description of a simple NDE is from my own files
and dates from 1973. Notice how the experience is in-
distinguishable from more typical out-of-body experiences. Such
phenomenology as entering a tunnel, meeting spiritual guides, or
entering a brilliant light played no role in the episode.

Twenty five years ago I was seriously sick and was rushed to the hospital in a very serious condition from loss of blood caused by a haemorrhage. In this weak condition the doctor decided on an exploratory operation. As he gave me ether and I drifted into a deep sleep, I felt as though I were going to die. The sensation was not painful, but as though I felt a tugging and pulling as in a game of 'tug-o'war.' Finally a little light hovered over my still form and all my senses were transformed into this small light ... I, or rather this little light, flew around the operating room watching everything that was taking place. I soon tired of this and flew right through the window and not feeling any pain but rather a glorious free sensation.

Sometimes the percipient will perceive him/herself draped in an etheric duplicate curiously resembling the physical body. Even more bizarrely, some people even witness the 'release' of this etheric double from a completely independent observational perspective. This relatively uncommon phenomenon is described in the following case, which I also collected in 1973:

Sometime during the night, although I was unconscious, I saw the hospital room with doctors surrounding Dr G. who was at my bedside, bending over me, listening to my heartbeats with a stethoscope, her fingers on my wrist taking my pulse. At the same time I saw, over my body, lying on the bed, another body of me suspended in mid-air in the exact position, hanging from the ceiling by what seemed to be a cord attached to my navel. I seemed to be an observer, but from where, I cannot say. All I know is that I saw two bodies of myself. I watched this sight for some time.

How can we best explain these temporary out-of-body excursions? Ever since the 1960s, researchers and parapsychologists interested in the out-of-body experience have tried building psychological models for the phenomenon. These theories can be grouped into four main categories:

1. Some experts believe that OBEs probably represent dreams. Considerable research has shown that people can learn to identify when they are dreaming. This phenomenon is called lucid dreaming, and some experts on the experience believe that the OBE is merely a special form of it. Since extrasensory perception can take place in dreams, these experts don't find it surprising that OBEs sometimes contain veridical elements.

2. Other psychologically-oriented parapsychologists feel that

OBEs result from bizarre forms of imagery. Perhaps people regularly undergoing OBEs have special mental powers to produce rich subjective experiences for themselves, which give rise to the phenomenon. A related theory is that people facing out-of-body experiences symbolically relive their own births during the episodes. The birth hallucination model could explain, for instance, the simple NDE case previously cited in which the witness saw her etheric duplicate body complete with a psychic umbilical cord.

3. More psychoanalytically-oriented is the 'disturbed self-concept' explanation. Researchers supporting this theory for the out-of-body experience believe that it takes place when we lose experiential contact with our own bodies. During our day-to-day lives we experience our physical bodies through proprioceptive stimulation, i.e. internal sensations emerging from within the body itself. This network of sensations can be disrupted by stress, while under the influence of psychedelic drugs, or during meditation. When they lose this (primarily unconscious) contact, some people may panic and mentally recreate their sense of embodiment, complete with an etheric duplicate floating in space.

4. Since out-of-body experiences often take place in threatening situations, some psychiatrists believe that the OBE is a narcissistic fantasy employed to offset the terror of imminent death. Dr Kastenbaum's explanation for the NDE (examined in Chapter 8) is a rough variant of this theoretical position, though it was originally proposed to explain OBEs in general.

Despite the cleverness of these conceptual models, they simply can't explain everything psychology and parapsychology know about the out-of-body experience. Purely psychological theories can't explain, for example, why some people report significant *physical* sensations while leaving and returning to the body. Dream theories can't explain the phenomenon either, since some OBEs take place while the percipients are resting or meditating. Nor can most simplistic psychological theories explain the extrasensory factors embedded in some OBE and NDEs, typified by the examples reported in the previous chapter. The discerning student of the OBE can throw birth models into the trash-bin, too. Dr Susan Blackmore conducted some excellent research in the early 1980s which demonstrated that people born through Caesarean section report OBEs just like everybody else.

Since my space is limited in this chapter, the foregoing summary of several popular explanations for the out-of-body experience has been extremely superficial. (For a more detailed look at these conceptual models and their limitations, the reader might wish to read my paper 'Psychological models of the out-of-body experience—a review and critical evaluation', which appeared in the *Journal of Parapsychology* in 1982.) Since 1982, researchers such as Susan Blackmore, Harvey J. Irwin, and Glen O. Gabbard have proposed second-generation psychological models for the OBE, but even these theories can't completely overcome the difficulties outlined in the previous paragraph. The primary problem with these recent conceptualizations is that evidence directly challenging *any* psychological theory has been collected by experimental parapsychologists. The findings of this research have been unfairly ignored even by some students of the OBE perfectly familiar with it.

For the remainder of this chapter, let's examine the considerable body of experimental OBE research, which likewise probably solves the mystery posed by simple NDEs.

Early experimental research on the out-of-body experience

By 1970, most experimental parapsychologists knew that the out-of-body experience represented something more than a pedestrian hallucination. This discovery was originally made by Dr Charles T. Tart, then a young psychologist at the University of California, Davis, whose ingenious research constituted the first systematic experimental study of the OBE within the laboratory setting. The impetus to the research came when Dr Tart initially met his subject, whom he called Miss Z. in his report, whose true identity has never been revealed. She was a college student in her early twenties with a history of chronic nocturnal out-of-body episodes. The psychologist was interested enough in her claims to recruit her for a laboratory experiment.

For the specific purpose of this experiment, Dr Tart used a sleep laboratory which included a lab room filled with psychophysiological equipment and a separate sleep chamber. The sleep chamber included a bed upon which the subject could recline while her brainwaves and other physiological functions were monitored through leads connected to the equipment in the lab room. The key to the experiment, however, was a ledge in the chamber located on the wall overlooking the bed. It was Dr

Tart's plan to place a randomly selected five-digit number on the platform. He hoped that Miss Z. would leave her body while sleeping, float up to the ledge, and then report the number back to him. Since an intercom connected the sleep chamber with the laboratory room, the subject merely had to call out the digits to Dr Tart upon waking.

Dr Tart conducted four sessions with the student over an eight-week period, and nothing extraordinary took place during the first three experiments. But during the fourth, Miss Z. reported a brief OBE to the experimenter at 5:57 in the morning. She had floated to the ledge where she spotted the number, which she correctly reported to the experimenter. This was the last session designed to explore the subject's out-of-body experiences, since Miss Z. soon moved from Davis and could no longer participate in Dr Tart's research.

When he later checked his polygraph readings, Dr Tart discovered that Miss Z. generated extremely strange brainwave activity during her OBE observations. The rhythms she exhibited couldn't be categorized either as sleeping or waking patterns, but were something in between the two. These electrical tracings served to confirm that something unusual transpired when the subject reported herself out-of-body.

By the time he reported this experiment in 1968, however, Dr Tart had found a small problem with the experiment that couldn't be overlooked. Working with a colleague, the psychologist discovered that the digits could have been seen fraudulently since they reflected from a clock in the room. If the subject had smuggled a flashlight into the room, she could have spied the numbers by judiciously illuminating the clock. Of course, there wasn't a shred of evidence that Miss Z. had employed such a procedure, but the discovery did compromise an otherwise exciting and successful experiment. It should be mentioned, though, that the fraud hypothesis cannot explain the unusual brainwaves the subject exhibited during her out-of-body state.

Despite the partial success of this pioneering experiment, no other researchers tried to replicate it using similar EEG monitoring or other sleep laboratory technology. Few parapsychologists or experimental psychologists were really interested in the out-of-body experience in the 1960s, and gifted OBE subjects were difficult to come by. Charles Tart certainly never found a subject equal to his student volunteer, even though he conducted similar research with Robert Monroe, who later gained considerable fame with his autobiographical *Journeys Out of the Body* in 1971. These experiments were not completely successful, however, and the experimental study of the OBE fell into oblivion for a few years.

Experiments with Keith Harary at the Psychical Research Foundation

Out-of-body research enjoyed a renaissance of sorts in the early 1970s thanks to a fortuitous legal battle. Back in the 1940s, an eccentric Arizona prospector named James Kidd had disappeared, and he was declared legally dead in 1967. What few people realized was that the miner had left behind over $175,000 in cash and stocks, which Kidd specifically designated for research into the soul's survival of death. Several psychics, organizations, and foundations petitioned the court for the money, which was finally given to the American Society for Psychical Research in New York. They in turn divided the windfall with the smaller Psychical Research Foundation in Durham, North Carolina. This organization had been founded in 1960 for the express purpose of promoting survival research, and their staff decided to explore the byways of the out-of-body experience with the money. (Similar research was designed in New York, but it will be bypassed in this chapter.)

It was at this point that a Duke University undergraduate named Keith Harary (then called Blue by his friends) entered the picture and changed the face of OBE research forever. It was my personal good fortune to take part in this research, which considerably revised my thinking on the phenomenon.

Keith originally came to Durham from New York to study psychology and learn parapsychology. His family background included both Jewish and Egyptian heritages, perhaps a combination that forced him from his body early in life! Keith had been undergoing such experiences for several years and didn't know what to make of them. One of his goals in coming to Durham was to visit J.B. Rhine's parapsychology laboratory, which had moved off the Duke campus in 1967. Studying out-of-body experiences wasn't the type of research in which Rhine's laboratory was engaged, so the staff suggested Keith offer his services to the Psychical Research Foundation. Since that organization had recently received funds to explore the out-of-body experience, they were delighted to meet Keith, who was soon recruited to help design their research and be their principal experimental participant.

The staff of the Foundation were happy to find that Keith not only reported repeated OBEs, but could consciously induce them. The task of organizing and implementing the experiments immediately fell to the Foundation's research co-ordinator, Dr Robert Morris, a rather cerebral psychologist with a penchant for parapsychology.

Before continuing with a discussion of this research, some comments should be devoted to the phenomenology of Keith's out-of-body journeys. Since he can induce and prolong these episodes, he has enjoyed a wide range of out-of-body states. Some of his etheric excursions resemble the type of OBEs regularly reported by the general public. For example, the following report which he provided for me represents this sort of experience:

> Late one evening, while relaxing in bed, I gradually noticed the sound of a television in the next room along with the sound of water forcefully rushing in the bathroom down the hall. Intrigued and mystified by the sounds (my roommate was vacationing out of town and I had not left the television on or the water running), I decided to investigate. When I noticed my body still lying on the bed behind me after having felt myself get up, it became obvious to me that an OBE was occurring. My form seemed to be almost identical to that of my actual body, but the reality which I experienced appeared to have been 'rearranged.'
>
> During the experience, the atmosphere felt strangely 'charged' while the lighting in my apartment was not as I would have expected it to be.

Keith also found that the furniture in the room was not positioned correctly. He returned to his body merely by focusing on it.

'The feeling was as if I had been directly transported from one point to another,' he concludes, 'not as if I were awakening from a dream.'

Other experiences Keith reports tend to be more surrealistic and resemble the kinds of perceptions reported during eschatological NDEs. The following report, for example, represents this dimension of Keith's out-of-body skills. Notice the transpersonal and otherworldly elements of the experience which tend to mimic more prototypical NDE cases:

> I had been lying on my bed trying to keep myself awake long enough to study effectively for my upcoming college midterms. It was becoming increasingly difficult for me to keep my eyes open. Finally, I fell back upon the bed and when I did so almost immediately found myself having an OBE in which I felt as though I were flying through space at an enormous speed. When I slowed down in the experience, I found myself floating somewhere out in outer space. I cannot hope to describe the experience as vividly as it occurred to me.
>
> All around me I could see planets and smaller particles in rhythmic motion. My vision seemed to at once focus in front of me and at the same time cover a three hundred and sixty degree radius. All of my 'senses' were perceiving in similar intense fashion. I could 'hear' a wonderful harmony which seemed to accompany every movement of every particle. I felt a sense of complete unity with all that I was experiencing. Every particle felt as though it were part of my self. When I moved the sounds and the movements of the particles around me seemd to move in a balance to my movements. When particles moved, I seemed to move in balance to their movements. And the overall harmony within which this all occurred also moved in balance to our movements. There was at once the feeling of being my own focal point and at the same time a feeling of being all of the particles and harmony and movement that surrounded me. I felt free of mundane concerns and worries. I felt not only that I was experiencing Nature, but as if I *were* Nature, expressing itself as an incredible balanced, harmonious movement of the Universe.
>
> Then, I remember thinking of myself lying on the bed in my room back at college. It seemed that it was time to return to that perspective. In a few moments I felt a jolt in my physical body and opened my eyes to find myself lying on the bed. I felt a complete sense of compassion for the everyday world. I looked at my books lying where I had dropped them and almost laughed at the seeming stupidity of studying Earthly knowledge from books. I felt energetic and almost jumped up out of bed to run outside. It had seemed that several hours had passed but actually only about five minutes had. I told myself to relax and go to sleep, which I did, hoping that I could find my way back to that harmonious experience in the other OBE.

Since Keith's out-of-body journeys resemble both simple and eschatological NDEs so closely, I think the results of our research have a direct bearing on our ultimate explanation for the NDE. For that reason, I would now like to summarize in considerable depth the research conducted with him in Durham between 1973 and 1974.

The first experiments in which Keith participated at the Psychical Research Foundation were target studies, in which he tried to project his consciousness from the Foundation's office building to its laboratory next door. In order to provide a suitable target for Keith to see, large letters or figures were placed on a board located in the lab's kitchen. Dr Morris and his associates hoped that Keith would 'see' the letters while disembodied and report them back correctly. The first target study was booked for the evening of 13 February 1973. Keith prepared himself by lying down and relaxing on a bed in the office building and then projected next door. When he returned to his body moments later, he told Dr Morris that while projected he spied a circle and a flowerpot in the second building. The specific target for this session turned out to be a circle sketched on the board.

Several more of these experiments were scheduled and Keith sometimes scored exceptionally well with them, though his successes were usually sporadic and inconsistent. Figure 3 shows the results of a particularly good target study, which was never officially reported by the Psychical Research Foundation. For this session, the experimenters in charge of choosing and displaying the target letter improvised a bit. What resulted was a diagram more than a target. Reproduced here for the first time is a drawing of the target and the corresponding sketch Keith executed upon returning to his body. The result of this session was stunning and reveals the impressive level of Keith's observational powers while out-of-body.

While these little experiments were encouraging, they didn't seem particularly suited to Keith's out-of-body perspectives, since he often reports problems with optical perception. So the researchers decided to change the focus of the experiments. Could their subject make his out-of-body presence *known* to people stationed in the target area? they wondered.

This exotic idea seemed worth exploring, so several of the Foundation's volunteers and staff members were randomly selected to sit in the meditation centre for the subsequent series of tests. This building was located 30 yards or so to the rear of the office and lab. For each of these experiments, Keith would send his projected self to the centre while reclining on a bed in the laboratory or office. His task was to 'see' the people sitting there and then report his observations to Dr Morris. In the meantime the volunteers tried to 'detect' when Keith was visiting them. For

Figure 3
Results of a Target Study with Keith Harary

I. Target used for the session of 21 March 1973:

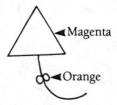

II. Keith's reproduction based on his out-of-body vision:

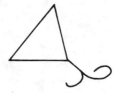

When Keith returned to the body, he reported that the target was 'like number 4' and that it consisted of two colours, including magenta.

the first of these sessions, for example, three members of the team were placed in the meditation centre and the results were encouraging. Keith successfully projected to the building and correctly reported back who was there and their exact locations. But he couldn't keep up this level of success in subsequent sessions.

Despite Keith's growing disenchantment with these experiments, some of the staff and volunteers did begin reporting strange experiences of their own. Sometimes they successfully 'guessed' when Keith was visiting them in his ecsomatic state. A few of them either subjectively sensed his presence or observed odd lights or shadows in the room. Since the experimental observers never knew the *exact* time Keith would be flying-in to the centre, the fact that these sensations often precisely matched the time of his out-of-body excursions is significant. The following report, for instance, was given to me by Dr Robert Morris, whose personal detection experience occurred when he was chosen to sit in the meditation centre.

> During one of these periods I experienced the feeling that Blue was in some sense there. It was not a strong impression, but it did impel

me to make note of it at the time. My experience was totally internal—no sensations, visual or otherwise, involved. I thought of Blue, thought about the possibility that Blue might be having an OBE at the time. I felt very comfortably warm inside, a good feeling, as I would if I knew I were being visited by a friend. The feeling lasted no more than twenty to thirty seconds. I realized that I knew the odds were 50–50 that Blue was in fact experiencing an OBE at the time and that my description's main value was therefore the comparability of its details with other descriptions obtained under more impressive circumstances.

It soon became obvious that these detection experiences were more reliable than Keith's OBE vision, but Dr Morris soon ran into trouble. It didn't take long before the experimental observers became too self-conscious with the task to correctly 'detect' Keith, so Dr Morris began thinking about substituting animals for the human observers. Such a proposal would take the burden of responsibility from Keith, who would no longer be forced to make concise observations during his OBEs, remember them, and report them upon returning to his body. The suggestion was enthusiastically accepted by the young Duke student and soon the first pilot studies were designed.

But what kind of animals should be used? That became the central issue of the experiments. For the first detection study, Dr Morris and his colleagues used gerbils and hamsters placed in a wire cage measuring 6in by 6in by 6in. Since ball bearings separated the platform from its base, the cage jiggled when it moved. The entire contraption was then hooked to a polygraph which kept an objective record of the movements. Dr Morris worked from the premise that the rodents would speed up their movements in the cage if frightened—such as when perceiving a phantom visitor in the room.

In order to keep the experimental conditions properly controlled, Keith was driven to the Duke University campus and placed in a special laboratory room. He had little difficulty making the flights back to the Foundation, but the little rodents never seemed to respond to his etheric presence. This failure didn't discourage the experimenters, however, since they realized that hamsters and gerbils are placid creatures. Rarely do they react violently to people, which may have compromised the philosophy behind these detection studies and the rodents' responses. This explanation for the results of these pilot sessions certainly seems reasonable to me. I remember visiting the gerbil cages in the lab building each morning during my stay in Durham. When I flicked on the lights, the little creatures took hardly any notice and did not seem scared. They would merely stand erect on their hind legs lackadasically, meander to the front of the cages and look at me—mixing idle curiosity with considerable indifference! That's when I think I first realized I could never become an experimental psychologist, too often required to shock or otherwise harm these gentle little creatures.

Since the gerbils and hamsters obviously weren't successful OBE detectors, Dr Morris quickly changed his strategy. Since Keith had been pretty isolated when he first came to Durham and had not yet made close friends, he and the psychologist decided he needed some pets. It didn't take long before the Duke undergraduate became the proud father to two delightful kittens. The more playful and personally responsive one was named, Spirit, while the other (procured to keep the first company) was correspondingly named Soul. The two felines pretty much had the run of the PRF's laboratory building, where Keith was then living. Their rambunctious romps certainly gave the Foundation a feeling of informality, except for the fact that its financial manager, whose office was near Keith's room, soon became allergic to cats. But everyone compromised and it was the financial manager, not the cats, who ended up being restricted while in the building!

Keeping the kittens in the building was also significant for parapsychology, since they eventually took part in some landmark experiments.

Dr Morris was hoping that the kittens would be more reliable OBE detectors than the small rodents used previously, and to implement the next series of tests he constructed an oblong shuffleboard-shaped platform (with raised sides) marked into 24 10-inch squares. The board was designed to monitor the kittens' behaviour, similar to the way the jiggle platform had been used in the preceding experiments. The goal of the experiments was to determine whether the kittens would change their behaviour when Keith projected to them. An entire series of such sessions were run with Spirit (who seemed more responsive than Soul to Keith) in the following manner.

Keith would be taken to the Duke campus while an observer, or observers, were left behind in the Foundation's laboratory with the kitten. The kitten was placed on the platform and roamed freely for several minutes, vocalizing frequently. The laboratory phone would ring four times during the upcoming experimental session. Several minutes elapsed between rings, which were signals to the observer to monitor the kitten's movements and vocalizations for a prescribed period of time, usually encompassing little more than three or four minutes. Now during two of these periods, randomly chosen for Keith by a computer, the student would try to leave his body and visit the laboratory. During the *other* two monitoring periods Keith merely lay back and mentally pretended to project to the kitten. The observers watching the kitten never knew which were the experimental periods and which were the controls.

Despite the elaborate design and precautions used for these detection studies, the results were stunning. Spirit was a typically energy-charged kitten who liked to scamper on the platform when left there; but during those periods when Keith projected to him, little Spirit would calm down, hardly move at all, and stopped meowing. This pattern was repeated each time the experiment was conducted, and soon the observers could easily determine when Keith was making his projections to them: the kitten's behaviour was that noticeable and even predictable.

Even though the primary focus of these experiments was the kitten's behviour, the observers could sometimes sense Keith's etheric presence themselves. Some of them started to claim detection experiences similar to those reported during the early phases of the project. Jerry Levin, for example, was a young technician employed by the Psychical Research Foundation to help monitor the sessions. During one of the kitten experiments, he was asked to monitor a thermistor to see if Keith's out-of-body presence could be physically detected in the experimental room. Paying close attention to the equipment didn't prevent him from personally experiencing Keith's disembodied visitation:

> I was just at the end of the first warning period when I saw a black streak in the periphery of my vision. Phenomenologically, the sensation appeared to be a thin black line about a foot away, between me and the polygraph. It was as if it were a fast moving black point leaving an after image behind. The streak was about the length of a pencil and lasted no more than a second. It was a very well-defined sensation which faded quickly. My impression was that the streak was an after image of some metallic part of the polygraph—there was a dim

light in the room. I noted briefly the time and character of the sensation and went back to monitoring the polygraph. After the experiment was over we learned that the OBE had just started at the time
of my detection response. That was my only detection during that
session.

Keith later reported to Dr Morris that his OBEs had been
unusually vivid for this session. One of them (which coincided
with Levin's observation) lasted for five minutes in which Keith
experienced himself in the form of 'a large glowing ball of
greenish tinted light which appeared to be about the size of a
standard beach ball'.

I should mention that Keith often experiences himself in this
or similar form, and during my stay in Durham I personally
witnessed this phenomenon. The incident took place shortly
before I left to return to my home in Los Angeles. It was
somewhat after 3 a.m. and I woke from sleep and remained
perfectly conscious for a few minutes. I was turning over to
return to sleep when a reddish ball of light suddenly materialized
in my room. Within an instant it shot through the room in a
parabolic trajectory and disappeared, while I leapt from my bed
to make a written note of the time. I learned the next day that
Keith vaguely recalled trying to project to me when he retired—
some time between 3 and 3:30 a.m.[1]

Personal experiments with Keith Harary
My own consultancy with the Psychical Research Foundation
began in the summer of 1973 when the kitten experiments were
approaching completion. When my plane landed near Durham,
both Keith and Dr Morris were there to greet me and drive me
back to the Foundation. I really didn't know what to expect from
the young psychology student. Even though I was still a young
researcher myself, I had long since had my fill of self-proclaimed
psychics. Most of these people like to talk incessantly about
themselves, their wondrous powers, and metaphysical philo-
sophies. I was delightfully surprised to find that Keith didn't
share these tendencies. He struck me as being shy and

---

[1] Keith didn't readily recall trying to project to me when I first saw him the next
morning. When I told him that I had experienced something unusual in my
room during the night, his memory came back to him. Keith specifically claimed that the projection trial took place around 3 a.m. without any prompting
from me.

remarkably reticent about discussing his psychic world. While driving into Durham from the outskirts, Keith seemed more interested in showing me the beauties of North Carolina than talking shop.

In order to save money, Keith was at this time living in the Foundation's second building and I was given a room in the meditation centre. Since this building was just 30 yards away from the others, getting to the laboratory each day presented little problem. (I merely had to scoot by the huge paper wasps' nest by the door, since Keith insisted I did not remove it or bother the insects.) Keith and I became very good friends during the next few weeks. The strong rapport we built during this time probably contributed to the success of our experiments.

My introduction to the experimental work with Keith was scheduled for my first evening in Durham, for Dr Morris had set up a pilot experiment to see if dogs would react to Keith's out-of-body presence.

The session began when the psychologist and I took the subject to an engineering building on the Duke campus, while an observer stayed in the meditation centre with the reluctant canine, who had thrown up earlier in the evening *en route* to the Foundation—hardly an auspicious beginning for the session! Keith entered a sealed booth in the room at Duke in order to prepare himself for the out-of-body journey. Several minutes passed before he signalled to us (through an intercom) that he was ready to project. Several more minutes passed before he stirred in the booth, which signified his return from his etheric perambulations. I was somewhat surprised when I watched Keith emerge from the booth moments later. Whatever the nature of his OBEs, they certainly took a significant toll on him both physically and mentally. He literally staggered from the booth looking as if he'd been drinking. His gait was unsteady and his speech was slightly slurred, and it seemed that his chest hurt him. It didn't take him long to recover, though, and he explained that he had successfully seen the dog.

The dog, on the other hand, never had a chance to respond to Keith's visitation. The poor canine, perhaps still upset from the drive, fell into a deep slumber early in the session and slept through our subject's projection!

Since my job with the Foundation was to recommend experiments or changes in their protocols, I immediately evaluated the kitten, hamster, and dog experiments and reported my impressions of them to Dr Morris. While it was obvious that the kitten work looked promising, it seemed to me that better results could be obtained using less domesticated animals. Kittens and lab animals don't react much to people, since they habituate easily to us. But what would happen if we employed animals that dislike people? I made this recommendation to Dr Morris several times and found him extremely receptive to the suggestion, since a fellow Foundation staff member had previously expressed similar ideas. I soon learned that their consultant researcher was Graham Watkins, a psychologist with a special interest in toxicology. I had met him a few days before and now learned of his penchant for snakes. His favourite 'pet' was an incredibly nasty black rat snake which he had found lying in the road outside Durham several weeks previously and brought back, unaware of its viciousness.

Some snakes (such as boa constrictors) enjoy human companionship, but an undomesticated snake will strike repeatedly if restrained by a gloved hand. The snake usually stops after a few minutes on realizing the futility of the strategy, becomes calmer, and will eventually get used to the situation. But not this snake! Graham's pet exhibited a ferocious dislike of people and would never stop biting when held. It seemed a perfect candidate for our detection studies, so two sessions were immediately planned.

The first of these experiments took place on the evening of 26 July. I remained with the snake and with a second observer in the Foundation's laboratory building. The reptile was placed inside a special room in a glass terrarium, where I could watch it through an observation window. (The lights illuminating the terrarium kept the reptile from seeing or responding to me.) Keith was taken over to Duke from where he would try to project back to me or the snake. Bob Morris and I used the same four-period observational protocol as had been used with the kitten work, with each critical period signalled by a telephone ring.

I really didn't know exactly what to expect, since I had had little experience with snakes, but Bob and Graham tried to help me as best they could.

'See if the snake becomes agitated,' Bob instructed shortly before leaving with Keith for the Duke campus.

'What does a snake do when it gets upset?' I asked.

With a psychologist's typical nonchalance, Bob merely suggested that I see if its respiration increased.

This proposal was hardly helpful since I've never seen a snake hyperventilate. 'How will I know if he's breathing faster?' I enquired.

'That's easy,' explained Bob. 'His heart rate will increase.'

What a wonderful plan, I thought to myself. I don't even know where a snake's heart is! So I decided just to observe the creature carefully and record any unusual behaviour it might exhibit.

Before the formal experiment began, I watched the snake for several minutes and made written notes on my observations. The reptile merely explored its cage and never showed any unusual behaviour. When the phone rang for the first time, I watched the snake closely for three minutes, but nothing exceptional happened. But when the phone range for the second time, the snake immediately responded in a rather bizarre fashion. Reprinted below is a statement I wrote in 1973 describing the snake's actions, which is based on the notes I made the same evening that the experiment took place:

> Shortly after the beginning of the second experimental period, the snake began to speed up its activity rate and, stretching out completely, burrowed under the shavings at the bottom of the cage. The snake had done this during the preexperimental observation period while it explored its new home, but not with such violence or speed. After quickly burrowing, the snake stared upward at the top of the cage, resting its head, throat forward, on the glass side. There it remained motionless for a moment, then quickly slid up the side of the cage (the side closest to me) until it was halfway up the glass. It then gnawed and bit wildly at the glass as though attacking something, or trying to 'eat through' the glass. This lasted for about twenty to thirty seconds. The snake then suddenly became calm again. This reaction occurred right in the middle of a three-minute experimental session. Prior to the experiment the snake had on two occasions opened its mouth and placed it against the glass. However, in both cases these reactions lasted only for a few seconds at most with no concomitant speed up of activity rate. After the violent reaction, the snake only opened its mouth on one other occasion.

When Keith and the experimenters returned from Duke later that evening, we compared notes. It seems that Keith had projected to the snake and me right within the second experimental period. Keith had even tried to enter the cage with the creature.

He made a second, but less vivid out-of-body excursion to the PRF during the fourth period.

Even though the snake hadn't responded during Keith's second out-of-body attempt, it was clear that its critical responses were strikingly unusual. When I described them for Graham, I asked him whether such gnawings could be considered normal for a snake.

'They're about as usual as the snake taking its tail in its mouth and cartwheeling around its cage,' he replied.

Clearly something extraordinary had occurred, so we immediately decided to replicate the experiment.

Our chance came several days later when Graham returned to the PRF with his prize snake. The results weren't at all spectacular this time, though, since the creature became uncooperative. The recalcitrant reptile immediately buried itself in the terrarium's shavings and slept through the entire proceedings —despite my pounding on the observation window, trying to wake it!

Target studies return to Durham
Even though Keith had performed excellently with the snake, I remained disappointed that I never took part in the Foundation's original target studies. While it was obvious that the earlier experiments were problematic, the psychology student sometimes succeeded with them extraordinarily well. I was keen to perform some target sessions of my own, since the results of a single successful experiment simply *look* more impressive than 'detection' or behavioural studies.

Keith never shared my enthusiasm for target studies, probably because the first PRF experiments in OBE vision had been poorly designed and implemented. But through some gentle coercion I finally convinced him to co-operate in such a session. My chance came one evening when the behavioural studies were in abeyance and Graham and Bob were trying to design other experiments.

Some years before, Graham had invented a curious device for studying the response of birds to magnetic fields. This odd-looking contraption consisted of a round cage with a bottom composed of depressible, pie-shaped planks. When the bird was placed in the cage, it depressed the planks whenever it moved, and a permanent record was printed out on a chart. The bird

couldn't escape from the rotund device since its top was screen-
ed over. Graham wanted to use the cage for our research with
Keith, since it superseded the platform Dr Morris used in the kitten work, which relied upon an experimental observer. So on 14
August we scheduled a pilot experiment to see if Keith felt com-
fortable working with the equipment, while I used the session to
conduct a target study with Keith's somewhat reluctant permission.

When Keith and the other experimenters went to Duke that
evening, I randomly picked several objects from the laboratory to
place inside or near the cage. I placed a large bottle sandwiched
between two frisbees on top of the device. Since I was still working in the music industry back in 1973, I had brought an oboe
with me to keep in practice. The long, black, wooden instrument
was positioned inside the cage, balanced on top of its rectangular
black case.

Dr Morris phoned me at 9:45 from Duke to synchronize the experiment. I was secretly hoping that Keith would make his
presence known to me, but I failed to detect his out-of-body
visitation during the forthcoming session. Keith's OBE to the
Foundation took place at 10:11 p.m. and he returned to his body
three minutes later to report his observations to Bob. Below is the
report Dr Morris wrote from Keith's rather disjointed, disoriented impressions. Since he had just returned to his body
when he made these comments, his adjustment to the real world
was still incomplete. The italicized portions of the report represent the correct responses he made to the target display.

> Got down deep, flip over there, real deep when there, TV looked on.
> Looked around room, above and around apparatus. Hard to see.
> *Round flat object like plate to front right in apparatus. Maybe glass.*
> Hard to remember. *Something black and square diagonally.* Unclear.
> *Saw two things; both might have been same thing. Something tall stan-*
> *ding in middle.* Might have created a kitten. *Long pencil on top.*
> *Something round.* Not a piece of wood, *maybe a frisbee on top.*

After making a few personal comments, Keith concluded, '*Maybe
saw bottle.* Shoe on top, to the right.'

Keith's impressions and language were not concise, but that
was understandable considering his dazed condition upon returning to the body. But it is still remarkable how correct his impressions were when we sort through his rambling comments.

His description of a 'round flat object like a plate' obviously referred to the frisbees, and he even correctly saw them in duplicate. Since they were the most conspicuous aspects of the target display, it is interesting that he immediately focused on them. It is remarkable that he correctly named the objects though he tended (earlier) to confuse them with the bottle standing between the discs.

Since Keith was generally unfamiliar with woodwind instruments, I don't think it is surprising that he couldn't specifically name the oboe and its case. But his remark that there was something in the cage like 'a long pencil' probably obliquely referred to the instrument.

When I read this report, my first impression was that Keith had successfully seen the target objects but not with normal depth perception or stereoscopic vision. It also looks as if mirror vision complicated his observations. So whatever faculty was operating during his out-of-body perceptions during this session, the rules of ordinary optics didn't regulate it.

This target experiment was the last session I designed with Keith before returning to Los Angeles, and it concluded my brief stay with the Psychical Research Foundation. I have not, however, summarized the entire story of the work done there with Mr Harary and his out-of-body skills. The complete project stretched between 1973 and late 1974 before the funds for the research were finally exhausted. Many more experiments were conducted with Keith, and to describe them all would take more space than this chapter allows. I have previously given a more definitive description of this research in my book *In Search of the Unknown*, which I reprinted in my anthology *Mind Beyond the Body*. These experiments included some pilots to physically detect Keith's out-of-body presence at the target location using thermistors, photomultiplier tubes, and so forth. More cleverly designed cat detection studies were also executed, which reached their peak when a laboratory technician 'saw' Keith's etheric double on a television screen monitoring the room to which he was projecting!

In general, the Psychical Research Foundation's living detection studies obtained better results than those attempts to physically detect his out-of-body projections. No consistently reliable detections using the thermistors and other equipment were ever isolated, but curious recordings were often noticed from these devices, especially the first time each piece of equipment was introduced. During my first observations with Keith when Dr Morris used the dog, for instance, Keith—secure in his chamber at Duke—was hooked to polygraph leads since we wanted to keep a record of his brainwaves. Graham Watkins deliberately left two of the leads unattached to Keith's head during the experiment. These wires were simply left in the booth to record the background radiant input from the chamber. It was later discovered that the background electrical noise in the booth decreased both times Keith reported leaving his body. While the exact interpretation of this finding is unclear, it suggests that the physical space surrounding Keith was modified when he projected his body back to the Foundation.

Implication for the NDE

While the experiments summarized in the preceding sections may seem irrelevent to the study of the NDE, I feel they have a significant bearing on it. The research conducted in the early 1970s with Keith Harary represents the most systematic study of the OBE in a single subject ever undertaken. While Dr Morris and several other staff members never could decide which explanation for the OBE best explained their results, I never found myself in that situation. My own feeling is that, in general, our results show that the OBE is the genuine projection of consciousness from the body. The Foundation's two-year project certainly indicates that some out-of-body experiences cannot be explained psychologically.

Most parapsychologists probably wouldn't support this type of sweeping conclusion and would prefer to endorse Dr Morris's more neutral position. Certainly there were problems with Keith's out-of-body performances, especially since his successes were sometimes inconsistent. But if we look at the collective results of the target and detection studies, I feel the research supports a 'separationist' (or literalist) interpretation of the out-of-body experience. No psychological or proto-psychological theory of the OBE appears equally tenable.

I pointed out earlier in this chapter that Keith's out-of-body experiences differ little from the related experiences reported by many people in their day-to-day lives. They differ only in that Keith, for some mysterious reason, can control his out-of-body projections and prolong them. Now if the NDE represents merely a specific form or expression of the out-of-body experience, any explanation for Keith's experiences would probably subsume the former. The results of the Psychical Research Foundation's research likewise bear on those rare 'veridical' OBEs summarized in the previous chapter. So it really does begin to look as if simple NDEs represent some sort of genuine separation of the consciousness from the body.

But can this separationist theory for the OBE explain eschatological NDEs, with their mysterious tunnels, spiritual guides, and heavenly landscapes? This is the critical issue facing the student of the NDE and will be dealt with in the next chapter.

11.

Journeys to the Beyond— Explaining Eschatological NDEs

Mrs Iris Lemov's NDE took place when she lapsed into a coma while recovering from some routine surgery.

'I was brought back to my room after surgery and was speaking to my nurse,' she reminisced in 1979, 'when a strange separated feeling between my body and my brain occurred. High above my body I floated wondering why so many doctors were around my bed and why they were doing a venal cut-down when I told them not to.'

The surprised witness tried to speak to the physicians, but they remained impervious to her. Mrs Lemov specifically noticed how pale she looked before she was sucked into a black tunnel.

> I felt frightened and excited as I neared the end of the tunnel. I felt peace, without pain, and free. The light at the end of the tunnel was bright but easy on my eyes. The valley I came to was a sight to behold. There was velvety green grass and calmness. Music coming from nowhere made me feel comfortable and I began to feel as if I belonged. I saw figures of people dressed in shrouds coming toward me and called me by name. This man with a white beard told me to go back—your family still needs you—enjoy your life. This beautiful man was my grandfather who died two years before I was born. To have had the chance to meet a man I've heard so much about makes the experience unforgettable—but to have the opportunity to find about the mystery of death was a true learning experience for me.
>
> If we all could have the opportunity of seeing my valley during the course of our lifetime, how much more purposeful our lives would be.

Mrs Lemov doesn't explain in her report how her experience ended, but later learned that her heart stopped beating during the episode.

'Death no longer frightens me and I am going on with the process of living,' she continued in the November 1979 issue of *Anabiosis*. 'My experience helps me in everyday life and also in dealing with the patients I work with as a medical assistant.'

The description of the otherworld offered by Mrs Lemov is typical of a great many eschatological NDEs placed on record, especially after 1975. But while the predominant pattern of these cases is consistent, details within the experience often vary.

Probably the most common form of eschatological NDE is the incipient journey, in which the percipient floats down a tunnel towards a bright light where he/she encounters God or some other spiritual presence. Other witnesses seem to float peacefully but nebulously within a misty void. Such experiences are usually pleasant for the dying person and sometimes resolve into a more elaborate otherworld journey. Most of these people find themselves in a beautiful meadow or similar romantic setting where it is common for these lucky witnesses to meet their deceased relatives, who firmly but lovingly send them back to earth.

Typical of the eschatological journey is the powerful reality of the experience for the percipient. Never for a moment, even upon recovering, does the percipient consider whether the incident was real or not. He or she remains convinced that some new reality was contacted during the experience and never falters in that belief.

But can the critical student of the NDE be so sure? We have the same problem evaluating NDEs that we have analysing other peak, mystical, or spiritual experiences. Being primarily ineffable, the impact they have on the survivor can never be properly shared with others. While we can evaluate the subject's written or oral testimony, we can never share in the personal meaning of the experience. For this reason, NDEs must forever remain uniquely personal and subjective events. The situation is probably best explained by Ms Helen Nelson, who became a very vocal advocate of NDE research because of her own experience. She explained in 1979 that 'trying to describe my clinical death experience is like trying to capture the Mona Lisa or the lustre of a Rembrandt with a very limited artistic ability'.

At least with simple NDEs that take place within the 'real' world of the operating room we can look for possible veridical features.

But there is simply no way to legitimately verify the eschatological observations made by some NDErs.

When trying to build a theoretical model for this type of NDE, several contradictory factors should be kept in mind. Some components of the otherworld journey seem to be objective, while others probably represent mythical or culturally determined aspects of the experience. The possible objectivity of the eschatological NDE is supported by the following facts:

1. Some eschatological NDEs begin with an out-of-body episode, and there is every reason to believe that the OBE is an objectively (ontologically) real experience.
2. Some aspects of the eschatological NDE can be 'shared' by other people witnessing the clinical death. I will be returning to this remarkable claim shortly.
3. Descriptions of the afterlife realm remain fairly consistent from percipient to percipient.

On the other hand, there are features of the eschatological NDE that few people would take literally:

1. Descriptions of the otherworld differ from culture to culture, often expressing the background or expectancies of the percipients.
2. During the eschatological voyage, the subject may have blatantly visionary experiences such as seeing the end of the world. It would therefore seem obvious that the entire experience is primarily subjective, perhaps psychologically created from within the experiencer's own psyche.

Any theory designed to explain eschatological NDEs has to incorporate these disparate facts and findings. So for the next few pages, let's try to discern which specific features of the eschatological journey are objectively 'real' and which probably exist solely within the percipient's mind.

Objective features of the eschatological NDE: two possible examples

The previous chapter focused on showing that the OBE probably represents the objective projection of consciousness from the body. Little more need be said on the subject in this chapter. But there are other aspects of the NDE that point to its objective existence.

Some people who have remained at the bedsides of the dying have occasionally shared in their NDEs in minor ways. Sir William Barrett (whose research on deathbed vision cases was summarized in Chapter 3) was the first to collect and publish such reports, and he included a chapter on the subject in his *Death-bed Visions*. These were primarily reports from people who saw—through clairvoyance or the sixth sense—the escape of the soul from the body. The British researcher explained that 'many well authenticated cases are on record where the relatives of a person, watching by the death-bed, have seen at the moment of death a cloudy form rising from the body of the deceased and hovering for a time in the room and then passing away'.

It is extremely difficult to evaluate such experiences, since they sound so unbelievable, even though similar cases sometimes get reported in our own sophisticated times. I know of a case in California where a mysterious glow emanated from the body of a deceased hospital patient. The light faded with time but was observed repeatedly by the hospital staff. But in the long run, the types of experiences collected by Barrett and others can be explained psychologically, and may relate to an extraordinary phenomenon currently called 'fantasy-proneness' by psychologists. The fantasy-prone person is capable of superb powers of mental imagery and can typically 'create' phantoms so powerful and realistic that he or she sometimes mistakes them for real people. Fantasy-prone individuals also tend to make exceptionally good hypnotic subjects and spend considerable time engaging in daydreams.

The discovery of the fantasy-prone individual was probably first made by Dr Morton Schatzman, a British psychiatrist who informally introduced the concept in 1980 in his book *The Story of Ruth*. Ruth was a young patient constantly plagued by the phantom form of her cruel father. Dr Schatzman helped her understand the subjective nature of the figure, but then discovered that she could conjure up such figures at will. He even scientifically demonstrated the realistic nature of the forms in the following way: by the use of formal EEG monitoring, the psychiatrist found that Ruth's brain stopped responding to a flashing light if her fantasy creation stepped in front of her eyes. Even a properly hypnotized person told to conjure up a 'ghost' probably wouldn't respond in this spectacular manner! In the United States, considerable research on the fantasy-prone individual has become the special project of Dr T.X. Barber, whose previous research on waking and hypnotic suggestion is famous.

The concept of the fantasy-prone person probably explains some of Sir William Barrett's cases and similar reports placed on record by other researchers. Deathbed visitors invariably become highly involved emotionally in the scenes they witness. Who wouldn't be caught up in such a situation, perhaps holding the hand of a dying friend or relative? Some of Barrett's Victorian witnesses were probably fantasy-prone subjects, capable of unconsciously projecting 'visions' of something (the soul?) leaving the body—visions so realistic that they mistook them for reality. Perhaps they were responding to the 'take away' visions simultaneously reported by the patients, visions we know to be extremely common among the dying.

I have gone into the subject of the fantasy-prone individual since few contemporary NDE researchers have tackled the subject of Sir William Barrett's cases. I hope I've shown that such reports—rare today though still made from time to time—result neither from lying nor from delusion, but from a little-known power encased within the human psyche.

Despite this possibility, there remain a few cases that can't be easily explained by the concept of fantasy-proneness. Ms Margaret Moser is, for example, a nurse in Jamaica, New York, who made some extraordinary observations while taking care of one of her terminal patients. She first reported her experience to Dr Karlis Osis, when the Latvian-born psychologist was conducting his original survey of deathbed observations by physicians and nurses in 1959 and 1960. Dr Osis never published her story, but it later fell into the hands of Susy Smith, a popular writer of psychic books who (before her retirement in 1978) published the story in two of her books, *The Enigma of Out-of-Body Travel*, and later in her *Life Is Forever*. Ms Moser recalled:

> In the winter of 1948–49 I nursed a very sick old lady, Mrs. Rosa B. She was a very clever, well-educated, and highly-cultured immigrant from Odessa, Russia, who had lived for many years in New York City. She was residing at that time at the Savoy Plaza Hotel on Fifth Avenue, and up to the last she was mentally competent.
>
> Early one afternoon I had put my patient to bed for a nap and was sitting at my little table beside the window writing in her chart. I was facing her bed, the door at my back. Mrs. B. had been asleep, but suddenly I saw her sit up and wave happily, her face all smiles. I turned

my head toward the door, thinking one of her daughters had come in; but much to my surprise it was an elderly lady I had never seen before. She had a striking resemblance to my patient—the same light blue eyes, but a longer nose and heavier chin. I could see her very clearly for it was bright daylight; the window shades were only slightly lowered. The visitor walked toward my patient, bent down, and, as far as I can remember, they kissed each other. But then, as I got up and walked toward the bed, she was gone.

Mrs. B. looked very pleased. She took my hand and said, 'It is my sister!' Then she slept peacefully again. I saw the same apparition twice later on, but never as clearly and always from another room. But every time she came the patient was obviously elated.

At Mrs. B.'s funeral service some weeks later, I positively identified a gentleman as being the son of the apparition, because he had his mother's nose and chin and looked so much like her. I asked one of the daughters about it, and she said that he was her cousin.

If this story is true, it is remarkable, and possibly points to the objective existence of the 'greeting figures' commonly seen by people having NDEs or deathbed visions. Of course, Ms Moser's report is merely an interesting story and relies exclusively on her own word. But in my years working in parapsychology, I have heard similar tales from many reliable, intelligent people with no motivation for lying to me. So while such reports or observations can't *prove* anything, they suggest the possibility that the spiritual guides seen by the dying represent some sort of genuine spiritual 'reality'.

We obviously need to collect more stories of this calibre before drawing any conclusions from them.

The second possible objective feature of the eschatological NDE is the beautiful music reported by the fortunate percipients. Witnesses undergoing both simple and eschatological NDEs often report hearing these heavenly sounds, which they claim surpass any earthly music known to them. It is relatively unusual for the reporters to describe the music in terms of a specific mode, such as singing or orchestral; the music simply seems too different from anything ever before experienced by these etheric travellers. If the percipient enjoys an otherworld journey, he or she usually hears the music emanating from the higher worlds as if projected directly from the atmosphere. The following two brief NDE reports describe this transcendental music.

The first case was originally collected by Dr Robert Crookall in the 1960s. The percipient was a British teenager, who was extremely ill in bed when the NDE transpired.

> I was only sixteen years old, ill in bed. I told mother I thought I was going to faint ... I felt myself drifting away from her. Suddenly I realized a feeling of great excitement, wonder, and delight surpassing anything I had ever experienced as I felt my body weightless and floating upwards in a golden glow towards a wonderful light around hazy welcoming figures *and the whole air was filled with beautiful singing*.
>
> I floated joyfully towards the voices and the light and then I heard my mother's voice calling me ... My whole being revolted against going back. Her voice grew nearer and to my great distress, I felt myself slipping away from that wonderful light and merging into a dull black cloud where my heaviness of body returned ... My mother thought I had died; I had seemed to stop breathing ... I am now forty-two and the wonder of it still remains.

Many similar reports have emerged in the literature since the Moody revolution of 1975 and, in fact, the following report originally appeared in *Life After Life*. This experience took place when the percipient suffered a ruptured appendix.

> I got up and walked into the hall to go get a drink, and it was at that point, as they found out later, that my appendix ruptured. I became very weak, and I fell down. I began to feel a sort of drifting, a movement of my real being in and out of my body, *and to hear beautiful music*. I floated on down the hall and out the door onto the screened-in porch. There, it almost seemed that clouds, a pink mist really, began to gather around me, and then I floated right straight on through the screen, just as though it weren't there, and up into this pure crystal clear light, an illuminating white light. It was beautiful and so bright, so radiant, but it didn't hurt my eyes. It's not any kind of light you can describe on earth. I didn't actually see a person in this light, and yet it has a special identity, it definitely does. It is a light of perfect understanding and perfect love.
>
> The thought came to my mind, 'Lovest thou me?' This was not exactly in the form of a question, but I guess the connotation of what the light said was, 'If you do love me, go back and complete what you began in your life.' And all during this time, I felt as though I were surrounded by an overwhelming love and compassion.

Dr Margot Grey found in her British study that 11 per cent of her NDE survivors reported hearing this 'music of the spheres'. Some of these reports appear in her excellent book *Return from Death*.

Whatever its core nature, this impressive music is a common feature of the NDE. But is it a real property of the otherworldly realms or merely a hallucinatory component of the NDE? My own feeling is that this music is an objective part of the experience since, on rare occasions, people visiting the dying have heard it too.

Sir William Barrett in Great Britain and Ernesto Bozzano in Italy were the first researchers to publish detailed cases of this phenomenon. Barrett even devoted a chapter of his posthumously issued *Death-bed Visions* to the subject, often basing his commentary on earlier cases collected, investigated, and published by the Society for Psychical Research. He focused his chapter on the strange harmonies often reported by the dying themselves, but pointed out that this music is occasionally reported by people visiting the patients as well.

Probably the most interesting case of this sort was published by the Society in the 1880s. The report focused on the pseudo-death experienced by a British gentleman named John Britton, a deaf mute dying from rheumatic fever. Because his hands were very swollen, he could no longer signal to his relatives, and everyone expected him to die. The patient's brother-in-law, Mr S. Allen, joined the household vigil when he was summoned by the family doctor. He became the first person in the household to hear the music, when he and his wife heard beautiful singing while staying in the room directly below Britton's chambers. They determined that the music came from upstairs but could find no normal source for it. Mr Allen later stated in writing:

> We found Jack lying on his back with his eyes fixed on the ceiling, and his face lighted up with the brightest of smiles. After a little while Jack awoke and used the words 'Heaven' and 'beautiful' as well as he could by means of his lips and facial expression. As he became more conscious he also told us in the same manner that his brother Tom and his sister Harriet were coming to see him. This we considered very unlikely as they lived some distance off, but shortly afterwards a cab drove up from which they alighted. They had sent no intimation of their coming, nor had anyone else. After Jack's partial recovery, when he was able to write or converse upon his fingers, he told us that he had been allowed to see into Heaven and to hear most beautiful music.

On the basis of this testimony, it seems that John Britton probably left his body, saw his relatives coming to visit, and then experienced some sort of eschatological journey.

The original records on this case were collected by the Reverend L.S. Milford, the master of Haileybury College, who turned them over to the Society for Psychical Research. Since both the primary witness and his wife heard the music, the phenomenon probably wasn't due to fantasy-proneness on Mr Allen's part.

Several similar accounts were published by Ernesto Bozzano in his monograph *Phénomènes psychiques au moment de la mort,* which has never been translated into English.

Since the publication of Barrett's book and Bozzano's short monograph, the subject of this curious music has completely dropped from psychical research. I explained in Chapter 3 that there are probably two reasons for this. For one thing, very few NDE researchers or parapsychologists have shown any interest in such reports. But probably more important is the fact that the social psychology of death has changed radically since Victorian times, when Bozzano and Barrett were collecting their cases. Few people today die surrounded by their loving relatives in the comforting setting of their own bedrooms. Approximately 80 per cent of the general public die in hospital rooms, which constitute sterile environments probably too impersonal to give rise to psychic phenomena. If more people died in their own homes, I think the types of cases highlighted by the early psychical researchers would most likely experience a revival.

Despite this change in the social structure of the death experience, I became interested in the subject of transcendental deathbed music in 1968. (Since my passions back then were both parapsychology and music, it seemed a natural enough subject to tackle!) I eventually placed letters in two popular psychic publications requesting readers to contact me if they'd ever heard this supernormal music.

I received a flood of correspondence which included several NDE cases in which this fascinating 'music of the spheres' was heard, and one of my cases closely resembled the typical cases published previously by Barrett and Bozzano. The report was contributed by a gentleman from Ohio, who stayed at his stepmother's side when she was dying in 1954. While he was at her deathbed he heard soft music in the room. 'It was very angelic and, as they say, out of this world,' he explained in his letter. 'It was very calm and peaceful and beyond that which is produced on this plane.' I later placed this report in my second book on transcendental music, *NAD, Vol. 2: A Psychic Study of the 'Music of the Spheres'*, published in 1970.

Interestingly enough, the witness's sister entered the room during the experience but failed to hear the music. So whether the music was, in this particular case, in some sense objective or the result of fantasy-proneness is difficult to say, but I think the collected reports published by Barrett, Bozzano, and myself suggest that this psychic music is partly objective—perhaps a genuine property of the otherworldly realms contacted during the dying person's eschatological journey.

Subjective features of the NDE

Even if the NDE is partly objective, certain features of the eschatological journey appear to be subjective and probably visionary. It is difficult to take some components of the eschatological vision literally since so many cultural factors partially programme it.

Despite the claims of some NDE researchers, there is no strong evidence that the prototypical NDE is a cross-cultural phenomenon. We don't have enough data from different cultures to make such a claim, and in fact, the limited cross-cultural studies placed in the literature point in the opposite direction!

The cases collected by Dorothy Ayers Counts from Papua New Guinea (see Chapter 8) do not include many of the NDE's core features, such as leaving the body and entering a tunnel. Since this analysis was published, similar data have been compiled by J. Timothy Green, who earlier replicated Dr Ring's core features model of the NDE while working with a sample population of NDE survivors in Southern California. Mr Green later became a school psychologist in Guam and ferreted out some 'return from death' reports from the island's indigenous Chammaro culture. While one of his witnesses reported something similar to a prototypical NDE, the other cases were much less impressive. 'None of my respondents mentioned being out-of-body (although it may be implied), seeing their body from a position outside of it, tunnels or dark areas, lights or entering into the light,' he reported regretfully in 1984.

Mr Green concluded his report by saying, 'My sense is that there are more cases of NDEs on Guam and, if I am successful in documenting more NDEs, I will report more fully on them at that time.' But that was the last anyone engaged in near-death research heard from the psychologist!

Remember, though, that Mr Green only collected a handful of cases; too few, in fact, to base any conclusions on. But some of his accounts curiously resembled Ms Counts's Melanesian cases, in which the dying patient often walked a road to the Great Beyond instead of floating through a tunnel. This type of feature is conspicuously missing from Western cases, where encountering a tunnel or barrier to the next world is commonly reported.

Another possibly subjective element in the eschatological journey is the spiritual figure so often contacted by the NDE percipient, either within the Great White Light or in the paradisiacal realm. This spiritual guide is often perceived as the literal Jesus, God, a formless spiritual presence, or sometimes takes the form of a deceased relative. It sometimes seems like the perceived figure is created in response to the observer's bias. Most significant is the large number of people who either encounter or interact with the historical Jesus. Dr Michael Sabom, Dr Margot Grey, and some Christian-oriented NDE writers have each published similar cases.

The following report, for example, is part of an eschatological journey collected by Dr Grey during her research in Great Britain. In her book *Return from Death* she doesn't, unfortunately, offer her readers much information on the medical background to the case, but only states that the informant was declared dead before his resuscitation, which culminated in the following typical otherworld journey:

> I arrived at a place—it's very hard to put this into words, but I can only describe it as heaven. It's a place of intense light, a place of intense activity, more like a bustling city than a lonely country scene, nothing like floating on clouds or harps or anything of that sort. While I was there I felt at the centre of things. I felt enlightened and cleansed. I felt I could see the point of everything. Everything fitted in, it all made sense, even the dark times. It almost seemed, too, as if the pieces of a jig-saw all fitted together. You know how it is with tapestry, how you see the back of the tapestry and all the interwoven parts, then when the tapestry's turned over you see how it fits into place. Suddenly I saw how all my life fitted together at that point. I could have been there for ever and ever. I saw Jesus Christ. I was aware of him by the print of nails in his hands and his feet and I remember I was very amused. I thought it was a joke at the time, it

made me laugh, and other people laughed with me; I think there must be humour in heaven.

Very similar is a case reported by Marvin Ford in his book *On the Other Side*, which takes a predominantly Christian approach to the study of NDEs. Just like the gentleman who responded to Dr Grey's request for cases, Ford's correspondent recognized Jesus from the obvious wounds in his palms. Dr Sabom's example of this same phenomenon resulted from an operating room NDE, in which the patient experienced a simple out-of-body episode before Jesus materialized by his side. The spiritual figure then escorted the percipient to the otherworld realm.

Modern religious scholars know, of course, that the historical Jesus probably wasn't crucified through the palms of his hands but through his wrists. This was the common Roman means of execution and evidence for the practice is evident on the skeletal remains of victims. So it's doubtful whether Dr Grey's subject, Marvin Ford's witness, or Dr Sabom's patient experienced the 'real' Jesus. What they were probably seeing was a representation of the religious figure presumably extracted from their own minds. In light of cases such as these, it begins to appear that the eschatological journey resembles a vision more than a literal journey through death.

People undergoing NDEs even tend to meet idealized figures from their own pasts, who often reappear in the guise of spiritual guides. Raymond Moody even published a case in 1987 in which the percipient met the famous singer Elvis Presley, who served briefly in that capacity!

This case is fascinating since it shows the manner in which the NDE is partly programmed by significant experiences from the patient's earlier life. The witness was Beverly Wilkins, whom Dr Moody met in Nebraska in 1980. Her experience occurred when her heart stopped beating while she was undergoing emergency surgery. Ms Wilkins first experienced herself floating up and over the operating table. She looked down but remained indifferent towards her body. In typical NDE style she entered a tunnel and floated towards a lovely white light and subsequently entered the paradisiacal realms. She was walking through a bucolic pasture where she met several deceased relatives and finally saw Elvis Presley, who spoke to her briefly before she returned to her body. Dr Moody points out in *Elvis After Life* that

Ms Wilkins once met the singer briefly during a concert tour. She had obviously been impressed by the meeting, which probably programmed her later eschatological encounter.

That the eschatological NDE (whatever its nature) contains blatantly visionary components can't be denied. This fact became obvious when Dr Kenneth Ring began collecting prophetic NDE cases in which the percipients were shown their futures or the future of the world. Some of these NDE survivors were shown apocalyptic scenes of coming cataclysms which will (presumably) ultimately destroy our planet. Dr Ring tends to take these cases rather literally, a point he makes in his fascinating book *Heading Toward Omega*. The typical pattern is for the percipient to undergo an otherworld journey and encounter God or a similar spiritual presence, who then 'grants' the upcoming revelation to the subject. The following example of this phenomenon is from Dr Ring's small collection of prophetic NDEs. The reporter experienced a return from death in 1967 during which such a prophecy was delivered to her.

> The vision of the future I received during my near-death experience was one of tremendous upheaval in the world as a result of our general ignorance of the 'true' reality. I was informed that mankind was breaking the laws of the universe and as a result of this would suffer. This suffering was not due to the vengeance of an indignant God, but rather like the pain one might suffer as a result of arrogantly defying the law of gravity. It was to be an inevitable educational cleansing of the earth that would creep up upon its inhabitants, who would try to hide blindly in the institutions of law, science, and religion. Mankind, I was told, was being consumed by the concerns of arrogance, materialism, racism, chauvinism, and separatist thinking. I saw sense turning to nonsense, and calamity, in the end, turning to providence.
>
> At the end of this general period of transition, mankind was to be 'born anew,' with a new sense of his place in the universe. The birth process, however, as in all the kingdoms, was exquisitely painful. Mankind would emerge humbled yet educated, peaceful and, at last, unified.

I find it difficult to take such revelations literally, even though I have the greatest respect for Dr Ring's work on the subject. Such previews of the planet's future destruction reek of a common Western religious sentiment. These prophetic NDEs seem to represent visionary translations of the 'Repent for the End is Near' message of the Western religious tradition dating back to early Christianity. Deep down within the psyche, I think each of us is concerned with our planetary survival and this concern could easily emerge during any powerful psychological experience.

Since the apocalyptic vision is undoubtedly a subjective component of the eschatological journey, it seems obvious that similar components could cloud every phase of the experience.

Can we explain the eschatological NDE?

Where do these contradictory findings lead us? Is the NDE a journey to the afterlife or isn't it? Is the experience objectively real or not? Does the NDE demonstrate that consciousness survives death, or is it a cosmic delusion?

There exist no simple solutions to these important questions, so to offer the reader some facile conceptual model for the NDE wouldn't be fair or proper. I don't think that either psychology or parapsychology really knows for sure what the NDE represents. But in the remaining pages I will try to explain what I think the NDE—especially the eschatological NDE—*could* represent.

The experimental studies outlined in the previous chapter, especially the work with Keith Harary, constitute strong evidence that the out-of-body experience is the real projection of consciousness from the body. This fact by itself suggests that some elements of the simple NDE are objective, but it is difficult to extend this finding to the complexities of eschatological journeys. Simply speaking, I feel that the core NDE and the subsequent otherworld journey represents *an intense visionary experience unfolded for the dying person when he/she enters an out-of-body state*. It is, in other words, some sort of revelation that takes place when the 'soul' separates from the body. I think this theory can explain many problems with the NDE that simpler 'separationist' theories cannot:

1. The out-of-body vision theory explains why the NDE is composed of both objective and blatantly subjective components.
2. This conceptual model is consistent with the 'second-level' visionary experiences some NDErs report—e.g. seeing popular religious figures and receiving apocalyptic prophecies.
3. Since part of the NDE is purely visionary, the fact that cultural factors and expectations partially programme its content is understandable.

4. The out-of-body visionary theory explains why NDEs sometimes occur spontaneously when the percipient isn't in a life-threatening situation.

I first began developing this theory when I noted something fascinating in the statistical findings of Kenneth Ring, Michael Sabom, and Margot Grey. I was constantly struck by the fact that people with prior knowledge of the NDE experience it less commonly in the face of death than previously ignorant individuals. This single finding is probably the most widely replicated effect in the literature, having now emerged in three separate surveys. This finding doesn't seem to make sense if the 'core' and the eschatological NDE represents a completely objective phenomenon. So I began conceptualizing the NDE in terms of a religious revelation and not really a literal journey into death. But at the same time, I never closed my eyes to the fact that some simple NDEs were possibly genuine releases of consciousness from the body. The eschatological journey, therefore, probably represents a 'tiering' effect within the NDE, in which the visionary components 'envelope' consciousness when it is projected from its shell.

It seems fairly obvious that NDEs take place when the percipient or patient needs to know that a future life exists. Let me emphasize, however, that just because there is a psychological need for experiencing the eschatological journey, that doesn't mean that the experience is a convenient fiction—a final bedtime story, to use Dr Robert Kastenbaum's colourful metaphor. *It is highly likely, even probable, that the visionary components of the NDE point to a greater spiritual reality.* Since we cannot directly perceive this reality while the body still lives, perhaps we experience a symbolic preview of it. It is for this reason that the percipient's observations will be coloured by his cultural background and religious expectations.

(Let me say, though, that I don't discount the possibility that some NDEs represent direct contacts with the Great Beyond. Cultural tradition may cloud the witness's perceptions, so that he or she 'sees' or interprets the observations in the form of familiar objects, settings, landscapes, and so forth.)

It is also for this reason that Ring, Sabom, and Grey found that their uninformed subjects experienced NDEs more frequently than people familiar with the phenomenon. Dying or close-to-death patients already familiar with the soul's final resting place (by virtue of their knowledge of the NDE) would have a lesser need for the revelation. Needless to say, this conceptualization of the eschatological NDE also explains why people undergo NDEs when they merely *perceive* themselves to be dying. Since the OBE/NDE vision is predominantly created by psychological urgency, whether or not the patient is physiologically near death becomes irrelevant.

In a sense, my conceptual model for the NDE is similar to Dr Carol Zaleski's theory that NDEs represent symbolic spiritual journeys. She presents this theory in great and eloquent detail in her book *Otherworld Journeys*.

As we saw in Chapter 2, Dr Zaleski believes that the modern NDE is a contemporary expression of the Christian eschatological vision, whose roots date back to the thirteenth century and even much earlier. While the eminent scholar eschews the belief that NDEs are objectively real, she entertains the possibility that it points to a greater spiritual reality, perhaps one which originally gave rise to the tradition. My explanation for the eschatological NDE and some aspects of the 'core' NDE is similar, but I think the visionary components embedded in the experience only transact when a genuine OBE is taking place. The eschatological journey may be a symbolic revelation, but it primarily takes place when the percipient casts off the body's encumbrances.

This separationist OBE/visionary model is also roughly similar to the predominantly Jungian conception of the NDE championed by Dr Michael Grosso, a philosophy instructor at Jersey State College. For his understanding of the NDE he draws on the great Swiss psychiatrist C.G. Jung's famous concept of archetypal thinking. Jung posited that there exist universal symbols buried deep in the psyche. These symbols constitute a particular way of thinking common to every race and culture, which he labelled the Collective Unconscious. Dr Grosso believes that the NDE probably represents an archetypal experience in which the percipient, while enjoying a drastic change in consciousness, relives an archetypal voyage into death.

In explaining his conceptualization of the NDE, Dr Grosso writes as follows:

> Research on near-death experiences may be uncovering data which empirically support the hypothesis of an 'Idea' or 'Archetype of Death'—a collective psychic structure whose function is to assist a

human personality during a major crisis of individuation. According to Jungian theory, such an archetype would represent and contain the racial memory and wisdom of mankind. The collective experience of the human race has come up with this as the best possible way to die. The archetype is a paradigm—an old Platonic term—for how to die. It is optimally functional for dying in the same way the lung through evolution has become optimally functional for breathing. Near-death phenomena point toward an archetype or paradigm for a *healthy death*—a somewhat paradoxical expression, I admit.

The advantage of this explanation is that it saves the important subjective phenomena; the experience of ineffable unity, transcendental elation, and so forth. For, as Jung claims, the archetypes are merging phenomena with numinous overtones. It also accounts for the transformative effects of NDEs, which seem to involve release from the limitations of ordinary, space–time bound individual existence. Yet there remain two thorny problems for the hypothesis of a death archetype. First, what is the fate of *personal* consciousness in this archetypal transformation of death? Second, what are we to make of the psi components of NDEs? The genuine paranormal effects obviously occur in a specifiable space–time framework and seem to involve awareness of particular deceased individuals.

Dr Grosso's answer is that superpersonal structures, such as the psyche, probably survive death since they transcend the physical world. But he doesn't feel that a pure survivalist theory for the NDE is called for, considering the current level of our research findings.

'Explaining NDEs is obviously a large undertaking,' he comments in a paper published in 1981 explicating his position. 'The most that can be said now is that they cannot be adequately accounted for by any of the reductionist theories, but that to invoke either Jungian or outright survival hypotheses would be premature.'

While Dr Grosso suggests that his theory is consistent with personal survival, he clearly doesn't believe that the NDE represents direct evidence *for* immortality. 'One is rendered free—in a Jamesian, pragmatic way—to accept the survival hypothesis, for such a belief is consistent with the near-death phenomenon,' he concludes. 'But the great question of who we are and what our fate is after death is still open.'

My own theoretical model for the NDE is consistent with Dr Grosso's speculations, but it extends them a step further and more openly towards the survivalistic interpretation. It is not clear whether Dr Grosso believes that the NDE really represents the release of 'something' from the body, which is the basis for my own separationist OBE/visionary theory. While I personally would not interpret the specific observations made by eschatological NDErs in terms of Jungian archetypes, I see nothing wrong with relying on the Swiss psychiatrist's language. Where I part company with Dr Grosso is in supporting a much more survivalistic interpretation of the eschatological vision, since I believe it points to a more fundamental spiritual reality within the universe. Symbols cannot emerge unless they represent something real, tangible, and greater to what they seem to signify for us and spiritual symbols probably conform to this psychological rule.

That the eschatological NDE represents a symbolic 'sneak preview' of the soul's ultimate resting place may strike the reader as wildly unparsimonious, but I think this conceptualization explains two further troubling findings in near-death research:

(1) When a person dies, his/her consciousness probably survives and enters a realm surpassing anything we could possibly imagine. Perhaps the soul is prepared for this eventuality through the eschatological vision—in which the properties of the next world, such as its landscape, are revealed to us. But since some sort of cosmic rift has occurred between the 'real' world and the Beyond when the NDE takes place, it isn't surprising that bystanders sometimes share these perceptions. For reasons I can't fully explain, some people visiting a dying person undergoing an NDE perhaps sometimes momentarily share in the experience. The bystander, perhaps due to his close spiritual bond with the patient, suddenly 'taps into' the eschatological realm and simultaneously gets a glimpse of the Beyond.

This part of my separationist OBE/visionary theory explains those extraordinary cases where the patient's friends see 'welcoming' spirits of the dead or hear the music of paradise.

(2) If there exists a spiritual dimension behind the NDE, knowledge of the higher realms is probably coded directly into human consciousness itself. Many religions teach that each of us is inherently connected to the universe and to each other on some grander level. (This concept has even been enthusiastically endorsed by some theoretical physicists, such as David Bohm in his celebrated book *Wholeness and the Implicate Order*.) It would

follow that knowledge concerning the higher worlds and the Great Beyond might leak out spontaneously when people take psychedelic drugs or otherwise change their states of consciousness. Such encoded visionary episodes might even be catalysed spontaneously, resulting in experiences such as John Skilton's eschatological journey—which took place suddenly while the Florida resident was unloading some lumber from a train.

So the fact that NDE-like experiences emerge from psychedelic drug use or in other contexts does not undermine their importance or the meaning of the core experience.

So while the NDE may not be a literal journey through death, there is little doubt in my mind that it points in that direction. The eschatological NDE is basically a sacred promise in which the soul's final resting place is symbolically revealed to us. It is not merely a transformative psychological experience, but a deeply spiritual encounter with some sort of Ultimate Reality—a reality buried deeply behind the NDE's metaphoric language.

Epilogue

Mrs Helen Nelson of New Britain, Connecticut, underwent her personal NDE in 1975, which changed her life for ever. She had been suffering from back problems for years, but ignored the chest pains she felt one bright Sunday afternoon. The pain grew progressively worse and she felt faint, so she finally called her physician but never completed the call. Her body was found four days later by her son, who broke down her door when she didn't respond to his knocks.

Some time later Mrs Nelson regained consciousness in an emergency-room, where she watched the staff work on her body. 'I remember it as clearly as if I were right there at this moment,' she later recalled in an interview published in the September 1981 issue of *Vital Signs*, a digest issued by the International Association for Near-Death Studies. 'I remember being up there in a corner, sort of looking down as they were working on my body.'

Mrs Nelson was slightly annoyed by the commotion and didn't care when she heard the physician say, 'She's gone.' For the next thing she knew, she was floating down a tunnel:

I could feel myself going through this tunnel, being drawn through this tunnel. And there was this light at the end. God, it was so bright! As I neared it I could feel the warmth enveloping me. I could feel ... it was like velvet suddenly creeping over me, the softness and this warmth. And I suddenly got into this spot and it was like a jolt and I'm standing and I'm looking around me and I see all this beautiful golden light! Again I have to say, if you can ever remember being touched by warm velvet, that beautiful caressing feeling.

Mrs Nelson found herself in a marble building, where she felt the presence of God. Spirits of the dead floated in the building and she spotted several of her deceased relatives, including her parents:

> They seemed to welcome me. They looked as they looked when they were quite young.
>
> I know we communicated a great deal. But I don't remember exactly what was said. I know I was given a tremendous knowledge, a tremendous understanding of reality. Every once in a while it's like a faint whiff of perfume, I get an inkling of it. And it's so delicious!

As she watched in growing astonishment, her father finally spoke to her, calmly but forcefully. 'Helen, you have to go back,' he said.

Mrs Nelson reached towards him and pleaded, 'No, please let me stay. I want to stay here. I don't want to go back. I can't bear any more pain.'

But her father was unmoved by her plea. 'There is something very important you have to complete,' he replied.

The next thing Mrs Nelson experienced was a rushing feeling mixed with considerable pain:

> I felt as though every limb, every bone in my body was being crushed or torn from me. I saw a lot of energy, a lot of electrical energy. It was like a BANG! I heard someone saying, 'Helen, Helen.' And I looked up and noticed my two ministers and my doctor. I kind of chuckled! I wasn't aware I had all the life supports going and I couldn't speak. But I chuckled. I thought I was at my funeral! Because I knew I had died! The reality that I was alive wasn't there yet.
>
> Then back into the coma. And that's what it was for quite some time—in and out of coma. The moment I would come out of the comatose state it would hit me what had happened.

Summing up her experience today, Mrs Nelsen says, 'I came out of this near-death experience with the one positive knowledge that is constantly magnified in my life, and that is that love is the innermost core of our entire being, the core of what life is really all about.'

Nobody can say for sure whether Mrs Nelson really visited the higher worlds or whether she felt the literal presence of God. Nor is it possible to know whether she spoke with her father or merely with the voice of her own psyche. But no matter what explanation best encompasses her journey (and similar reports), it's clear that the experience of death is probably extremely pleasant. To feel the emotions granted to Mrs Nelson certainly outweighs the pain of dying.

Most people who survive NDEs lose their previous fear of death. The constant theme reiterated in all their stories is that whatever fate befalls the soul, death itself should be confronted without fear or trepidation. Once we stop fearing death so much, maybe we can begin to live more fully and compassionately. That was the lesson Mrs Nelson learned through her close encounter with death, and it is a lesson we should emulate in our own lives.

For studying the long-range meaning of the NDE is essentially an exercise in living, not dying.

References

Chapter 1

Armore, Daniel. 'A first-hand account of an NDE'. *Revitalized Signs*, October 1987.

Bradshaw, Rick. 'Personal reflections on near-death experiences'. *Anabiosis*, August 1979.

Gallup, George, Jr. *Adventures in Immortality*. New York: McGraw-Hill Book Co., 1982.

Grey, Margot. *Return from Death*. London: Arkana (Routledge & Kegan Paul), 1985.

Lovell, Tracy. 'Personal accounts of near-death experiences'. *Anabiosis*, August 1980.

Moody, Raymond, Jr. *Life After Life*. Atlanta: Mockingbird Books, 1975.

Chapter 2

Epstein, Perle. *Kabbalah, the Way of the Jewish Mystic*. Garden City, NY: Doubleday, 1987.

Grof, Stanislav and Joan Halifax. *The Human Encounter with Death*. New York: Dutton, 1977.

Plato. *Republic*. London: Penguin Books, 1955

Ring, Kenneth. 'From Alpha to Omega: ancient mysteries and the near-death experience'. *Anabiosis*, 1987, 5, 3–16.

Zaleski, Carol. 'Evaluating near-death testimony: a challenge for theology'. *Anabiosis*, 1987, 5, 17–52.

____ *Otherworld Journeys*. New York: Oxford University Press, 1987.

Chapter 3

Barrett, William. *Death-bed Visions*. London: Methuen, 1926.

Bozzano, Ernesto. *Phénomènes psychiques au moment de la mort*. Paris: Editions de la B.P.S., 1923.

Clarke, Edward H. *Visions: A Study of False Sight*. Cambridge: Riverside Press, 1878.

Cobbe, Frances P. *Peak in Darien*. London: 1882.

Crookall, Robert. *The Study and Practice of Astral Projection*. London: Aquarian Press, 1960.

_____ *More Astral Projections*, London: Aquarian Press, 1964.

Gurney, Edmund, Frank Podmore and F.W.H. Myers. *Phantasms of the Living*. London: Trübner & Co., 1886.

Hyslop, James H. *Contact with the Other World*. New York: Century, 1919.

_____ *Psychical Research and the Resurrection*. New York: Small, Maynard & Co., 1908.

Lundahl, Craig R. and Harold A. Widdison. 'The Mormon explanation of near-death experiences'. *Anabiosis*, 1983, *3*, 97–106.

Myers, F.W.H. *Human Personality and Its Survival of Bodily Death* (2 vols.). London: Longman's, 1903.

_____ 'On indications of continued terrene knowledge on the part of phantasms of the dead'. *Proceedings of the Society for Psychical Research*, 1892, *8*, 170–252.

Osis, Karlis. *Deathbed Observations by Physicians and Nurses*. New York: Parapsychology Foundation, 1961

_____ and Erlendur Haraldsson. *At the Hour of Death*. New York: Avon, 1977.

Richet, Charles. *Thirty Years of Psychical Research*. New York: Macmillan, 1923.

Chapter 4

Grey, Margot. *Return from Death*. London: Arkana (Routledge & Kegan Paul), 1985.

MacMillan, R.L. and K.W.G. Brown. 'Cardiac arrest remembered'. *Canadian Medical Association Journal*, 1971, *104*, 889–90.

Moody, Raymond. *Life After Life*. Atlanta: Mockingbird Books, 1975.

_____ *Reflections on Life After Life*. Atlanta: Mockingbird Books, 1977.

Ring, Kenneth. *Life at Death*. New York: Coward, McCann & Geoghegan, 1980.

_____ 'Frequency and stages of the prototypic near-death experience'. In *A Collection of Near-Death Research Readings*, edited by Craig R. Lundahl. Chicago: Nelson-Hall, 1982.

Sabom, Michael. *Recollections of Death*. New York: Harper & Row, 1982.

Sabom, Michael and Sarah S. Kreutziger. 'Physicians evaluate the near-death experience'. In *A Collection of Near-Death Research Readings*, edited by Craig R. Lundahl, *op. cit.*

_____ 'Near-death experiences'. *Journal of the Florida Medical Association*, 1977, *64*, 648–50.

Chapter 5

Bush, Nancy Evans. 'The near-death experience in children: shades of prison-house reopening'. *Anabiosis*, 1983, 3, 177–94.

Gabbard, Glen O. and Stuart W. Twemlow. *With the Eyes of the Mind*. New York: Praeger, 1984.

McCarthy, James B. *Death Anxiety—the Loss of the Self*. New York: Gardner Press, 1980.

Morse, Melvin. 'A near-death experience in a 7-year-old child'. *American Journal of the Disabled Child*, 1983, *137*, 959–61.

Nagy, Maria. 'The child's theories concerning death'. *Journal of Genetic Psychology*, 1948, 73, 3–27.

_____ 'The child's view of death'. In *The Meaning of Death*, edited by Herman Feifel. New York: McGraw Hill, 1959.

Chapter 6

Collier, Barbara. 'Ketamine and the conscious mind'. *Anaesthesia*, 1972, 27, 120–34.

Domino, E.F., P. Chodoff and G. Corssen. 'Human pharmacology of CI–581, a new intravenous agent chemically related to phencyclidine'. *Federation Proceedings*, 1965, 24, 268.

Grinspoon, Lester and James B. Bakalar. *Psychedelic Drugs Reconsidered*. New York: Basic Books, 1979.

Johnstone, R. 'A ketamine trip'. *Anaesthesiology*, 1973, 39, 460–61.

'Ketamine and back'. *High Times*, 8 August 1978.

Leary, Timothy. *Flashbacks*. Los Angeles: J.P. Tarcher, 1983.

Lilly, John. *The Scientist*. Philadelphia: Lippincott, 1978.

McCarthy, D.A. 'History of the development of cataleptoid anesthetics of the phencyclidine type'. In *PCP: Historical and Current Perspectives*, edited by E.F. Domino. Ann Arbor, Mich.: NPP Books, 1981.

MacMillan, R.L. and K.W.G. Brown. 'Cardiac arrest remembered'. *Canadian Medical Association Journal*, 1971, *104*, 889–90.

Moore, Marcia and Howard Alltounian. *Journeys into the Bright World*. Whistlestop Mall, Mass.: Para Research, 1978.

Ring, Kenneth. *Life at Death*. New York: Coward, McCann & Geoghegan, 1980.

Siegel, Ronald K. 'The psychology of life after death'. *American Psychologist*, 1980, *35*, 911–31.

Smith, J. '...caught up into Paradise'. *Vital Signs*, June 1983, 7 and 10.

Stafford, Peter. *Psychedelics Encyclopedia*. Los Angeles: J. P. Tarcher, 1983.

Chapter 7

Brice, D.D., R.R. Hetherington and J.E. Utting. 'A simple study of awareness and dreaming during anaesthesia'. *British Journal of Anaesthesia*, 1970, 42, 535–41.

Garfield, Charles. 'The dying patient's concern with "life after death" '. In *Between Life and Death*, edited by Robert Kastenbaum. New York: Springer, 1979.

Grey, Margot. *Return from Death*. London: Arkana (Routledge & Kegan Paul), 1985.

Moody, Raymond. *Reflections on Life After Life*. Atlanta: Mockingbird Books, 1977.

Rawlings, Maurice. *Beyond Death's Door*. Nashville: Thomas Nelson, 1978.

Sabom, Michael. '*Beyond Death's Door*: a book review'. *Anabiosis*, 1979, *1* (3), 9.

Welch, Thomas. *Oregon's Amazing Miracle*. Dallas: Christ for the Nations, 1976.

Chapter 8

Alcock, James E. 'Psychology and near-death experiences'. *The Skeptical Inquirer*, Spring 1979, 25–41.

Anabiosis. 'Denver cardiologist describes findings after 18 years of near-death research'. *Anabiosis*, May 1979, 1–2.

Cook, Emily Williams, Ian Stevenson and Nicholas MacLean. 'Is near-death experience a misnomer?' Paper presented to the 10th International Conference of the Society for Psychical Research, Cambridge, September 1986.

Counts, Dorothy Ayers. 'Near-death and out-of-body experiences in a Melanesian Society. *Anabiosis*, 1983, *3*, 115–36.

Gabbard, Glen O. and Stuart W. Twemlow. *With the Eyes of the Mind*. New York: Praeger, 1984.

Green, J. Timothy and Penelope Friedman. 'Near-death experiences in a Southern California population'. *Anabiosis*, 1983, *3*, 77–96.

Greyson, Bruce. 'Organic brain dysfunction and near-death experiences'. Paper delivered to the 135th Annual Meeting of the American Psychiatric Association, Toronto, May 1982.

_____ 'Empirical evidence bearing on the interpretation of near-death experience among suicide attempters'. Paper presented to the annual convention of the American Psychological Association, Los Angeles, August 1981.

_____ 'Toward a psychological explanation of near-death experiences: response to Dr Grosso's paper'. *Anabiosis*, 1981, *1*, 88–103.

Kastenbaum, Robert. 'Temptations from the ever after'. *Human Behavior*, September 1977, 28–33.

_____ *Is There Life after Death?* London: Rider, 1984.

Landis, Carney. *Varieties of Psychopathological Experience*. New York: Holt, Rinehart & Winston, 1964.

Lindley, James H., Sethyn Bryan and Bob Conley. 'Near-death experiences in a Pacific American population: the evergreen study'. *Anabiosis*, 1981, *1*, 104–25.

Noyes, Russell, Jr. and Roy Kletti. 'Depersonalization in the face of life-threatening experiences'. *Psychiatry*, 1976, *39*, 17–27.

Overton, D.A. 'State-dependent learning in drug states and atrophine-like drugs'. *Psychopharmacalogia*, 1966, *10*, 6–31.

Stevens, William Oliver. *The Mystery of Dreams*. London: George Allen & Unwin, 1950.

Chapter 9

Alment, E.A.J. 'Consciousness during surgical operations'. *British Medical Journal*, 1959, 2, 1258.

Atwater, P.M.H. *Coming Back*, New York: Dodd, Mead, 1988.

Blackmore, Susan. *The Adventures of a Parapsychologist*. Buffalo, NY: Prometheus Books, 1986.

Brice, D.D., R.R. Hetherington and J.E. Utting. 'A simple study of awareness and dreaming during anaesthesia'. *British Journal of Anaesthesiology*, 1970, 42, 535–41.

Brunn, J.T. 'The capacity to hear, understand and to remember experiences during chemo-anesthesia: a personal experience'. *American Journal of Clinical Hypnosis*, 1963, 6, 27–30.

Clark, Kimberly. 'Clinical interventions with near-death experiences'. In *The Near Death Experience—Problems, Prospects, Perspectives*, edited by Bruce Greyson and Charles P. Flynn. Springfield, Ill: Charles C Thomas, 1984.

Flynn, Charles P. *After the Beyond*. Englewood Cliffs, NJ: Prentice-Hall, 1986.

Froelich, Warren. 'Hartford research suggests coma victims retain awareness'. *The Hartford Courant*, Tuesday 23 May 1988.

Green, Celia. *Out-of-the-Body Experiences*. Oxford: Institute of Psychophysical Research, 1968.

Grey, Margot. *Return from Death*. London: Arkana (Routledge & Kegan Paul), 1985.

Kohr, Richard L. 'Near-death experiences, altered states and psi sensitivity'. *Anabiosis*, 1983, 3, 157–76.

Millar, Keith and Neal Watkinson. 'Recognition of words presented during general anaesthesia'. *Ergonomics*, 1983, 6, 585–94.

Ring, Kenneth. 'Precognitive and prophetic visions in near-death experiences'. *Anabiosis*, 1982, 2, 47–74.

_____ *Heading Toward Omega*, New York: Morrow, 1984.

Sabom, Michael. *Recollections of Death*. New York: Harper & Row, 1982.

Schmeidler, Gertrude and R.A. McConnell. *ESP and Personality Patterns*. New Haven, Conn.: Yale University Press, 1958.

Chapter 10

Blackmore, Susan. 'Birth and the OBE: an unhelpful analogy'. *Journal of the American Society for Psychical Research*, 1983, 77, 229–38.

Gabbard, Glen O. and Stuart W. Twemlow. *With the Eyes of the Mind*. New York: Praeger, 1984.

Harary, Stuart Blue (Keith). 'A personal perspective on out-of-body experiences'. In *Mind Beyond the Body* edited by D. Scott Rogo. New York: Penguin, 1978.

Morris, Robert L., S.B. Harary, *et al.* 'Studies of communication during out-of-body experiences'. *Journal of the American Society for Psychical Research*, 1978, 72, 1–22.

Rogo, D. Scott. 'Experiments with Blue Harary'. In *Mind Beyond the Body*, edited by D. Scott Rogo. New York: Penguin, 1978.

_____ 'Aspects of out-of-body experiences'. *Journal of the Society for Psychical Research*, 1976, 48, 329–35.

_____ 'Psychological models of the out-of-body experience—a review and critical evaluation'. *Journal of Parapsychology*, 1982, 46, 29–46.

Tart, Charles T. 'A psychophysiological study of out-of-body experiences in a selected subject'. *Journal of the American Society for Psychical Research*, 1968, 62, 3–27.

Chapter 11

Barrett, William. *Death-bed Visions*. London: Methuen, 1926.

Crookall, Robert. *More Astral Projections*. London: Aquarian Press, 1964.

Ford, Marvin. *On the Other Side*. Plainfield, NJ: Logos International, 1978.

Green, J. Timothy. 'NDEs in Chammaro culture'. *Vital Signs*, 1984, 4, (1–2), 6–7.

Grey, Margot. *Return from Death*. London: Arkana (Routledge & Kegan Paul), 1985.

Grosso, Michael. 'Towards an explanation of near-death phenomena'. *Anabiosis*, 1981, 1, 3–26.

Lemov, Iris. 'Personal reflections on near-death experiences'. *Anabiosis*, 1979, 1 (3), 5–6.

Moody, Raymond. *Life After Life*, Atlanta: Mockingbird Books, 1975.

_____ *Elvis After Life*. Atlanta: Peachtree Publishers, 1987.

Ring, Kenneth. *Heading Toward Omega*. New York: Morrow, 1984.

Rogo, D. Scott. *NAD, Vol. 2: A Psychic Study of the 'Music of the Spheres'*. Secaucus, NY: University Books, 1970.

Schatzman, Morton. *The Story of Ruth*. New York: Putnam's, 1980.

Smith, Susy. *Life is Forever*. New York: Putnam's, 1974.

Wilson, S.C. and T.X. Barber. 'The fantasy-prone personality'. In *Imagery: Current Theory, Research and Application*, edited by Anees A. Sheikh. New York: Wiley, 1982.

Zaleski, Carol. *Otherworld Journeys*. New York: Oxford University Press, 1987.

Final Note

The scientific study of the near-death experience is an unfolding drama, with exciting new discoveries coming to light each year. To keep abreast of new findings in near-death research, the International Association for Near-Death Studies offers its members both a newsletter and a scholarly journal. For information regarding the Association, readers may write to IANDS at the Department of Psychiatry, University of Connecticut Health Center, Farmington, Connecticut, USA 06032. Alternatively, one can contact the British wing of the Association at IANDS (UK), The Old School House, Hampnett, Northbach, Glos. GL54 3NN.

Because near-death research has never enjoyed much public funding, scientific studies of the NDE have sometimes suffered. To preserve and support new research into the subject, researchers at the University of Connecticut have organized the non-profit University of Connecticut Near-Death Studies Fund. To learn more about the Fund, readers can write to Dr Bruce Greyson at the same address.

Index